A M GE of INCONVENIENCE

A Marriage of Inconvenience

ByMeliora J Schoenberg & David B Gibb

An historical novel in three parts

Emily Emma Maude Jackson (nee Hall)

(Cover: The author wearing Emily Emma's teacoat)

Cover Design by Deft Design

Preface

The tale is one handed down through the generations of my family. Yet, with all such tales that are passed on by word of mouth, the facts become more ill defined and clouded with times' passage. My connection with the "unlikely heroine" is illustrated by the brief extract of my family tree which follows.Perhaps I was more interested or more affected by all I learned of Great Great Aunt Emily than were my sister and late brother. The story narrated by our mother instilled in me such a sense of sadness. Of unfairness as to how Mrs Jackson was treated and depicted by society at that time.

I have felt that this is not simply a story bookended by the governing principles or morals of the late Victorian age and neither is it purely a series of events which heralded the advent of the suffragette movement and then employed by academics and students (mostly in North America) for various historical/political theses.

Just as during the 1980's with the paparazzi or these days with the monster of social media, Great Great Aunt Emily became the innocent victim, the scourge of her locale and the object of pillory in the national press. I employ the adjective "innocent" through unashamed family bias yet even had Emily transgressed in a manner that I, for one, cannot understand then she would not and did not merit the odium heaped upon her.

There have been small publications of this story before now and I am grateful to those authors. However, I have always sought to have on record what I feel is a more personal tribute to the memory of Emily. I sit in my Croft. Across from my armchair there is a large wooden seat used by Hartley Baldwin. Aunt Emily's clock is here as is her Macassar Ebony box...............

Meliora J Schoenberg

****

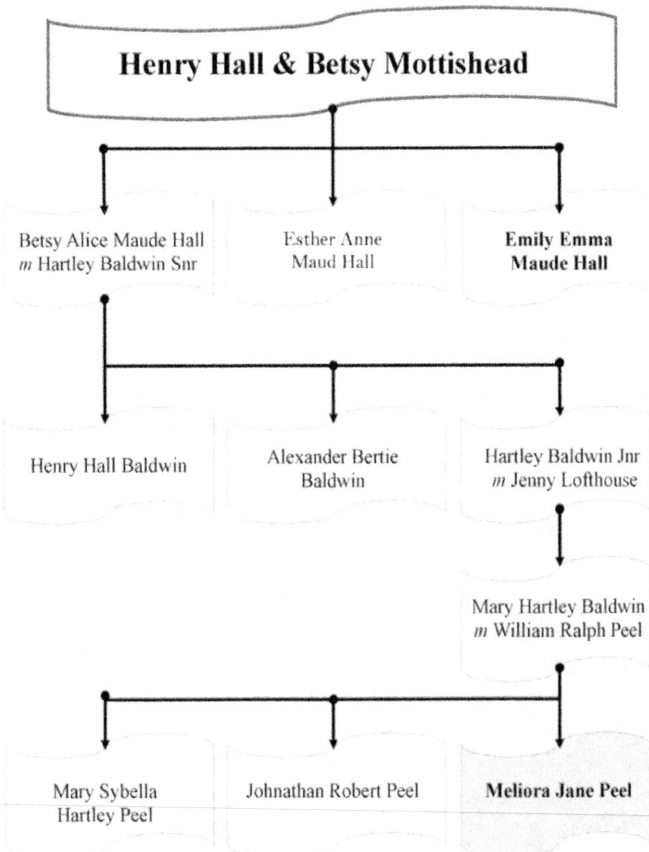
Henry Hall & Betsy Mottishead
Betsy Alice Maude Hall
m Hartley Baldwin Snr
Esther Anne
Maud Hall
Emily Emma
Maude Hall
Henry Hall Baldwin
Alexander Bertie
Baldwin
Hartley Baldwin Jnr
m Jenny Lofthouse
Mary Hartley Baldwin
m William Ralph Peel
Mary Sybella
Hartley Peel
Johnathan Robert Peel
Meliora Jane Peel

PART ONE

The Abduction

Three men crouched in a carriage drawn by a pair of stunning black horses. As the horses stood quietly outside the lychgate of the eighteenth century church only the sound of their metal shoes clinking on the cobblestone could be heard. They jostled from one hind leg to the other, impatient to be on the move. The harness and chains rattled as they shook heads in the March sunlight. By now they were used to waiting. This was the third time the horses had been driven to Whalley on a Sunday morning. The narrow road outside the church of St Mary Magdelene was quiet as there were very few passers by. The date was Sunday 8th March 1891.

The church clock struck 12 noon and the organ music wafted through the now open doors of the church. The first of the congregation made their way out into the spring sunshine.Curious looks were directed at the smart carriage and horses stationed so near to the church. Clitheroe was a small parochial town and it was most unusual for anyone to attend the morning service by way of a carriage.

This mission had been planned for many months with the precision of a military exercise. In command of the operation was Jackson. A man used to such covert manoeuvres, he had fought in the Maori wars in New Zealand and further had seen action in the American Civil War. Jackson was present along with his accomplices, Dixon Robinson and his brother William Robinson.

The two Robinsons alighted from the carriage. They loitered by the vehicle as if immersed in conversation between themselves when truly they were speaking in soft tones to Jackson who remained hidden from view within the carriage. The predetermined plan involved William rapping on the side of the carriage the moment their quarry, Emily, came into view.

As the congregation spilled onto the roadway many glanced in the direction of the mysterious carriage and pair before continuing on their way. The parishioners seemed, to those waiting by the carriage, to take an age to make their way out of the church, along the footpath to the lychgate and thence to the road. Poor Jackson began to wonder if Emily was indeed at the Church or if his spy had made a mistaken observation. There was a sudden rap on the side of the carriage. It was William's signal. Jackson's foreboding instantly turned to joy when his eyes caught sight of Emily, his wife, in the frame of the large wooden church door. Immediately he pulled shut the carriage curtain. Jackson dare not risk being spotted by any of the congregation as they went by the carriage making their way sedately homeward from the service.

By holding back the curtain a little though Jackson could observe his estranged wife. She was arm in arm with her elder sister Betsy. She looked happier and, to him, lovelier than ever. His wife, the woman he had married and yet a wife he had never lived with. Jackson had sent William to stand by the side of a building until the two sisters walked by. Emily and Betsy were chatting avidly with each other unaware they were being watched. Unaware they were now being followed.

William signalled his brother. Dixon strode boldly up the path and also positioned himself behind the sisters. When Emily and Betsy reached the lychgate Jackson leapt out of the carriage and, with fixed piercing stare demanded of his wife." You will come with me". For a brief moment Emily did not identify the stern and aggressive voice. Then she looked up and felt a wave of horror and disgust as she found herself face to face with.............her husband.

Emily at once recognised his long thin face and the cold staring eyes. This was the man she had married two years previously. It was indeed Edmund Haughton Jackson.

Jackson stood in Emily's path. "I want you to go home with me now" he said firmly. Emily let out a scream. His decision was made. It was time for action. This was to his mind to be a facile capture and victory. Life in Lancashire for this brave and resourceful ex soldier had been too quiet these few months. His circumstances had become grave in that he could barely keep himself in bread and butter. This was no different to a combat mission. Time now to capture his wife.

Jackson grabbed hold of Emily's arm. "You are my wife" he yelled employing the tone of an Army Sergeant Major. Taking a grip of her sister, Emily stared at Jackson in a clear voice for all to hear articulated "I will not go with you". The attention of the gathered churchgoers was focused upon the growing disturbance. They were not going home. They stood stock still.

Emily clung desperately to Betsy. Jackson fought hard to keep hold of his wife. The voices of the protagonists continued to rise. The onlookers though were silent. There had never been such a spectacle to behold. And on a Sunday!! Within the restrained crowd there was a common curiosity. What was all this about? By dint of fate there was amongst the onlookers a reporter with the Clitheroe Times. The reporter could not believe his luck. Nothing like this had happened before in this normally quiet, traditional and sedate town. With such enthusiasm the reporter proceeded to note every single detail of the drama which was unfolding before his eyes.

Jackson began to pull Emily away from Betsy. He was quite amazed at her strength and resistance. Betsy was purple with rage and desperately clung onto her sister. Voices continued to be raised. The tussle became more violent.

"Hold me fast Betsy, don't let him take me away" screamed Emily. Momentarily the sisters caught Jackson off guard and he had to give ground but a further effort by Jackson saw him dragging the sisters in the direction of the carriage. Emily struck Jackson's nose with her elbow and there was blood on his face. At this point in the struggle Jackson's scarf which had been covering his face was pulled down for all to see. There was a sudden intake of breath from the crowd and some there were heard to utter in shock "Haughton Jackson".

Jackson wrestled on regardless, blood streaming from his nose.

'Please help us" Emily beseeched the onlookers. However, the crowd were mesmerised by the drama and not one of them was prepared to enter the fray. Dixon Robinson pushed forward to assist Jackson. With arms tightly round her sister, Betsy would not relax her hold and hung on for grim death. Dixon managed to grab one of Betsy's hands whereupon he bent back her fingers so hard that she was in excruciating pain and had to let go her grip upon Emily. Walking backwards towards the carriage Jackson dragged Emily forwards as if in some dreadful, slow and fateful dance.

Emily and Betsy still pleaded for help but the ears of the crowd remained deaf to their entreaties.

Dixon then gave Betsy another hearty push whereupon she fainted, landed heavily on the ground and was left lying there motionless. William Robinson, though a doctor, seemed unaware of Betsy's plight. He was disgusted by all the brutality he was witnessing. To the bystanders he said "It's no use. It's no use." He left the scene muttering about some patient he said he had to visit.

The carriage had an iron step halfway between the ground and the door. Jackson had his back to the carriage but he dared not let go of his wife in order to get up the step. She might escape. Emily was certainly not making his life easy.

In desperation Jackson shouted to Dixon who was still standing rather arrogantly over poor Betsy. 'For God's sake Dick, help me."

Emily managed to shove her assailant backwards into the carriage. Jackson landed on his back. Emily's force though propelled her forwards and she tumbled on top of her by now prone husband. What a sight for the gawping remains of the congregation. Emily's legs protruded from her undergarments and, with her dress dangling from the carriage door, her petticoats fluttered in the breeze.

Dixon rushed forward and pushed Emily's legs and garments into the carriage and slammed the door shut. He ran to the offside door, jumped in and urged the coachman to make haste. The coachman, with whip and voice, spurred the horses into action. The coach set off at a spanking pace down the road towards Blackburn.

Betsy slowly came to. She caught sight of Dixon's hat on the ground nearby and immediately the struggle she had endured was recalled. As her vision cleared Betsy saw the rear of the coach disappearing round the far bend in the road.With the help of a bystander Betsy struggled to her feet. She hobbled back to her home at Prospect House in Church Brow just down the road from the church. Once home her husband, Hartley Baldwin, dispatched the maid to find Dr Musson. Betsy sat with her arm aching and her head pounding.

"Haughton Jackson has taken my poor sister" she sobbed. Hartley listened incredulously as his wife tearfully imparted the dreadful events of the morning.

When Dr Musson arrived her injured hand was bathed and bound up and he reassured her that nothing was broken. She was told to rest. Betsy therefore retired to her bedroom. In the peace of her room Betsy closed her eyes certain that Hartley would soon be back with Emily.

Once he had made sure that his wife was comfortable Hartley went downstairs. He gathered a few friends including his son, Hartley junior, and the coachman of his sister-in-law, Esther. Once assembled this "posse" set off by carriage to Blackburn where it was assumed Emily had been taken.

****

Haughton Jackson had been obsessed with reclaiming his wife. She belonged to him, didn't she? In his mind there had been a conspiracy in Clitheroe to deny him what was legally and morally his. His only allies were his sister Isabel and his friend Dixon Robinson. Jackson had had Emily secretly watched as she and her sister paraded around Clitheroe. On several occasions he had sent Dixon to follow them and report back to him.

Jackson suspected that Emily's brother-in-law, Hartley Baldwin, and his own solicitors were playing a game. Jackson though could not wait.

"To hell with them all. I want my rights and I will have them" he confided to Isabel.

There was much plotting and many long talks. They were like a secret team.

"For two pins I'd pick her up and carry her off willy-nilly. Then we will see who is master"

Not that Jackson needed any bolstering but Dixon Robinson the articled Clerk volunteered:

"A man has a legal right to possess his wife's person. It is Emily who is breaking the law."

Jackson had considered picking Emily up when she was on one of her shopping trips into Clitheroe or while she was walking. Yet Emily was always escorted on her outings. This infuriated him. He began to believe that Emily was being kept a prisoner by her family specifically to keep her away from her lawful husband and his attentions.

No. There were too many people around for a snatch like that. It was Dixon who first suggested that they should try to abduct Emily on a Sunday when she left the church. It could be done discreetly and there would not be a great number of locals around. Whilst Isabel viewed it as very risky the belief she expressed was that it was high time this wife of Jackson was put in her place.

The plan started to take shape. The plotters would have a carriage and horses at the Church gate and, as Emily came out of the church at around noon, they would invite her or, if necessary, compel her to get into the carriage. The carriage would then drive off at great speed to West View, No 2 Rover Street, Blackburn where Isabel would be ready to receive their willing or unwilling captive.

Emily had previously mentioned that she was not a regular at the church anymore. He did not know why. They dare not let anyone know of the plot or even let out any hint of what was afoot so they had to play a waiting game. The carriage and horses would be ready at Whalley which was a small distance from Clitheroe. A faithful spy would be posted at the rear of Clitheroe Church. If this spy identified Emily attending the service at 11 am a message would be sent to those waiting at Whalley and that would be their chance.

Dixon, ever the tactician, suggested that his brother William Henry Robinson be present in case anything went wrong. William was a doctor and could be useful if the escapade went awry and anyone got hurt. This was agreed.

On two successive Sundays, Emily had not attended the morning service. It must have seemed to Jackson that he'd never possess his wife. He had waited with the others in Whalley for two hours on each occasion only for the scout to report a "no show" both times.

Jackson began to wonder if his plan had reached the ears of the cunning Hartley Baldwin, Emily's brother-in-law. For, when he had been courting Emily, he had hinted that Hartley may have placed eavesdroppers at the pair's most intimate and secret rendezvous.

The coachman could have spilled the beans. Yet what beans could he really spill? He had been told nothing. By the time the coachman appreciated the true purpose of the presence of the coach on a Sunday the "snatch" would be well underway and it would be too late for him to tip off anyone. The coachman was a Clitheroe stableman. He got paid for what he was asked to do and that was that. Afterwards the coachman did revel in making sure everyone in Clitheroe and Blackburn knew what had happened and his part in the drama.

As to whether Hartley Baldwin had got wind of the exploit and had asked Emily to stay away from church, Jackson preferred to dismiss the notion. It was but the luck of the draw that she was not there.

So it came to pass on that Sunday the coach was drawn up in Whalley for the third time. Jackson, once more, watched and tensely waited for the spy.

"Well?" demanded Jackson of the spy when he presented himself. The reply came "She's there".

Dixon Robinson pressed money hurriedly into the hand of the spy before joining Jackson who was already seated within carriage alongside William. The moment had arrived. The carriage occupants were silent. Each focused on the task now so near at hand as the horses galloped along the road getting closer and closer to Clitheroe.

****

Emily was obliged to sit with her two captors. Exhausted after the physical exertions of the struggle she felt very sore. Her arms were bruised and swollen, black and blue from the shoulders to the elbows. Her chest was painful. She was shocked. She was very angry.There arose also from within her an increasing sense of fear.

Next to her Jackson was feeling flushed with the success of his plan. He now felt in complete control of everything. Momentarily he shook his fist at his wife as a symbol of his "victory".Emily recoiled a little and whispered "Surely you are not going to hurt me? I cannot talk or even think."

She implored him "Give me time to recover."

Oblivious to the effect of all he had just put Emily through, Jackson said rather nonchalantly:

"You are not yourself" and proceeded to offer her a sip of brandy from his flask. Emily refused and said firmly "I want nothing from you. I will take nothing from you".

This response seemed to incense Jackson. He adopted a commanding tone.

"I shall allow you no communication with your friends. Any letters you write, I will see. I shall also open and read any letters you may receive from your family and it will be for me to decide whether to give them to you or not."

Emily turned away from her husband. By now she could not bring herself to look at him. She was nervous and confused. What did Jackson next plan for her? From the carriage windows she could see they were in Blackburn yet the streets were not familiar. Suddenly, gripped by the thought that, as was not uncommon in these Victorian times, he might be taking her to a mental institution, she enquired in a faint voice "Where are you taking me?"

Jackson spat out the words "West View". Emily was not reassured. Though very anxious, her eyelids weighed down by tiredness and stress could not remain open any longer.

****

The carriage went over a deep rut in the road. The bang as the nearside wheel crashed into the hole brought Emily out of her troubled sleep. They drew up outside West View. Though there were few people about in the street at this time those that were observed nothing untoward at the comings at West View.

Jackson knocked at the door of his sister's house and then returned to the carriage where Dixon was assisting Emily down the step. She was too dazed and too weak to resist or try to run away.

Susan had been the family maid at West View for all of eight years. She had been told to expect Haughton Jackson and his wife. Susan was a little nervous. She had not seen Emily for a long time. She opened the door and saw the two men both with a hold on Emily walk in step with each other to the door and into the house. Susan shut the door behind them and then went to fetch a decanter of port. In normal circumstances it was not the maid's position to do this but she had noticed how flustered Emily had seemed when she entered the house and, having been repeatedly told by her mistress to make Emily welcome, it just seemed the right thing to do.

Emily had been "escorted" into the drawing room. This room was comfortably furnished with large buttoned armchairs and a library of books on one side. In the middle of the wall a roaring fire crackled as the flames licked up the chimney.

Emily was relieved to be offered a seat in one of the armchairs. Susan approached with the port. The captive was offered a glass but Emily raised a hand to gesture refusal of this refreshment. Next Isabel swept into the room.

"Ah, Mrs Jackson here you are." Isabel leant forward to greet her sister in law with a familial kiss. Instinctively Emily drew back then uttered in a quiet but clear tone:

"Yes and you know how I have come and why I am here"

Isabel fired back in the manner of a Victorian headmistress "My brother has done what he has a right to do. You have brought this entirely upon yourself'.

Jackson, staring downwards towards his wife, then asserted:

"You.....you are a low, base born but educated creature. You are a puppet and you are a fool."

He appeared to work himself into a frenzy. His sister later described Jackson's behaviour in the drawing room as being that of a man quite beside himself with passion. In fact, he was simply full of himself and his victory. His wife was at last under his control, in his prison. He was going to savour this moment. Jackson strode this way and that across the drawing room floor berating Emily about her dereliction of duty, about how she had made him look a fool and that he would tolerate such insubordination no more. He lambasted her sisters as cruel and evil specimens.

Suddenly, the tirade ceased and Jackson stood still. In a clipped manner and indicating with his right index finger he said to Emily:

"Take off that bonnet".

She looked up at her husband with a long cold stare and unexpressive face. Angrily Jackson stepped towards her and seized the bonnet with both hands. The bonnet was secured to her hair by two six inch long hat pins and fixed under her chin by ribbons. Dislodging the bonnet was not simple. Jackson pulled the bonnet one way and then the other with increasing force.

Emily shrieked "You are strangling me". Just as the pins began to shear into her head Jackson wrenched the bonnet free and hurled the item into the fire. As the flames consumed the bonnet he grinned at his wife with a combination of both rage and triumph.

Even Dixon was taken aback at his friend's actions.

"Haughton, you are going now beyond the bounds of reason" he shouted.

Jackson took no notice. He stood upright immediately in front of Emily and with hands on his waist said curtly "Sit there until I tell you that you can move."

One by one they retired from the drawing room leaving Emily by herself. The door was pulled shut.

The Siege

Emily knew where she was and why she was at West View. Yet it was all just so unreal.Was this but a tormented nightmare or was she truly a prisoner in this house? She felt alone and surrounded by "enemies". Emily daren't think of her husband's next designs upon her for they were bound to be cruel and hurtful. She gazed far into the fire. Her eyes became mesmerized by the dancing of the orange and yellow tongues lapping around the thick logs. Her thoughts drifted back in time. The light hearted and carefree times she had found with John Anderton. Before then were the days of playful innocence shared with the sisters who she loved so much. For this moment she relived such happy times and the name of Haughton Jackson was expunged from her consciousness.

Bang! Bang! The noise of someone knocking at the front door startled Emily and brought her back to her nightmare. The knocking continued but there was now, as well, the sound of footsteps and hushed voices outside the drawing room. She heard Jackson's voice but not what he was saying. Suddenly Jackson enquired in a voice loud enough for everyone to hear "Who is there?”

"Robert Heston" proclaimed the caller in an equally loud voice. Esther Hall's coachman continued:

"I want to see Mrs Jackson".

Emily could contain herself no more. The notion that her rescue was at hand filled her with adrenalin such that she rushed from her chair, grabbed and pulled open the door to the drawing room and cried out :-

"I am here against my will. He burned my bonnet. I want to go home".

Instantantly, Jackson rushed over from the door and at one and the same time clamped a hand over Emily's mouth, seized her around the waist and carried her upstairs. He threw her like a sack onto a bed in the upstairs room and said "Stay here. I warn you if you leave this room without my permission you will pay for it." He stormed out, slamming the door shut and locking it before heading downstairs to deal with the ongoing disturbance outside.

Susan had been born and brought up in Wexford, had had a quiet upbringing and was not used to shouting and fighting and yet, in the hour or so since Emily and Mr Jackson arrived at the house she had witnessed all the events in the drawing room, a coachman banging and shouting at the door and Mr Jackson storming upstairs trying to physically control his wife. The volume of noise outside the house increased. Well, Susan had had enough. She was fearful that something awful might occur. She was fearful for Mr Jackson's safety. So although it was not her place to do so she telephoned the police.

The noise had attracted a few locals who had gathered outside West View. They did not know what was happening. As the crowd gathered together, the rescue party, upon seeing that Heston had not succeeded in gaining entry to the house, alighted from their transport. Each was carrying a stick. They appeared menacing to the spectators who meekly parted to allow the posse to progress up to the house. From the front window of her locked bedroom Emily, herself rather fearful at the commotion outside, looked down and recognised Hartley Baldwin at the forefront of what she now realised was her rescue party. She was elated. She jumped up and down at the window, hands banging against panes but, against the raucous hubbub outside, her attempts to attract attention proved fruitless.

In Clitheroe that Sunday at noon the peace had been disturbed. Now the citizens of this district in Blackburn were similarly witnessing raucous scenes. Hartley Baldwin struck the front door of the house repeatedly with his stick. It sounded like a machine gun with ample ammunition. Meantime the others in the posse darted up the side of West View around the back of the property searching for an access point. Jackson remained inside, for he had already made his next move.

Frustrated and furious, Hartley Baldwin suddenly turned about and smartly left the property. He was a well known figure in professional circles in Lancashire. Hartley Baldwin had influence. He took himself off to Blackburn Central Police Station where he demanded to speak to the Chief Constable. However, being as it was a Sunday, Chief Constable Lewis was not on duty. He was relaxing at his home.

This would not do. Not for Hartley Baldwin. He had no qualms about phoning the Chief Constable at his home which is what he proceeded to do. Whether he welcomed the interruption to his weekend or not the Chief Constable felt he could not refuse the request for assistance from Hartley Baldwin. They agreed to rendezvous at West View.

Upon seeing the Chief Constable approach with two constables, Hartley Baldwin instructed them:

"I demand that you break into that house and free the lady who is being illegally detained there".

As this demand was being made a small coach pulled by a white horse drew up nearby. A small uninteresting man got out. He was wearing a shabby brown suit and thin strands of greasy hair strayed over the collar of his shirt. He produced from an inside pocket an official looking piece of paper and handed it to the Chief Constable.

As soon as he had locked Emily in the bedroom, Jackson had urgently contacted his solicitor and explained the trouble there was and how an attempt was being made that very moment to take his wife away from him. The solicitor had immediately phoned his Clerk and instructed him to get to West View without delay.

The Clerk handed the Court Order to the Chief Constable. The Chief Constable took his time to read carefully over the document. Hartley Baldwin did not realise what was happening. He could not believe the police were not, there and then, hastening to rescue his sister-in-law.

The Chief Constable looked up from the document and said slowly and deliberately "In the light of this document, I cannot intervene."

"If you will not break down the door then I will" said Hartley turning once more towards the front door.

The Chief Constable raised his voice:

"Sir, I advise you not to do that. Please go home. If you take action such as you threaten to do you will be breaking the law. It does appear that this man Jackson has legal right on his side. As a solicitor you know about the decree I have just read and the rights it confers. Besides I must disperse this crowd. Your presence suggests to me that a serious breach of the peace might occur. You would surely not want that now would you Sir?"

Crestfallen and unhappy, Hartley Baldwin gathered his accomplices and retreated back to Clitheroe.

****

William Robinson was still affected by the violence he had witnessed in Clitheroe. As he was very concerned about Emily, he made his way to

West View as he knew she had been taken there. With some difficulty he navigated his way through the jostling crowd only to find the police constables wouldn't let him pass. It took him a good five minutes to persuade the officers that he was a doctor and he was there to attend upon a lady within the house.

A rather ashen faced Susan gingerly opened the door whereupon William encountered Jackson, his brother Dixon and Isabel huddled in deep conversation. As if to explain himself William said that he was concerned about Mrs Jackson's health and, as a doctor, he wanted to check on her.

Jackson simply rolled his eyes as if to say "Don't be so soft" but he did not object and so William climbed the stairs to find Emily.

He knocked gently upon the door. There was no response. He found then that the door was locked and so turned the key and slowly looked around the room. He saw Emily standing by the window. The colour had drained from her face. There were obvious signs of recent tears around her eyes and she looked very frail. William stood where he was as he did not want to alarm her by moving towards her.

"My dear you really must have something to drink"

Emily shook her head both ways saying "No. No. They will have drugged my food and my drink'.

Dr Robinson was more concerned about Emily's mental state. "You must have something. You will become ill if you neglect to nourish yourself."

Emily refused to take anything.

The doctor retired from the room but returned later at 5 30pm. He found Emily lying curled up on the bed albeit with her eyes wide open and staring at the ceiling. William poured her a glass of water asked "At least drink this?"

Emily replied "You drink it first. I will drink the rest"

Slowly and so that Emily could see clearly, William drank about a third of the water and emphasised a swallowing motion in his throat. Emily then held out her hand and he transferred the glass. Doctor Robinson felt great relief to then witness the "prisoner" sip the remainder of the water. It was, at least, a start. He felt his visit had been worthwhile.

In the evening William brought Emily a cup of tea. Once more he was made to taste the tea before Emily drank it.

"Please have something to eat, something light?"

Emily repeated her fear of being drugged whereupon William did his best to reassure her. He would see to the food himself. She could trust him for he was a doctor.

At this point Jackson entered the room. In an attempt to further alarm his wife, he simply announced that his solicitor was waiting for him downstairs as there was "business" to be sorted. Revived a bit by the tea she had had Emily spoke to Jackson albeit without looking at him.

"I would like to be able to see my solicitor, Mr Weeks."

"That is out of the question" retorted Jackson who promptly then left the room along with William. Emily heard once more the noise of the key being turned in the door of the "prison bedroom".

The evening thereafter was silent. There was no sound from the rest of the house as Emily, again, was left with her thoughts. Why silence even pervaded outside West View. No traffic. No voices. Even the birds appeared to have deserted the fully spread sycamore outside the bedroom window. The clock above the chest of drawers was broken. Darkness enfolded outside and Emily soon lost any sense of the time.

After 10 pm the rattle from the door told of the key being turned. Emily sat bolt upright in the bed hugging her legs. Her eyes were focused on the door as it slowly and silently pushed open. A woman appeared. She was tall and thin and wore what looked like a nurse's tunic. She barely glanced at Emily. The woman sat on the chair close to the window, put on a pair of metal rimmed spectacles and proceeded to read a book she had brought with her.

Was this lady a nurse or a guard posted there by her husband? Emily could not tell. Not a word passed between the two women. The chill of night descended. What thought Emily would be her fate? She could not sleep. She never did that night.

****

Robert Wagstaff was a well known figure in the circles of power and influence in Manchester. Even those who were not acquainted with "Bertie" as he was called could not miss him in a crowd. His portly build and deep booming voice by themselves brought attention upon him. Outwardly a jovial man he had cultivated this manner in order to encourage the trust of others who would then share confidences.

On that Sunday that was so fateful for Emily, Bertie was in his office in Manchester. As editor of the Northern Daily Telegraph he had, as always, to supervise Monday's edition of the newspaper. Sundays were always difficult days. Unlike weekdays there were not Council meetings to report upon, decisions in Parliament to comment on and no commercial dealings at a weekend. As the Courts did not sit there was nothing colourful to report from that source. Accordingly, unless there was a big Royal event or a heinous crime committed on the Saturday or Sunday, it was usually quite a task for Bertie to fill the pages for Monday's news hungry Mancunians.

At about 3 pm Bertie was scanning his eyes over an article about a meeting of a group of women that had taken place in a Church Hall in the north the city. This did not seem worth printing. Bertie thought to himself -"Votes for Women"? What a load of stuff and nonsense.

Just then Taylor, his assistant editor, entered the room. He had a perplexed expression on his face.

"Well" enquired Bertie.

Taylor responded hesitantly.

"Sir, I have just spoken on the telephone to our freelance man in Blackburn. You know Joe Mantle? Anyway, he seems to think that a woman has been abducted outside the church in Clitheroe and driven against her will to Blackburn. He's not sure but has heard in the street that the abductor was the lady's husband. Of course, it may not be true. Anyway, it's not possibly the sort of thing we want."

There was a noticeable silence. Bertie assimilated what he had just been told. It was true his newspaper did not report "tittle tattle", yet Bertie always had a sixth sense for a story and this sense was telling him there was something in this. Also, he was keen to reject what he thought as the boring article about the Church Hall meeting!!

"I want verification of what is going on. I need to know who is involved and where this woman has been taken to. To make tomorrow's edition I need information by 6.30 pm this evening.

The Editor of the Northern Daily Telegraph had his answer within half an hour. For, a phone call from one of Bertie's police informants told of a disturbance at Rover Street in Blackburn involving people from Clitheroe. There had been another communication to the Manchester newspaper from the freelance reporter in Clitheroe. He spoke of injury to the sister of the woman abducted and also named the woman who had been kidnapped.

In his usual loud voice, Bertie said "Well. Well. Well. Emily Emma Maud Hall."

This could not have appealed more to Bertie. For some years previously, Mr Wagstaff had suffered his only public humiliation when, having recklessly permitted the publication of an article alleging certain wrongdoings within Clitheroe Town Council, he was threatened with being sued for substantial damages. He was made to print an unreserved apology in his newspaper and put the sum of £1000 to a Clitheroe Charity. His nemesis at that time was the Mayor of Clitheroe none other than Mr Henry Hall - Emily's father!

Bertie summoned all his reporters and contacts. They were to interview all the witnesses in Clitheroe. A reporter was to make haste to Rover Street. He was going to turn the tables on the Hall family but, given his previous experience, he would ensure he stayed on the right side of the law this time.

Mr Wagstaff took charge of the article himself.

There was another call from the police informant. This was the "meat" on the bones of the story Bertie was hoping for. For the police had been shown a decree of the Court granted to the husband requiring that Emily reinstate her husband's conjugal rights. The only conclusion that could be reached was that Emily had refused to obey the Court order and her husband, to get his wife to comply, had had to carry her off. Yes. Bertie's sixth sense had again been found correct. This was a BIG story. This would sell many copies of the paper. This would indeed be a form of revenge.

The printing presses rolled. "The Abduction of a Wife at Clitheroe - Interesting Romance" was the headline.

****

On the evening of the Sunday of the kidnap, Jackson had spent much time in serious conversation with his "Council of War". Along with Dixon Robinson he had been round the house twice making sure that all entrances and potential access points to West View were locked, bolted or barricaded. Whether it was the police or Emily's family the townhouse had to be made impenetrable. Strict instructions were given to Susan the maid and the Nurse that no one was to be admitted to the property under any pretext and that, for the moment neither of them could be allowed to leave the house. In the circumstances these servants were allowed to make phone calls to their family and friends whenever necessary. It was hoped this state would not endure for very long.

Jackson had seen off the first "attack" by Hartley Baldwin but he knew this was just the beginning. He had spoken at length to his solicitor so he was convinced that he had both the moral and the legal right on his side so far as the taking of Emily was concerned. However, he was unsettled by the knowledge also conveyed by his solicitor that warrants had been issued for the arrest of himself, Dixon and William for the assault upon Betsy Baldwin.

"Why should they want to arrest me? I had nothing to do with all of this. I need to go and speak to the police and clear my name." panicked William. "It is outrageous that I, a doctor, am being accused of causing bodily harm. What will my patients think?"

"Be quiet" snapped Jackson. "Whether we like it or not we are in this together. No one, not even you can leave this house" he said staring at William.

"What about my patients?"

In a more conciliatory tone Jackson approached and put a hand upon the doctor's shoulder. "Do not worry unduly my friend. There was such a melee at the church the police will have no evidence of any assault. It is but a ruse to try and get us out of the house and thereby allow Hartley Baldwin to take my wife away from me again. It will all be over soon".

In the background there was the sound of someone clearing their throat. Jackson glanced across to the door. "Well, what is it?" he enquired seeing the maid standing there.

"It is Michael. He arrived to see you about one o'clock. As you weren't here he stayed in the kitchen with Shammy. With all that has happened since you got back here sir, I thought you'd other things on your mind. Now though Michael says he has to go home."

Jackson heaved a sigh, just another thing for him to deal with. "Tell Michael I will see him shortly."

Jackson turning back to the others in the room said;

"We have to organise supplies. Isabel, can you draw up a list of the essentials we shall need? Give the list to Dixon. Dixon, contact the supplier and place the necessary order."

"But that means opening the door? Is that not dangerous? How long are we supposed to make provision for?" enquired Dixon.

"Just do it, please" Jackson said dismissing the questions. Then, upon seeing curiosity remaining in the eyes of the others he said "Get prepared for one month."

He strode out of the room leaving the others in a state of some disbelief.

****

The kitchen at West View was not a large area but was perfectly adequate for the needs of Isabel's normally modest household. An iron range along the far wall, ample wooden worktops, a large shelved pantry going off to the left and suspended from the ceiling a wooden pulley. There was a solid table with 3 chairs in the middle of the room. At one of the chairs sat a fair haired youth. He had bright red cheeks and with his curly locks appeared younger than his actual twenty years.

Michael had met Jackson some twelve months ago. Shammy, the wire haired fox terrier had run off whilst Michael was walking in woods near to his father's rectory. Michael had looked everywhere for the dog. After more than an hour, he headed home despondent and upset.Then, on the path by the river leading to the rectory, this tall smart man appeared clutching a rather wet Shammy. Jackson claimed to have witnessed the dog losing his footing and rolling into the river whereupon he plucked the small creature up and back onto dry land.Whether true or not Michael was just overjoyed to have Shammy back and Jackson became his hero. It wasn' t unusual for Michael to appear at Rover Street on a Sunday for Michael did not have friends (other than his dog) and his own father was always busy at church.

For his part, Jackson did not discourage Michael's visits. Jackson had always dreamt of having a son - instructing his male heir about life, manhood and the ways of the world. Obviously, Michael was not his son but, for Jackson, a young man who looked up to him was the next best thing.

That Sunday though Michael was bored. He had been shown by Susan to the kitchen as Jackson was not at home. He had been told he must keep an eye on the range and make sure it was topped up with coal whenever necessary. He must have been there for 4 hours at least. He was hungry but his upbringing and nature meant he would not help himself to food without being invited to.

Shammy was curled up by the range. The sound of approaching footsteps caused the dog to become alert. He stood up. As the footsteps grew louder Shammy barked and raced to meet the visitors to the kitchen.

Jackson entered the room with his sister.

Normally Jackson would have bent down and made a fuss of the dog but, on this occasion, he was very much preoccupied. He went straight to Michael, put a hand on his shoulder and said "I'm sorry Michael as you may have heard, there's been a lot going on today though nothing for you to worry about. However, Shammy and you must stay at this house for now as it's not possible for you to go home. Please telephone your father and let him know. If there's a problem then speak to me. Susan will find you a room upstairs. We will organise some food shortly. Now, off you go."

Michael, looking quizzical but lost for words, followed Susan out of the kitchen. The little dog gave a whimper and trotted off.

Jackson then turned to his sister. "We have a problem. Mrs Blanchard went out this morning to meet her nephew in Manchester. Now she will not get into the house. Would you and Susan be able to prepare food for all of us?"

It may be imagined this request amounted to impudence. After all Jackson was a guest in Isabel's house and it was only by virtue of his actions that the cook, Mrs Blanchard, was not able to perform her duties in the kitchen. Isabel was though very close to Edmund. He had always exercised a brotherly charm over her and whilst she would not obsequiously do his bidding she was not easily offended by her younger brother. It was also the case that West View was not her house. She stayed there by grace and favour of her elder brother Raynsford. Indeed, Raynsford had encouraged her to accommodate Edmund. He had even provided Jackson with the carriage employed in the abduction of Emily. Isabel had no experience of catering. She responded that she would organise something.

Time was passing. It crossed Jackson's mind that he should see and speak to Emily, but no, why should he? He had so much to do and much to think about. Between them, William and the nurse could deal with his recalcitrant wife.

Jackson proceeded to the basement of the house. There he found some suitable pieces of rope, wood, old pulleys and tools. He was a practical man and set about his task. He remained in the basement until after midnight. When he emerged the house was devoid of noise. He made his way quietly up to the ground floor and then upwards to his room. From the first floor he chanced to glance outside. The remnants of the crowd were now drifting way. He spotted two constables on duty at the front of the house.

The exertions of this momentous day had taken their toll on him. He was weary. Jackson did not know what the next day might bring but, unlike his wife along the corridor, he quickly enjoyed the onset of a very deep sleep.

****

At dawn on the Monday morning nothing much had changed outside Rover Street. Emily's bedroom was filled with a double floor length window looking out across the street to Granville Terrace. Her guard, the nurse, had left the room at 6 am. Exhausted but relieved to be by herself, Emily pulled herself off of the bed and went towards the window where she pulled back the damask curtains and gazed out. She spied the police constables on duty but they did not look upwards. It mattered not for the police had not rescued her yesterday and there was no reason why they should do so today.

Emily tried the window but it was locked. She so wanted some fresh air. The branches on the tree nearby swayed in the gentle wind which made her even more eager to ventilate the room. About to turn round she noticed a figure at the window of the first floor flat across in Granville Terrace. Emily rubbed her sleepy eyes and focused and saw that the figure appeared to be waving. She could hardly believe it for there, so relatively close to her, was her sister Esther. She never questioned what Esther was doing there or why she was there, Emily just felt better for she was not totally alone. Emily smiled and waved and gestured across the street. She went to the bedroom door only to find, of course, that it was locked. The prisoner wanted someone to tell her what was going to happen and yet she did not want to see anyone.

Elsewhere at West View others were stirring. Dixon Robinson was in the kitchen. The previous evening when it was apparent there would be difficulties catering for everyone, Dixon had put his best foot forward and impressed the inmates with a mutton stew and dumplings he had served up. Before he had gone abroad with Jackson, Dixon had done a bit of travelling and had learnt to prepare food for himself and his travelling companions. He was now setting about breakfast.

Next to appear was Michael. Dixon found a raw sausage and flung it over to Shammy.

"Excuse me sir" said Michael. "I cannot stay in this house. I have to get to my work or I will lose my job."

"Now that is not up to me, you will have to speak to Mr Jackson."

****

Meanwhile at Clitheroe, Hartley Baldwin was pacing up and down in his living room. Betsy had risen but had not yet changed into her day clothes. She sat in her armchair in her dressing gown with a cup of tea on the table by her side. Betsy knew better than to interrupt her husband when he was so obviously working out what had to be done. In any event she herself was still in pain and discomfort from the attack upon her the previous day.

"Why cannot the police arrest the felon?" muttered Hartley. "The assault upon you was outrageous."

'Now, now, dear it was not that bad. It is Emily we have to try and help. At least Esther managed to rent the flat in Granville Terrace. She'll be able to get a message to us if anything happens."

"That's not the point." grumbled Hartley. "We cannot just sit around doing nothing. We said to your late father we would look after Emily and we must keep our word"

Just then Charnock, the Baldwins' butler entered the room.

"Excuse me, Sir" and held out a tray with the post and the morning paper on it.

"Thank you, Charnock" and turning back to his wife Hartley said "I'll go to the office soon. I will speak to my people, and, if we can go back to Blackburn this afternoon we will. I will not let Jackson think he has won. I cannot let Emily imagine we have abandoned her."

Betsy was concerned, though she did not show it. She knew her husband was a clever and careful man. He was a proud man but he was not a street fighter. She did not want to see Hartley dragged down and getting into deep trouble on account of a bounder like Jackson.

Hartley sat back into his armchair and opened the newspaper -The Northern Daily Telegraph. Instantly he tensed, sat bolt upright and exclaimed:

"I do not believe this. It is all over the front page...........an Interesting Romance..............what poppycock......what a man will do for love..........I cannot read any more of this. It is all lies. We might have to sue."

"Please calm down. This is not like you Hartley. You can always speak to the newspaper and put your side of the story."

"Certainly not, this is a private matter. Family washing does not get aired in public. At least mine does not. The Telegraph has gone down in my estimation. I never thought it would lower itself to print such salacious rubbish." He paused and his eyes dropped to the bottom of the page.

"Now, I understand. That jumped up pipsqueak Wagstaff. Remember him? The very Wagstaff whom your father almost crucified fifteen years ago. He is responsible for this. We will never get a fair press from that man. I cannot wait here any longer."

Hartley bent down, gently kissed his wife and set off for his office.

****

There was a gentle knock at the bedroom door. The key was turned and William entered with boiled eggs, tea and toast for Emily.

"How are you?" he asked solicitously.

"I just want out of here" Emily said in a voice that was faint through tiredness.

"I know" said William." Had I but known yesterday all that was going to happen I would never have agreed to help. I am so sorry."

"Surely then you can help me get out?" said Emily trying to test the veracity of William's words.

"Madam, I cannot leave the house myself. My brother and Mr Jackson are quite adamant that no one can leave. It is why my brother is having to do the cooking. Now try your eggs"

Emily picked up and passed the spoon to William. She did not have to explain. He broke into the first egg, took the top onto the spoon and swallowed. He handed back the spoon before pouring a little tea into the cup and drinking that. He went to leave Emily to partake of her breakfast but as he left she asked in her quiet voice:

"Doctor, what am I supposed to do for clothes? I have no clothes here other than those I am wearing?" William was a bit taken aback. It had not crossed his mind. In fact, he found he was embarrassed and did not know how to respond. All he could say was "I will be back later."

****

Of the occupants at West View that morning, Jackson was the last to rise. After dressing and checking himself in the wardrobe mirror he went directly to the kitchen. When he appeared the talk amongst the others there ceased as if it was necessary to establish Jackson's mood before continuing. He did appear less prickly than he had been the previous day. He asked how everyone was then turned to William:

"And how is our favourite hostage?" he enquired with a smirk.

Dr Robinson saw no reason for Mrs Jackson to be referred to with such a lack of respect but bit his tongue. "She has had her breakfast and wants to know about her... em.....her wardrobe." He turned away.

"And what about you my boy?" he said smiling at Michael.

"Sir, I need to get to my work by this afternoon. I'm worried I might lose my job.

"Do not fear Michael. You will be at your work this afternoon."

The Robinsons were perplexed. If no one was permitted in or out of the house how was Jackson able to give such assurance to Michael?

Susan came to the door of the kitchen. "It is a phone call for you Sir." Jackson went away to take the call.

****

For want of something to do and without anyone to speak to, Emily sat at the dressing table and decided to write a letter. She had not decided to whom the letter would be addressed, one of her sisters? Her solicitor? She did not know. She wrote:

"Less than 24 hours ago my life was as I wanted it to be. The peace and serenity of the cottage where there was a beauty in the simplicity of everything. The ornaments and little pictures of little value yet each carried for me the sentiment of familiarity and the comfort of warmth.

With this cruel twist of fate I am as if covered in an ice cold shroud. I am possessed of no feeling, numbed by the walls of this prison. These walls which may possess colour to others but which are, to my eyes, stark and grey.

If I countenance my fate I shrivel inside. The nightmare of the asylum I try in vain to caste away. But I lack anymore the force of will or strength to arrest such course should this be the decree of my husband. And what if ....." Emily put down the pen.

Distracted by a hubbub outside, she moved once more to the window. It was hard for her to understand, for outside the house there seemed to have gathered from almost nowhere a crowd of some thirty or so persons - men, women and some children too. They were standing about. Most were talking amongst themselves and others just laughing. They were not moving. Emily stepped back from the window. She did not want to be seen.

****

Jackson returned from the phone and met his sister in the Drawing Room.

"You look troubled brother"

"I've had disturbing news. That was my solicitor. Apparently the taking of my wife yesterday is all over the Northern Daily Telegraph. I cannot understand it."

"Surely if the public know why you had to do what you did then this is good?"

"Isabel. You do not see. My solicitor says that the public will be drawn to this house like bees to a honey pot. There will be members of the press from all over the north and maybe some from London feasting on us like vultures. This is never what I intended. What is more the publicity maybe used by Hartley Baldwin. In fact, I'd not be surprised if, knowing the press hounds are about, he stages another rescue attempt."

Dixon appeared. Jackson assumed again the mood of a Commander.

"Dick, until I can make certain arrangements, I need you to go upstairs to the spare front room and keep a good look out on what is happening outside. If you see Hartley Baldwin or any of his cronies anywhere near the house let me know immediately. I'll likely be by the telephone in the study.

By the time Dixon arrived at his look out post, the crowd outside had swollen to about seventy people.

****

At Blackburn Police Station, Chief Constable Lewis was focused on preparing an address he was due to make on the coming Friday to a special meeting of Chief Constables at the Station Hotel in Manchester.

His dalliance with Mr Baldwin the previous day was furthest from his mind until the duty Police Sergeant came into the office, saluted and said:

"Sir, we have just heard from Constable Brown at Rover Street. It seems a crowd of around seventy have congregated outside the house at Number 2. It's not known if they are there to cause trouble."

The Chief Constable sighed. He was not a subscriber to the Northern Daily Telegraph and was therefore bemused and could not understand why anyone would congregate outside a private residence.

"Oh, very well then, in case there's a problem send another four men there. If there's no difficulty in half an hour then two of them should come back as they will be needed here."

The Chief Constable reverted to his proposed speech. However, within fifteen minutes, he was again interrupted. It was a young Police Cadet who had been assisting at the front desk.

He saluted.

The eyes of the Chief Constable looked up from his speech without his head altering position.

"Yes?

"Sir, we have had a call from the policeman at Clitheroe who understands that a group of about 100 from that town is planning to head this way for the Rover Street house this very afternoon."

Chief Constable Lewis was suddenly gripped with the image that followed from what he had just been told.

"This could turn out to be a violent and bloody riot. Get me Manchester Headquarters. We need reinforcements."

****

The old leather binoculars had seen better days. They had scuff marks. There were, by now, superior models on the market. This pair had been with Jackson during his service days in America and well travelled having also been used by their owner to survey the New Zealand countryside. The binoculars were now in the hands of Dixon

Robinson. He grabbed hold of them from the cloakroom as he made his way to his "look out" post.

Dixon's eyesight was perfectly good. He could view the street and crowd without any aid. The binoculars however made him feel important. They were in keeping with the appointment he had received from Jackson. It mattered not to Dixon what the adventure was, be it the pioneering to New Zealand, the kidnap of Mrs Jackson or, as now, the siege the young Mr Robinson was just content to feel he was Jackson's right hand man.

Robinson did though stray as his concentration weakened. With the binoculars he espied a terrier in the park chasing a much bigger sandy coloured dog. The owner of the large dog bawled at his pet's tormentor. The little dog stopped, stared, lifted its leg and then ran off in another direction.

The binoculars scanned the nearer buildings. Dixon held them steady catching sight of movement within an upper storey room in Granville Terrace. A young woman had risen from her dressing table and had discarded her nightgown. Dixon felt awful but could not persuade his hands to change the direction of the binoculars until the noise of a horn blasted out nearby. He immediately gathered his senses, pulled away the binoculars and looked down. He saw the green and gold livery of the wagon emblazoned on the side of which read "STONES of PRESTON, Greengrocers and Purveyors of Quality Meat & Fish". He had completely forgotten about the provisions order made the previous day. The wagon was trying to make its way through the crowd.

In something of a panic, Dixon rushed downstairs to find Jackson in the study.

"What are we going to do? That's the wagon from Preston with the supplies. We are going to have to open the door."

"No. We are not." said Jackson. "Come with me."

****

In the street, the curious mingled with the various press reporters. Some would debate what they thought were the rights and the wrongs of what had been in the Telegraph that morning whilst others, where there was space, sat around in little groups enjoying what was a very sunny morning. A man from a nearby district had set up a stall under one of the trees from which he sold refreshments and ice creams. The extra officers from Blackburn Police Station arrived. There was a hush in the crowd. The sight of this squad of Peelers suggested that more drama might be about to unfold. Was the house to be stormed?

There was no sign of urgency displayed by this new force. They stood at ease now in two separate groups and one Constable even went to the stall where he was handed a cup of tea. The general noise of the crowd resumed.

The Stones' wagon could only inch forward as, by and large, the horn had been ignored. The Police Officers managed, in time, to cordon off part of the crowd creating a narrow corridor for the wagon to move and park outside West View.

There was the sound of a thud above the crowd followed by a rattle.

"Look up there" said an eagle eyed man wearing a flat cloth cap. He pointed upwards towards a window on the first floor. It had been opened and figures could be observed moving near to the front of the window. Again there was hush.

A metal pole then protruded at an angle. This was followed by a mass of rope and finally a medium sized wicker basket. The fruits of Jackson's labours of the previous evening were now on display and about to be put to the test.

The basic pulley system allowed the basket to be slowly lowered to street level. A suspicious policeman waited and took hold of the basket when it was within reach. The officer found a brief note inside which read "Please load the provisions".

The note was passed to the man from Stones. He opened the wagon and started loading the basket. When it was fairly full of tins and packets of this and that a small burly man stepped forward and said to the delivery man "Hold on. I'll give you a hand."

They both took hold of the rope after the Stones man had waved up towards the window. At this point some in the crowd shouted "Heave" This shout became infectious and before long the whole crowd was chanting "Heave." "Heave."

The next load to be raised looked like fish. When it was about half way up the delivery man's hands slipped on the rope and the basket started sliding downwards.

"Ooops" was the crescendo from the spectators before the stocky little man managed to halt the descent and the basket moved once more in an upwards direction.

A pale man in a pale suit with a droopy moustache then came forward. As the storeman waved for the next basket lift, the voice of the pale man said clearly "Halt".

When the delivery man turned around there was revealed in the basket four bottles of wine and a box of very choice cigars and the pale man was very happy. The photographer from the Northern Daily Telegraph reckoned Mr Wagstaff would be very pleased with the shot he had just captured.

The Stone's man shut up the wagon. The crowd dramatically made a path for him to leave the street and cheered him on his way.

****

Emily was not the only one who picked up a pen that morning.

Having observed the ongoings from an armchair in the front window of the Granville Terrace flat, Esther elected during the subsequent lull to write a letter to her sister.

"My Dearest Em,

I miss you so much. The wrench of our being parted like this is great. It does though ease my personal angst that, in a silly way, I am here with you. I could not bear to be at the Cottage where my imagination would torture me so.

I feel guilty. Guilty, that I cannot help you. Guilty, that I cannot somehow drag you away from that monster. I can and do pray for you.

Please rest assured that Hartley will come up with something. He will not rest until you are back safe and well in the bosom of your family.

Can we have a little game? If you see me at my window, wave your right hand if you are well, wave your left hand if you are not good. And wave both hands if you are in grave danger. Of course I do not know what I could possibly do but I can let the others know.

Remember Em - You are not alone.

Your loving sister

Esther."

Just then there was a knock at the door.

Hartley Baldwin Junior entered the flat.

"Father sent me to check on you."

"Oh. I am fine. I have settled in well."

She proceeded to narrate all that had occurred that morning. How she had only managed one brief glimpse of her sister.

"Emily will not put herself in the window for all of those people to gawp at her".

Hartley Junior spotted an envelope addressed to Emily Hall.

"Do you want me to deliver that?"

"Oh. I do not know. Do you think it safe to approach the house? I was just going to post it."

"Leave it to me" assured the young man as he popped the letter in his pocket, kissed his Aunt on the forehead and left.

****

Baldwin Junior then mingled with the crowd. The only risk of his being identified was if either of the Robinsons or Jackson himself saw his face. Hartley Junior therefore ensured he was always surrounded by others and that he kept his head looking downwards. He reached the vendor's stall, engaged the stallholder in conversation and bought lemonade.

It was the most natural thing for a stranger to strike a conversation here, for everyone wanted to know and to talk about the abduction. Hartley Junior was though only half engaged in conversation. His eye was trying to plot a way to get past the policeman on duty at the front door to access the letterbox there. With his mind on what the vendor was saying and his eyes upon the policeman he failed to see the man approach him on his left side. The man wore an unironed shirt, sported unpolished down at heel brogues and when he spoke his breath was unpleasant.

"So what do you make of all this?" said the scruffy individual.

"Of all what?" responded Hartley.

"You know, Mr Jackson's demonstration of love. I mean who does she think she is? I have to find out the views of the man in the street. If you could then just tell me in your own words....."

Hartley Junior panicked. The scruffy man had by now produced his notebook. The young man realised he was in conversation with a journalist. How his father had that very day drummed it into the whole family- "On no account say anything to the papers. Neither attack Jackson nor defend Emily. Anything we say will be twisted. Do not give the vultures the satisfaction."

These words rang in Hartley junior's head. Yet he did not want to draw undue attention to himself. He thought quickly.

He then addressed the scruffy journalist, "Now I do not know which publication you are from although it does not matter. You see I am not local. I am not from these parts. I have just come upon all these people."

Holding out his hand in the direction of the stallholder, Hartley declared "Now this is the man you want to speak to. He knows everything and everyone. His views are very interesting".

Hartley Junior then tapped the shoulder of a passing lady "Excuse me" he said and put distance between himself and the newspaper man.

"Look up there" shouted a voice at the back of the crowd. This directed the gaze of many towards the same upstairs window. The basket had again been pushed outward but it was not empty. The audience could see a bit of white over the edge of the basket. Then as it got a bit lower a head appeared. Laughter broke out.

"It's a dog, It's a dog" they shrieked. Shammy looked petrified. He wailed at the world as he made his alarming descent.

As the basket got nearer to the ground, a figure moved towards it, removed Shammy and held the dog in his arms. Shammy calmed down and then licked the stranger's face.The basket was then lifted back up.

"What's next?" posed the crowd. "This is better than the circus" said a woman to her children by her side.

They did not have to wait for very long.

All eyes became fixed on the upstairs window. A pair of legs appeared first. With help from those inside the torso of a young lad was pushed out with his hands gripping to the rope for dear life.

The rope swung one way and then the other with Michael holding on. At first the crowd drew a collective breath as they feared a tragedy may then unfold. However, once the slow downward momentum was steady, they decided to encourage the young abseiler by singing in joyful unison "In for a penny, in for a pound" by Gilbert and Sullivan made famous the previous decade.

Very sheepishly, Michael, with the aid of a stranger, landed on the ground and was reunited with Shammy before scurrying off. The stranger retreated and, almost unseen, merged back into the crowd.

****

In charge of the rope and basket had been the Robinsons. As soon as they saw that Michael had landed safely Dixon returned to the study leaving his brother to pull up the rope, curl it up and put it with the pulley and the basket. He and Dixon had been so eager to unhitch the basket and get Michael ready for his escape neither had noticed the small white envelope stuffed in the comer of it. As he turned with the rope the sun caught the corner of the envelope and William then took hold of it, turned it over and saw the writing "Emily Hall".

William put the envelope into his inside pocket. Should he tell his brother about this? Should he inform Jackson?

****

In his office in Clitheroe, Hartley Baldwin sat going over in his mind the options he had as he saw them. He had had a long conversation with the Area Superintendent of Police. The warrant held by the police for the arrest of Jackson and his associates did not empower officers to enter the house. Surely, they could be "flushed out"? They would have to come out eventually. They have to leave to get food? He could simply play a waiting game and, when the door was opened, a band of Clitheroe men could rush in and retake possession of Emily. If it was properly planned Jackson would have no warning and the intruders would be in and out before he knew it. However the police would no doubt be obstructive. They'd hardly allow unwelcome visitors from Clitheroe to waltz into Jackson's house. This was a lot more problematic than perhaps had first appeared.

He had gathered though from his sources in the Police that there were "behind the scenes" conversations between the Authorities and Jackson's solicitors to try and prevail upon the miscreants to voluntarily surrender and attend the Court by arrangement. If so, would the police remain at Rover Street? Should the answer to that be in the negative then that could be his big opportunity?

Another option then presented itself to Hartley's legal mind. If the state did not allow a citizen to be imprisoned against his will indefinitely without recourse to a Court of Law, then surely this same rule, if properly presented, could be argued in support of Emily's freedom? Before he could follow through this chain of thought Hartley's secretary entered his office.

"Mr Baldwin, your son is waiting to see you."

Hartley got up, walked to the door and ushered Hartley Junior forward "Come on then. Come in." The office door was closed behind them.

"How is Esther? Is she alright in that flat?"

"Yes father. She seems fine. I was shown which room Emily is being held in."

This was important to Hartley Senior for if there was to be a rescue operation, he could work out by reference to archived plans the optimum route to precisely where his sister-in-law was being held.

Hartley Junior then reported how Esther had witnessed lots of stores being hoisted up into the house.

"Damn" swore Hartley "That means they can stay in the house for a long time. That is a blow".

Hartley Senior only half listened to his son's narration about the dog and the boy coming down the basket and rope. His ears though pricked up when he heard of how his son had put into the basket Esther's letter.

"Very good, my boy. Well done. If only we could find out if Emily got that letter then it might be possible for us to get messages to her."

The door opened. This time the Secretary said "That is Mr Heston to see you."

"Send him in" said Hartley.

"Good afternoon, Sir" said Heston then, seeing that it was Hartley Junior in his father's company the coachman continued:

"I have forty good men ready and willing to go to Blackburn and bring back Miss Emily."

"That is very pleasing to know Heston and I am grateful for your efforts. If I can work out a plan, I will let you know."

Hartley Senior was appreciative of Heston's loyalty. Mr Baldwin was though not unwise. Heston, when off duty, mixed in rather undesirable circles. These men he had secured would be ruffians spoiling for a fight or men who had reason to hate Jackson. They were not men filled with noble motivation. These would not be men blessed with any guile. He had to have regard to Betsy's advice. One false move on his part could not just tarnish but ruin his reputation and professional standing.

****

That afternoon Jackson was feeling quite pleased with himself. He had procured and had imported to the house the victuals both necessary and luxury to sustain the household. Further supplies could employ the same route. No attempt had been made thus far to stop the supply. There had been no mutiny from those incarcerated at West View. He had got Michael out of the way.

The telephone was a great invention he said to himself with a grin. Jackson could orchestrate from the end of the telephone or so it appeared to him.

One thing did trouble Jackson a lot. Twice the police had knocked on the front door to execute a warrant. Each time the door had remained bolted and the inmates silent. In telephone discussion with his solicitor, Jackson knew the warrant related to himself and the Robinsons, and that, if executed, they would be taken to Clitheroe. He knew the warrant was the main cause of the siege. Yes, he had to protect himself against any serious attack by Hartley Baldwin and his cronies. However, if he was arrested in terms of the warrant, how long would he be away from West View? He could not expect Isabel and the two servants to prevent Emily escaping or being rescued whilst he was absent. His solicitor conveyed that the police were interested in coming to an arrangement with Jackson for a form of voluntary surrender. Once more Jackson had to plot a strategy.

****

Emily heard the gentle tap at the door. She had been lying down with her eyes shut - not asleep. She pulled herself up as supper appeared on a tray. Dr Robinson was again the waiter.

Supper was faggots, potatoes and some not very appetising looking cabbage. The understandable conclusion was that Dixon Robinson was not "at home" in the vegetable department. By now Emily was slightly more trusting in that she did not insist upon everything being tasted. On this occasion she pointed to the faggots whereupon William took a fork and sampled the meat.

As she sat by the small table she began to pick at the food but still could not summon up any appetite. It was also the case that Emily did not like being watched as she ate. It was clear that, unlike on other occasions, William was not simply going to walk out of the room.

William sidled over to the window to try and peek out without being noticed below.

"There are still a lot of people out there."

Emily was in the mood to converse as she had not spoken to anyone that day.

“Why? I do not understand why anyone should want to hang about here.”

Dr Robinson then appreciated how cushioned from the world Emily had been these two days or so.

“Oh, this is all big news. The paper was full of it this morning, all about you and Mr Jackson. You are quite famous.”

Emily went white with shock. She abandoned her cutlery on the plate.

"Now, now "said Dr Robinson reassuringly "It will all blow over I am sure. There's nothing to worry about."

Nervously Emily enquired "But what, what can they possibly think is going to occur? What are they waiting for? Are they going to cheer when I'm taken away to the asylum? Is that it? Am I akin to a circus act?"

William could see that Emily was working herself into a frenzy. He wanted to put his arm around her but feared that such a gesture maybe misinterpreted. He gathered his own senses, held her shoulders and said in as confident a manner as he could:

"Look, Mrs Jackson. You are not and I repeat not going to be taken to an asylum. Mr Jackson does genuinely care for you I am certain of that. Anyway the crowd outside are waiting for him, not you."

Emily looked perplexed.

"Well, I don't know if I'm supposed to say or not. The police want to arrest Mr Jackson and also my brother and myself. It concerns your sister, Mr Baldwin's wife. She was hurt you see and we are all to be taken to Court."

Slowly Emily felt a bit reassured. This explained the crowd. This explained the police outside and the baskets of food being pulleyed into the house. Further it occurred to her that when Jackson was taken away she might be able to escape. She looked at William, smiled the briefest of smiles and returned to her supper. She was aware of William walking towards the door. He seemed to hesitate.

Emily said gently "Was there something else?"

"Oh, I do not see it matters" responded the Doctor as he pulled the envelope from his hand, placed it upon the mahogany dressing table and left the room.

With immediate curiosity Emily put down the cutlery once again, rose and walked to the dressing table. She recognised right away her sister's writing. She could not believe it. A warm current seemed to surge through her body as she picked up the envelope and as she did so the key in the door was roughly turned and instinctively Emily rushed over to the bed and buried the envelope under her pillow. It was hidden just in time. Jackson strode into the room.

"Emily. I must apologise for the fact I've so far been unable to speak to you."

Enthused by having seen Esther's writing and knowing of what she surmised might be Jackson's imminent arrest Emily was not cowed in her husband's presence.

"You presume that I desire to parley with you. I suggest that that is, in the circumstances, a presumption too far."

Jackson ignored this repulse to his approach.

"All being well I will sit down with you tomorrow afternoon. I am sure we will be able then to sort out what is to happen."

"What is to happen indeed? You kidnap me and hold me here without a by or leave. Now, only now, you want to consult with me? I had no say in you going to New Zealand. You gave me no choice when you demanded to return here. In Kensington I made my position clear to you but you do not listen. It is only what you say or want that matters so why should I think my views matter now. I have already said I require clothes but, as usual, no attention is paid to me. I still have only my Sunday attire."

"I was never told about your clothes."

Emily had to back down. It was William she had spoken to about the clothes. She did not want to get him into trouble so she quickly changed the subject.

"I think I have the right to speak to my solicitor."

Jackson could not allow this. He felt irritation and even rage rise at what he perceived as an impertinent suggestion. Was his wife inclined to alter the marriage settlement? He was about to lose his cool yet he knew that this may not be a good moment to lose his temper.

"We'll see. We'll see. We have lots to speak about. I am hopeful this can be resolved if only we can but drop our guard and speak honestly to each other. I will see you tomorrow. I promise."

Before Emily could challenge any of this Jackson slipped out locking the door behind him.

Emily extinguished the light in the room and gazed out of her "prison" window. Many from the crowd had by this time drifted off home but there were still about a couple of dozen loitering in the moonlight. Some were chatting to the police. The stall was closed up and the vendor had retired for the night. With the light off Emily could look upon the evening sky and be unseen by anyone below. She could be immersed in her thoughts.

The prospect of seeing Jackson and having to stomach his incessant demands made her stomach churn. It was indeed the last thing she wanted to have to endure. Imprisoned as she was Emily could not avoid the inevitable confrontation for Jackson held all the cards. Or did he? An idea began to form and yet, as this seed grew, the doubt as to whether she could carry it off grew in equal measure.

What if? What if? Emily mused to herself. Since his return from New Zealand he has witnessed her obduracy, her rejection and her bitterness. It will be exactly what he will expect from her the next day. Now, if Emily could devise a line to take that was less harsh, that would give her husband hope then would he be more benign and give her more freedom? Yet Emily found it hard to camouflage her true feelings. She could not become a convincing liar.

A second night in the Blackburn house, her mind in so many ways confused about how best to handle the next day. The omens for any sleep were, once more, not good at all.

****

Jackson that night had not dissimilar dilemmas to those of his wife. Given his predisposition all Jackson really wanted to do was enjoy the total control he then exercised over Emily. It was a total slight to him that not only did Emily refuse to do his bidding but that her failure to obey the Conjugal Rights Order was now a matter of public knowledge. He felt he was the object of public ridicule, the butt of people's jokes. It made his blood boil and it was all her fault.

What did he really want? In the short term he wanted to teach her a lesson, yet what of the longer term? He would prefer not to lose the comfort of the marriage settlement and the security her wealth cloaked him in. There were the other comforts a wife can offer which, though less of a priority in the grand scheme of his life, were not unattractive. If he hectored Emily too much he could ruin everything.

Was it all really irretrievable? Was he wasting his time? He had observed how determined Emily appeared to be. Should he alter his approach? Jackson was very uncertain how things would evolve. He did not though agonise over it all. No. What will be, will be. Unlike his wife, Jackson could disconnect his mind and allow sleep to take over.

****

Emily retired from her window vantage point. As she turned around she heard an owl hooting from somewhere upon the big tree. Then suddenly she remembered. She ran to the bed and threw herself onto it, her feverish hands raced about under the pillows. At once she felt the envelope and pulled it out. In the moonlight she could still make out Esther's writing. She closed her eyes and held the unopened letter to her chest as if it was her sister herself that she was hugging.

****

Tuesday was the third day of the siege. The sharp wind reminded everyone that in the North of England in March winter is never very far away. This was acutely so at West View. The property was built on the highest point on Rover Street and whilst aptly named for its frontage to the west, it was particularly exposed to the rigours of an easterly wind funnelling down over the Pennines.

For some reason the male residents were all awake and up early. They gathered at the kitchen table. Dixon prepared and served up his standard breakfast of eggs, toast and tea. Neither of the others dared complain lest they be asked to take over kitchen duties.

"You may be pleased to learn my solicitor reckons he has reached an accord with the police." This was, of course, Jackson speaking. "All being well we are to be allowed to travel to Clitheroe at our own convenience"

"You mean we will not be arrested. Not taken from here in handcuffs?"

"That is part of the deal. My solicitor has a barrister who will represent all of us. I cannot say exactly when this is to happen."

"But what will happen to us at Court?" Dixon asked with a taint of worry in his tone.

"My solicitor says all will be well. He will speak to each of us at the Court. Do not fret Dick. The solicitor knows what he is doing."

William had thus far remained quiet. He then piped up quietly "What about Mrs Jackson?"

This seemed to irritate Jackson. "It is of no concern to you Dr Robinson. The lady is my wife. I have made arrangements."

William was worried but felt he could not make any further enquiry upon the subject.

"Excuse me" said Susan as she appeared before the assembly in the kitchen. "That is your solicitor on the phone again, Mr Jackson."

****

First thing after his breakfast, Hartley Baldwin telephoned his office. He had one or two things to attend to. He would not be in to the office until later. He could be reached at his home but only on a matter of emergency.

Just then, as was part of the routine, Charnock appeared with the newspaper on a tray.

" No mail today Sir, just the newspaper".

Hartley had the previous day ensured the order for the Northern Daily Telegraph was cancelled. He would not suffer again the jaundiced articles by Wagstaff. Instead he ordered and was now presented with the Times. A good solid London publication read up and down the country and indeed worldwide. As he browsed the initial pages Hartley thought "This is more like it." It was when he turned to page 4 his eyes seemed to stop blinking.

He stared and stared. The report, under the headline "Clitheroe Kidnap-Latest" set out how Mr Jackson, it argued, was possessed of both the moral and legal right to physically prevail upon his wife to be with him. It was likely to prove an issue to be determined in the Courts, but what the article posed was what chaos would result to the social fabric if a wife could simply elect with no cause to disobey her husband? In this case Mrs Jackson would be best to reflect upon her stupid folly, reunite with her devoted husband and behave as she is expected to behave."

Hartley quickly turned to the next page. It was the letters page. Half the correspondents were writing in relation to the Rover Street affair. To a letter they were in support of Mr Jackson and what was referred to as his "romantic endeavour." Hartley allowed the paper to drop onto the floor and slumped back into his armchair.

****

Jackson whistled as he returned from the telephone.

"Someone's cheerful" observed Dixon.

"And with good cause my friend. I have just ordered half a dozen newspapers. Apparently, I am something of a hero. Just wait until Mrs Jackson reads them." he said with amusement.

Turning then to William he said "My good man. The papers should be here soon. I wonder if you would just go up and when the paper boy appears lower the basket?"

William did not care to be treated in this manner but, as he could not tolerate being in Jackson's company when he was so arrogant, he left the kitchen without demur.

****

Across the street Esther was again sat in her chair in the bay window of the flat. There was little of note that met her eyes so she would pass the time reading a book. After about twenty minutes or so, she heard a ringing from outside. A lad with a large bag over his shoulder was ringing a bell held in his hand and so obviously trying to gain attention.

The boy looked upwards. As had occurred the previous day, down came the basket. The boy seemed to know what to do. He removed the newspapers from the bag and put them into the basket.

As Esther followed with her eyes the upward climb of the basket, she caught sight of movement at another window. She stared over and saw quite clearly Emily. Emily was waving across to her. Esther stood up and frantically waved back. How pleased she was to have this communication with her sister. After a couple of moments Emily disappeared from view. It then struck poor Esther that Emily had been waving her left hand. Oh gosh. What did it mean? Was it left hand for alright or was it right hand. She had only written the note the day before but was now confused as to what the signals meant. The fact was Emily must have got her note. She could maybe chance another letter to her sister.

****

The early morning visitors to Rover Street were pleased when the vendor arrived and opened his stall. Before long tea was being brewed and cocoa was served. Ungloved hands were wrapped tightly round the hot cups as the need to keep warm was great. Another entrepreneur had turned up. Directed to Rover Street by Mr Wagstaff, the girl pushed her trolley to the middle of the street, the latest edition of the Northern Daily Telegraph sold like hotcakes. No need to encourage the Rover Street audience to buy the papers as they could not wait to digest "the latest". Quite apart from anything else it helped to pass the time and the articles always provoked conversation between the spectators.

A steady stream of people had headed up the hill so much so that the crowd quickly swelled. The gathering was far greater than the morning before. The new arrivals immediately spread the word. The rumour was that those holed up in the house were to give themselves up to the police. No one knew where this rumour came from. In a state of heightened excitement and anticipation the masses arrived. Some stood upon boxes to get a good view whilst others brought packed lunches as a sign they were prepared to "wait it out" so as not to miss a sighting of any of those they had, until now, only read about.

The crowd, as a group, was friendly enough however, the sheer weight of numbers persuaded the Constables on duty to call for reinforcements.

****

William was still irked by Jackson's manner as he stowed the basket and took hold of the newspapers. On his way down he decided to have another word with Emily, after all, Jackson couldn't stop him. The Doctor was his own man not a lackey to a bully. He unlocked the door and walked in.

"I apologise for not knocking Mrs Jackson".

However "brave" he made himself feel towards Jackson, he was still hesitant and uncertain in the presence of his wife.

"It is alright, Doctor. Please come forward. Is there something the matter?"

"No, Madam. Just something I think you should know."

Emily looked at William with an expression of modest passing interest and said quietly "Go on."

"Well remember I said how Jackson is due to be arrested by the police along with my brother and myself of course."

Mrs Jackson nodded.

"It seems that Mr Jackson may volunteer to go very soon."

Emily was now very interested.

"According to my brother the thing that stops Mr Jackson going is you. He is anxious that you might not be here when he gets back from Court."

"I see. What else?"

William looked at her reluctant to say anymore and fretting he had already spent too long in Emily's room.

"Oh, nothing else, I just thought you might want to know."

"Yes. Well. Thank you."

Once the door had shut behind the Doctor, Emily reflected on what she had been told. At times she found William's nervousness or reticence so frustrating. She always felt he was trying to tell her something yet would never get to the point or wanted her to guess what he was on about.

In her mind Emily was quite satisfied that William was genuine in that he had not been put up to speak to her and given a script by Jackson. For, it occurred to her there was no earthly reason for such a rigmarole over something that Jackson could quite easily tell her himself. She concluded therefore that Jackson's desire to get this Court business over with was true and, if so, the rest of William's messages were also true. She knew then the answer. Exactly how she will handle the promised meeting with her husband.

****

Jackson was back in the drawing room when Susan brought the newspapers. She had been handed them by William who still preferred not to be in the same room as Jackson. The papers were put on the table.

"Ask Mr Robinson Junior to join me."

"Yes Sir" replied Susan.

In a moment Dixon strolled into the room and without a word he picked up the nearest newspaper and threw himself into one of the armchairs. Jackson, from his chair, peered at him over the pages of the Manchester Herald which he had taken.

"You'll enjoy the read Dick. It's more than I could have imagined."

"Ha. Ha. It refers to you here as "a loyal soldier" and further down you are "a wronged husband"."

"Listen to this Jackson "Our Reporter interviewed Mrs Jones a Blackburn housewife who claimed to have relatives in Clitheroe with special knowledge of the family. Mrs Jones is firmly of the view that Mr & Mrs Jackson would have been and could be very happy but for Mrs Jackson's interfering and mischief making relatives."

"Hand me that paper".

Dixon obeyed.

Jackson re read the whole article.

"You know what, Dick with each passing day I feel even more vindicated. What will Mrs Jackson say about this? In point of fact, I feel now the press may benefit from a statement from my goodself."

Dixon then said pointedly "I thought you cursed the publicity? Are you seriously going to speak to them?"

"Let's just say I will hear what my wife has to say to me before I make up my mind."

****

For more than a day Isabel had, so far as she could, kept herself to herself. There was a small day room on the ground floor of the left wing of the house. She wanted to stay away from those who had invaded her home only because she was so used to her own company. She could pass the time in this room by reading or sewing. If her brother needed to consult her, she was available.

Isabel had no desire to interact with or befriend Emily. The woman had indelibly blotted her copybook so far as Miss Jackson was concerned and Isabel was not possessed of much measure of forgiveness. Once anyone crossed her, well, that was basically that.

Her brothers were different. She had never been very close to Raynsford. He had left the family home at an early age and eventually set up his home in London. Nevertheless, he had always looked after Isabel, ensured she was well and provided for. Edmund was different. She was well aware of his shortcomings. He was indeed something of a rogue and was hardly dependable. Even so he was quick witted, possessed of clever cunning and a charm that could persuade her to do almost anything for him. As youngsters they had played and sparred together. They were indeed as close as any siblings could be.

Isabel was kept abreast of most things by the loyal Susan.

Susan had offered her mistress to go and get her the papers to read but Isabel dismissed this suggestion.

"Susan, the newspapers simply want to make money at any price. It is pure sensationalism, exaggeration and untruths"

"I daresay it is my lady" replied Susan ingenuously as she herself could not wait to gorge on all the printed stories. Susan was not really educated. She did not understand some of the fancy words uttered by those in the house or the academic or some of philoshophical features in some of the posh papers. However, Susan enjoyed the letters pages and the bits in the less highbrow dailies.

Isabel said with a chuckle as she settled back into the book she was reading:

"Tell you this. Were I to read in the newspaper an article praising something I had done, I'd swear it was a lie!"

****

In front of the mirror Jackson brushed back his hair. With index finger and thumb he pressed back his fine thin moustache. He wanted to ensure he was at his finest for Emily. He sported a newly cleaned three piece blue suit. A silver fob watch was attached to the waistcoat. He dabbed a couple of drops of French Cologne behind his ears.

He was about ready.

The hall clock struck 12 noon. He was aware he had promised to meet his wife in the afternoon. Jackson had intended it to be a bit later but, in view of the fact his solicitor had arranged further discussion for 2 pm, he had to attend on Emily now. It was technically afternoon.

As he turned from the mirror he picked up the newspaper taken earlier from Dixon and removed and then folded up the relevant couple of pages before putting them into the inside pocket of his jacket.

"If she does not behave" he said to himself. "I can use the newspaper. When she reads this she will feel so very small" Patting his chest over the paper he said "This is my secret weapon".

As he left his room Jackson was devoid of nerves. As had been the abduction this next move was simply another strategy in another battle.

****

There was the now familiar noise of the lock being turned. Emily tensed inside, stood up and moved to the far side of the room as Jackson entered.

"How are you today, my dear?" he enquired with a smile. She looked at her husband but stayed silent.

"Please, Emily you must sit down."

Rather than risk Jackson taking hold of her arm and guiding her to the chair Emily did as she was bid and sat down. Once Jackson was seated in the other chair he leant forwards and said in a gentle tone:

"I need to know how you are. Are you eating?" He enquired solicitously.

For the first time Emily forced herself to look at Jackson in the face whereupon she spoke without any trace of bitterness or anger.

"I do not really understand. You confuse me so very much. On the one hand it appears you want to torture me and yet, at the same time, you profess to care for me and want there to be a future for us. Yet I ask myself how this can be so? Why should a man who cares for me lock me up in a room with neither company nor amusement?"

Jackson warmed to the soft tone of his wife's voice. It had been so long since he had heard anything uttered other than venom or rejection.

"I know it is difficult for you to grasp. What I have done is for your own good." Emily seethed inside but did not show any reaction as her husband continued:

"When I went abroad it is natural that you would rely upon your family for comfort and for company. You may even forget the times that you and I used to share together for, I accept, that reading my letters is hardly the same as the relationship we had before I embarked. It is patently obvious to me that the dependence you have had on your relatives has become an addiction and that only by cutting you off from that drug can you properly return to the way you were and appreciate the pleasure and reward in our marriage together."

Much later Emily looked back on this conversation. All she wanted to do was scream and run away from this man and how she managed to control herself she never really knew. All she had was the promise she had made to herself before the meeting that, whatever Jackson did or said, she would remain calm. This together with how she had planned things in her head allowed her to keep her focus.

"But I am cooped up in this one room. I might be able to get used to living here if things were a bit more normal. If only I could go downstairs. If only there was not that crowd outside. Were I but able to write to my sister. I do not need to actually leave the house."

When she wanted to Emily was able to make her eyes look soft and she did so at this moment looking across to Jackson.

Jackson did his best to assimilate this information. This could not be correct. Was Emily saying she would be content in this house? Was she hinting she may, after all, be content with him? Jackson could not accept this at face value.

"Are you saying you want to be with me?" he asked without frills. Emily was ready for such a question. For the very first time in about two years she addressed her husband by his name.

"Haughton, I was and I am gravely hurt by so much that has been said and done since we married. The honest answer to your question is that I do not know. Since you returned, we have only been in conflict with each other. You maybe right in that these last days by myself have given me time to think. I do need time. Perhaps I could stay here a bit longer. I can keep distant from my family and see how I feel? Just don't confine me in this room"

"I am not sure. If I had to leave the house for any reason you could slip out and go back to Clitheroe. How do I know you will not just run away? How do I know your family will not turn up and demand you go back?"

"If there is to be any future - and I am not saying there is - you have to trust me just as I have to trust you. So, if I tell you I am comfortable here, that we can try to get along and that if you leave the house for any reason I will not run away then you have to accept that. I will no doubt have Susan and your sister to chaperone me here."

Jackson was not entirely convinced by his wife's "soft eyed look" and pleasant words. However, it did propel him to rise from his seat. He stood behind Emily and caressed her neck with his fingers before bending down to give a chaste kiss on her cheek. Emily did not respond but equally she knew she could not recoil or it would prove that her words had all been a charade.

“I have enjoyed our little chat Emily, and I hope so much we can continue in this manner. I must go now."

As he was closing the bedroom door Emily said in a voice just loud enough for him to hear:

"Please come back soon".

The instant the door was shut she pretended to spit out those words.

Emily had survived but had she succeeded? She could not tell. As Jackson might leave for this Court anytime now she had to make preparations. She scrambled in the drawer to find the writing paper whereupon she wrote:

"Dear Esther,

I must keep this short. Only the Lord knows if this will reach you.

I believe my husband might leave for Clitheroe anytime now. If I am to be rescued from my current shackles it must be when Jackson is away from here.

I miss you

Love

Em"

On the envelope she put, "Miss Esther Hall, First Floor Flat, Granville Terrace, Blackburn" and then forced the envelope into the waistband of her underskirt.

****

Jackson looked at the clock. It was time to call his solicitor.

"Good afternoon Mr Jackson, I trust you are well" said the voice, once the Secretary had put him through.

"Get on with it man, what are the police saying? Do we have a guarantee of unhindered passage?"

"If we can give an assurance that you and the Robinsons will board the morning train to Clitheroe any day this week then the police will not arrest you."

"We prefer to go by coach rather than the train."

"I cannot think the mode of transport will make any difference".

"I need the police also to give you their word that they'll leave Isabel's house alone and will not seek to enter it whilst we are away."

"That has been confirmed to me. So when do you want to do it? When shall I tell the police you will leave the house? Thursday? Friday?"

" Make it tomorrow. Let us just get it over with. And before you go, did you get hold of McAllister?"

"He is ready. Just waiting word from me"

****

That afternoon Emily's body finally collapsed. Having sustained all the stress and strain since Sunday and having lain staring at the ceiling for two consecutive nights, it was time for her limbs and her mind to say "enough was enough". No noise from any crowd and indeed no command from Jackson could disturb Emily as she remained motionless and asleep on the bed for almost four hours.

Emily stirred at the sound of voices. They were outside in the corridor.

"I do not like it. I think it a trap".

Emily recognised William's voice.

."A doctor cannot be seen to be led away in handcuffs. My practice would be ruined. I do not trust the police."

"Well trust Mr Jackson" replied Dixon.

"I think I trust him even less".

"Come. Come. Brother. Jackson has been right so far. You just wait and see. The police will withdraw from here for that is part of the deal and tomorrow we can all stroll out with our heads held high. Wait and see if I am right. Now come and help me with the supper."

So, it is to be tomorrow. Emily became a little carried away, for, in her head, she convinced herself that by this time tomorrow she would be free.

****

Jackson was by the telephone in the study. He pulled out the newspaper from his pocket. The one he had not had to employ in his meeting with Emily. He read beneath the headline and mentally noted the Reporter's details. Next, he looked at the Editor's page, picked up the telephone and asked the operator to be put through to the newspaper. There was a click and a delay on the line before a woman's voice said:

"Manchester Herald, how can I help you?"

"I want to speak to Mr Jack Jones, your Reporter"

"Who is calling please?"

"I'd rather not say."

"I'm not sure if Mr Jones is currently available"

"Just tell him it is about this Blackburn business, the shennanigans at Rover Street."

Jackson did not have to wait very long. A young perky sounding voice took over on the other end of the line. In truth, Mr Jackson would prefer to have dealt with a more mature individual but if this was the Jack Jones who had done the article in the day's newspaper then this was the man he would deal with.

"Yes, Sir, I am Jack Jones. You have information about the siege?"

"Yes."

"Well, I have to tell you we get a few crackpots calling, such as folk who do not leave their name. Folk who want paid for what they claim to know. So, I have to ask you at the start, where exactly do you claim to have the information from? Have you been outside the property? How have you come by the information? As a journalist with a reputable paper I have to check my sources."

Jackson felt a degree of incredulity. This "wet behind the ears" youngster was professing to be a journalist. Referring to the Herald as "reputable"? Hardly! No. It was as if this Jack Jones was going through some check list dictated to him by his Editor.

"This is Mr Edmund Jackson speaking from West View in Rover Street."

There was a pause on the line followed by a stutter:

"Sir......just hold on.................I need to get a notebook...........don't go away"

"Hello. Mr Jackson" The voice was a more assured voice, a more senior type. "Marshall, Assistant Editor. I'm afraid Mr Jones had an appointment he had to go to. You can speak to me though."

Jackson felt better speaking to this Marshall and yet he felt sorry for the young Jones. He knew Mr Jones had been sent away so that someone else could "take the glory" of having spoken to the "hero" in the abduction story. Jackson recalled his days as a new recruit in the army. Once he had, by spotting an ambush saved a rout, only then for his Sergeant to have immodestly taken the subsequent commendation for himself.

"Mr Marshall. I shall speak to you on one condition. If you print anything I say to you just now you have to credit Jack Jones with it. Do you hear me?"

"But why so insist? I do not understand."

"You do not have to understand Mr Marshall. That is my condition. If not agreeable to you then I will go now and ring the Northern Daily Telegraph."

"Mr Jackson. Now don't do anything of the sort. If you say it has to be Mr Jones, then so be it. Now what is it you want to say?"

"Something, you need to know first, Marshall. I have Mr Dixon Robinson with me just now. He has just heard you accept my condition. Should you, on reflection, choose to renege on our accord then I will write to selected newspapers making it clear that you have invented everything and that the public can give no credence to anything printed in the Herald."

This was a brazen threat. Dixon Robinson was not with Jackson. It pleased Jackson though to exercise both the power and the control he perceived his new found fame brought.

"Yes. I understand."

There followed, not so much an interview but rather a press release. In other words, Jackson told Marshall what he wanted him to say and nothing more.

"My wife is back with me. She is not, as some would have it, being held here against her will. Mrs Jackson is free to leave West View whenever she wants, but she desires to remain here with me. She has told me so in terms both warm and affectionate. Her desire now is for us to be left alone to get on with our lives."

"Can I speak to Mrs Jackson?"

"Marshall. I am, like all husbands, entitled to and do speak on behalf of my wife."

"If what you say is true, why forever was it necessary to abduct her on Sunday?"

"It is now, unfortunately public knowledge that Mrs Jackson and I were, through circumstance forced apart. Indeed certain persons have tried to keep us apart. That though is now history. Mrs Jackson has come round."

"Can I ask?"

Jackson interrupted:

"No. I will be making no further comment to the press. Good day Mr Marshall." A click on the line notified Marshall the call was over.

****

Hartley Baldwin got home from his office at the usual time. After placing his walking stick in the umbrella stand he went to join his wife in the living room. The daily ritual continued with Charnock entering with a tray which he first lowered to Betsy and then to Hartley.

Mr & Mrs Baldwin partook of a sherry at this time of the day.

"Tomorrow is the day then."

"I beg your pardon?" said Betsy.

"The Chief Constable called me today. He tells me that Jackson and the others are in Court tomorrow. I know the prosecution team."

Hartley raised his glass.

'To justice" he toasted.

"Where is Hartley?"

"He is due back soon. Why?"

"I want him to go and tell Esther about tomorrow. For I'm sure she will want to attend the Court."

****

Emily had been anxious about William's visit. It would be just her luck if, instead of the doctor, Susan or someone else brought her food that evening. Even were it the doctor, could she trust him? She felt she had to.

Sure enough it was indeed William. The fayre he brought was steamed fish in hot milk with green beans and boiled potatoes.

"How are you tonight, Doctor?"

William was rather surprised for he'd never been welcomed like this by her.

"I am well Madam and I hope you are also."

"Doctor or can I call you William? I have to ask a favour."

William was intrigued and though he had no idea what this lady was about to say he felt a little nervous.

"Yes." he said.

"William. As you know I am not allowed out of the house. I need so much to get a letter delivered to someone nearby and I wondered if you could somehow organise this? "

"I am not sure Mrs Jackson."

Emily produced the envelope addressed to her sister. William immediately realised this was connected with the letter he had found in the basket and left in Emily's room. He did not really want to be involved in the family politics which he saw being played out. If he refused though would Mrs Jackson let his part in the earlier letter be known to others? For now, he was fairly certain it was a "little secret" between the two of them.

Emily held out the note to Doctor Robinson and looking with her "soft eyes" said "Please?"

William took the note quickly and buried it in his trouser pocket.

"I will try Mrs Jackson. For you I will try." He then left the room.

A Skirmish in Court

When Wednesday broke, in the Jackson household there was a relative frenzy as the men made their demands of Susan. Shoes were to be polished, shirts to be pressed. Could she look out a certain pair of gold cuff links? Extra towels needed? Why none of this had been anticipated and organised the night before was surprising particularly given Jackson's own pride in being prepared.

With Susan rushed off of her feet, Dixon was really stretched trying to prepare breakfast completely by himself. Still, he reckoned, this could per chance be the last such occasion. All being well Isabel's cook would be able to return at some point today or tomorrow.

Shortly before 9 o'clock Dixon joined Jackson in the study. The latter was standing to the side of the window in order to look out without being seen.

"Dick. Did I not tell you so? No sign of the police."

"Should we not be making our way then? We do not want to be late."

“All in good time." said Jackson "One of my contacts tells me that word has broken out all over Clitheroe and there's some hysteria there. By carriage we will never get to the Court by the appointed hour. So, it is the train for us. I have organised a first class carriage. After all "he added with a chuckle "we are the "stars" of this ridiculous show trial"

"I wish William would hurry up." Dixon said in his rather nervous way.

Just then William did appear. He looked rather flustered and was obviously having trouble fastening his silver cuff links.

"Sorry if I am late. That's me about ready for the off."

Dixon with hesitation asked "I take it we will be safe? I mean that crowd out there. They won't molest us?"

Jackson stared at his companion hardly believing in his timid streak.

"I hardly think they are a band of cutthroats out to lynch us. Anyway, I will take the lead. You two follow me when the time comes." Jackson then sat down.

It was William's turn to be curious.

"What exactly are we waiting for Mr Jackson?"

"Patience, my friend. Shortly you shall observe."

Susan then interrupted the group.

"Mr Jackson, Sir. Your sister would like a word with you."

Jackson rose and as he left the room he bowed to his companions in an exaggerated manner and smiled leaving both of them in a state of some perplexion.

****

"Yes. Isabel. You wanted a word?"

"Edmund, I want you to know I will be thinking of you and praying for the outcome we both want."

"Do not fret sister. It will all be a doddle, this Clitheroe thing."

"You must take this more seriously. This is not the time for you to wind people up. Remember there are some people out there who harbour malice towards you, people who do not wish you well. There are clever persons determined to outfox you."

"Isabel, I have no fear. You must not forget that they are but plodding bloodhounds whereas I am the wily fox!" He graced his sister with a chaste kiss upon her cheek and returned to the study."

****

There was a loud knock on the front door. Jackson checked out the window and rang the bell for the maid. Dixon looked alarmed.

The door opened whereupon Jackson said "Susan. Will you let these men inside?"

Dixon followed Susan as far as the study door. He heard the large bolt being slid open, the key being turned and upon seeing a shaft of daylight illuminate the entrance vestibule he witnessed about a dozen men enter West View. Each held a stick.

Jackson made his way past Dixon. He held outstretched his right hand as one of the men stepped forward and took hold.

"You are McAllister I assume? Make yourself and your men at home. You know your charge and duty? Until I return to this house, however long that might prove to be, you are to keep this property secure. No one and I mean no one must enter or leave this house. The lady of whom you will have heard is in the front right bedroom upstairs. I would not encourage you or any of your men to converse with her. If she wants anything then Susan here can deal with it."

"Understood, Sir" said McAllister. "We are professional bailiffs. You can rely upon us."

"Oh, I should have said that the kitchen is downstairs. It is fully provisioned."

Jackson then reached to the nearby hat stand and removed his top hat therefrom. He turned to the Robinsons behind him and as he lowered the hat onto his head he said:

"If you are ready gentlemen, let us depart."

****

As they witnessed the arrival of the bailiffs the throng outside were confused. They did not understand what was going on. Their curiosity was heightened and their senses trained and very focussed upon the "hostage house". So many pairs of eyes scanned the building from one window to another for any sign of anything happening.

It was a noise that turned all the heads. The noise of the bolt of the front door again being loosed brought everyone's gaze and attention to that door.

The newspaper description and drawing of Jackson had been so very accurate that there could be doubt as to the identity of the man first appearing from the house. As cheers rang out and resonated down the street the volume of the crowd was greatly increased. Jackson stopped for a moment to breathe in the adulation. In appreciation he raised his hat to the crowd before moving forward slowly and carefully towards the waiting carriage.

In Jackson's wake, Dixon Robinson looked positively dumbstruck by the reception of the public. William though appeared sheepish and uncomfortable. He tried to hide his face behind the hat he held in his right hand.

As he reached the pavement William caught hold of his brother's arm and shouted into Dixon's ear:

"I won't be a moment. I'm going to get a newspaper."

He made his way away from the carriage to where Wagstaff's girl was standing in the middle of the road with, as usual, a bag full of the day's Northern Daily Telegraph.

William took the paper held out to him by the girl but then suddenly grabbed hold of her arm. Hurriedly he said:

"There's a crown in this for you if you can deliver this note to the flat across there. No questions asked. Half a crown now and the rest tomorrow when I know you have delivered it."

The girl had followed William's eyes to the door of the building which contained Esther's flat and, being not unused to peremptory orders such as this, knew it was not her position to query the mission proposed. She snatched the note and the 2s 6d offered. William turned to go but, as he did so, the girl said sharply:

"Not so quick mister. I need three pence for the paper."

William rummaged about in his pocket, handed over the payment without a further word and rushed back over to the carriage.

Rather out of breath Dr Robinson hauled himself into the carriage and they were off. The cheering continued until the carriage had disappeared from sight on its way to the station.

****

Emily's attention was taken by the sudden cheering outside the house. She went to the bay window. She need hardly have worried about being spotted there for, to a man and a woman, the entire audience was intent on looking at her husband and the others. Emily was horrified at what she saw. She could not grasp why Jackson was being cheered to the rafters. What had he said? What lies had been told about her? There was no evident sympathy for her out there. Yet she was the wronged party. She was the captive prisoner. All that she observed then made her isolation feel worse. As Emily saw Jackson drinking in the applause and doffing his hat, she felt sick in her stomach. She retreated from the window. Something was not right. If only she could see a newspaper. If only she could speak to her sister. Her family would come to her aid. Surely they would, wouldn't they? Now Emily was not nearly as confident as she had been the night before

****

Mags - Wagstaff's girl - went over to the stall vendor.

"Keep an eye on my bag, will you?" she asked him. With the departure of the carriage the crowd had significantly dispersed. Precious few more paper sales would be made.

Mags wandered over the road. She was an observant girl. The person who had paid her the half crown was one of the important gentlemen from the house. Was the commission she had been given perhaps to do with some covert affair involving the gentleman? Mags could do a good job for him and there maybe more such commissions. She might uncover something and then Wagstaff would reward her for bringing him an exclusive.

She read the envelope. The script read "For Miss E Hall." Well she sounds like a single lady so perhaps the gentleman is a married man. Mags mused about all the potential scandals she could be being led to. No. If it be one of those passionate affairs she had read about in books, Miss E Hall would definitely not be the woman's real name.

Mags approached the concierge. "I'm looking for Miss E Hall."

"Who is asking?" The concierge was quick to notice that Mags, if not a ruffian, was certainly not the type that tended to frequent the flats she was charged to look after.

The concierge once more looked Mags up and down. She could be a trouble maker but the concierge could think of no good reason to impede her. With a grave stare she said in a clipped manner "Very well then. She is on the first floor, turn left and the second door along."

Mags bounded up the stairs. In her mind she believed she had outwitted "the guard" without giving away anything about her secret mission. She so wanted to knock on the door as she approached, to be able to see the face of the gentleman's lover when the door was opened. But no, it was not her place. If she was to be a trusted conduit for the gentleman, he had to be able to trust her, to trust her implicitly. She had to be content with slipping the note through the letterbox of the flat.

Mags passed the concierge who pretended not to notice her. Back out on the street, Mags knew that for however many more days she was told to go back to Granville Terrace she would not only sell her papers but she would keep a very close eye on anyone entering or leaving the block of flats.

What Mags did not know was that Emily's cry for help which she had just delivered would sit on the floor of that flat unopened and unread. Esther was not there to help her sister. She had returned to Clitheroe as bid by her brother-in-law Hartley. When the note was delivered in Blackburn, Miss E Hall was preparing herself to go to the Police Court to support her other sister.

****

The Police Court in Clitheroe was within the town's Police Station. It was not garnished with noble emblems of state and nor could it be said to resemble much more than a plain square room. It was equipped with a fixed bench on a slightly raised platform in front of which there was a wooden table and some chairs. A few rows of hard single wooden chairs completed the basic furniture that was on view.

In truth the Police Court only convened whenever necessary which was not very often. The crime rate in Clitheroe was very low. If any serious crime was reported then it would be dealt with by the Assize Court in Preston. The Magistrates in Clitheroe by and large dispensed justice in cases such as those of being drunk and disorderly, the occasional minor affray, petty theft and theft of cattle or sheep. Any large scale cattle rustling would bypass the Police Court to one at a higher level.

The room which housed the Police Court served other purposes. It was where the Women's Institute held monthly meetings. The local Watch Committee which convened in public used this room as did local voluntary groups for tombolas, beetle drives, bring and buy sales and the like.

On this particular morning the Police Court looked bare and drab apart from the aforementioned wooden furniture. A large wall clock showed the time as 9 o'clock and in the large and empty space the sound from the clock of each second passing by was clearly audible. The scene and the silence provided an eerie edge to the atmosphere. The peace and the quiet would not though last much longer.

****

This morning, Hartley Baldwin had risen early. He did not intend venturing to his office until after the Court Hearing. His involvement at the Hearing that day took the form of more than one role. His Firm had instructed Counsel for the prosecution namely a Mr McConnell. He had to greet Mr McConnell and ensure, in so far as he could, that this Counsel was properly briefed. Hartley also had to attend to look after and to support his wife as, after all, she was the Complainant in the charge of assault. Setting aside these professional and personal duties there was a need on Hartley's part to be there. He wanted to convey to Jackson by his demeanour and appearance that he would not give up, as he saw it, the fight for Emily. There was also the possibility that he would hear or notice something useful in what he felt would be the battles, as yet unspecified, in front of him.

Betsy gave no outward sign of being unnerved by having to go to Court. She had already established from her husband that the Hearing would likely be short in duration and that she would not be called upon to speak.

He had told her "They are basically going to be here under arrest. The Court will either remand them in custody to await trial which, I confess is highly unlikely, or bind them over on certain conditions and liberate them pending another Hearing at a later date."

"If that is so then I cannot understand why the town is so full of incomers and strangers, all heading down towards the square. Why so much interest if that is all that is likely to occur?"

Hartley sighed a bit and looked at his wife. "You know what people can be like, Betsy. The press has created a storm. They have made those involved in this kidnapping into exaggerated characters and fed the minds of the readers. This is an opportunity to view some of the persona in real life for the first time. We are all goldfish even Jackson and today the goldfish have to swim in the bowl that is Clitheroe Village. You will see. People who would never have given you a glance or a nod will now stop and stare if they see you in the street."

Charnock entered with his tray bearing the morning paper. Hartley Baldwin held up a hand in a stop gesture. "No Charnock, not today. I prefer not to read the paper on this particular morning. Thank you."

Hartley then put the hand into his waistcoat and pulled out and glanced at his fob watch.

"The Court opens at 11 o'clock with the hearing scheduled for 11 30. If we are to collect your sister on the way and get the two of you a good seat I reckon we should set off in about half an hour."

****

Jackson sat in the train compartment with his feet resting on the opposite seat. He seemed to be in a trance listening to the sound of the carriage wheels rushing along the rails and hearing the steam engine harnessing more power to progress the journey up the long incline leading to Clitheroe.

Sitting next to Jackson, Dixon mused "It is so good to be out of that house. How very odd. Though I am heading to the police in Clitheroe I feel freer than I did whilst cooped up in the house."

Neither Jackson nor Dickson's brother found the comment particularly humorous.

Jackson removed from his inside pocket a cigar. After cutting off the end of it, he struck a match with an ostentatious flick of his right hand. The match was held in position between his thumb and index finger with the other three fingers splayed widely apart. With cigar ready to be enjoyed he settled back into his seat and replaced his feet upon the seat as before.

William was horrified by this nonchalant behaviour. He, for one, was taking this Court business seriously. He was not without concern for himself. As a doctor the publicity of a Court hearing could damage or ruin his professional reputation. Yet there was Jackson, who had provoked the whole affair, sitting without any obvious care in the world. The doctor could not tolerate the accumulation of the cigar smoke within the confined space. He stood up and opened the window next to where he was sitting. As he put his head to the fresh air, Jackson quipped:

"Now, my good doctor. Watch out for bridges and tunnels. People tend to get beheaded after they have been to Court - not before!"

So as not to embarrass his brother, Dixon fought hard to and did succeed in stifling a hearty laugh. As always Dixon found Jackson so very entertaining.

****

Hartley and Betsy set off earlier than they had planned. They decided that rather than simply join Esther outside Shawbridge, they would prevail on her for a cup of tea and find out how she had managed to cope during her days in Blackburn.

The route to Shawbridge took them past the Newsagents shop. As they approached the shop Hartley suddenly stopped as if frozen to the spot. His eye had caught the Newsboard propped up by the shop door. The banner proclaimed "Siege Over as Couple Reconcile." Having earlier declared he would not read a paper that morning, now nothing would stop him as he abandoned his wife on the pavement and strode into the shop.

When he soon came out of the shop and onto the pavement, Betsy saw her husband's eyes dart right, then left and right again across the opened page of the newspaper. She tensed with the sense of concern she detected from him.

"Hartley, what is it?"

Hartley Baldwin remained transfixed by the article and whilst shaking his head replied to Betsy:

"I just do not believe this. This has to be a lie. I won't accept this. It says that Mrs Jackson, sorry, Emily has announced she is content staying at West View with her husband, how they are getting on so well and how she now wants to get on with her life."

He looked up. Betsy stared into his face trying to take in what Hartley had just said.

"Who wrote all of this?"

He referred back to the paper.

"Never heard of him. The name is Jack Jones Junior"

Hartley read a bit more before folding the paper neatly under his arm and saying "Come, my dear. We must make haste to speak to Esther. Perhaps she knows something that we do not."

****

This was a big day in Clitheroe. The eyes of the local residents and the press were on this town like never before. Reporters arrived in the town from Manchester first thing in the morning. Others from Preston and other northern towns followed soon after. At the Dancing Pony Inn two reporters from London were billeted having travelled up from that city on the late train the previous evening. Anticipating a bumper trade, many local shop owners had been up since before dawn in order to be able to get their stock ready and be open in time for the arrival of the first morning train at 7 15 am.

By 10 am the place was swarming with people. They spilled onto the roads and filled the public spaces. Every time a train from Blackburn arrived at the Railway Station there was a mini stampede to see if the notorious trio was arriving.

A brass band from Nelson had come to Clitheroe to entertain the crowds. They took up position in the bandstand at the park near to the Railway Station.

Apart from the shopkeepers it did seem as if everyone in the town and beyond had taken time off work just to be able to say that they were there the day Clitheroe was in all of the National Press.

Within the Town House, the Court usher checked that all the chairs were in their proper place.

The Magistrates for the day were Mr W B Dewhurst as Chairman and Mr J H Clarke. These two officials were in an ante room along with the Clerk of the Court. They were well aware themselves from reading the newspapers of why they had had to convene the Court on this day. The Jackson case was their only business.

"Your Honours" said the Clerk addressing himself to the Magistrates. "I'm advised that Counsel involved in today's case are Mr McConnell for the prosecution and, for the accused, Mr Waugh."

"McConnell, we know. He's from Liverpool is he not? Mr Waugh I have not previously come across" observed Dewhurst.

"He is from Bradford" said the Clerk.

"I know we cannot prejudge anything" said Mr Clarke "but for two Counsel and with all this attendant cafuffel over what my sources indicate to be a rather trivial matter, I am very perplexed. I cannot fathom it out. Folk must have more money than they have sense these days."

Clarke caught sight of Dewhurst's disapproving expression. He knew the Magistrates were forbidden to discuss a case before they had heard it. He immediately raised both hands "Do not worry. I will say no more."

The usher had a plan. As he saw it the most important people that day were not, as such, the celebrated accused but rather the press. They would report on Clitheroe to the whole nation and beyond. Accordingly, he had put a word in certain ears that if the press chanced to attend at the rarely used and normally bolted side door off a corridor leading to the Court room, he would admit them at precisely 10 50 am. They could then take up the "best seats in the house" before he opened the front door to the masses.

****

Once she had witnessed Jackson's tumultuous departure from West View, Emily was uncertain as to what to do. What was to happen next? If she was indeed to be rescued it maybe unlikely for a while yet, with William away, would she be served with any breakfast? With the watchers having, for now, dispersed Rover Street was empty. Emily decided to move one of the chairs over into the space in front of the window. At last, she could take in the view of the world outside with no fear of any voyeur staring at her. It was a relief from looking at the wallpaper for hours on end as by now she knew every single twist in the pattern. Once seated, there was a sense of peace that descended more than she had known since the kidnap.

She had not long sat down when the noise of the key in the lock caught her attention. The handle then turned and Susan entered.

"Good morning" said Emily courteously.

"I've just brought breakfast, Madam. With Master Robinson away I'm afraid it is only toast, some hot milk and some tea."

"That is fine."

"Excuse me, Madam. I've been asked by Mr Jackson to enquire of your clothes."

"I beg your pardon" said Emily

"Well, he asked Mistress Isabel if she would go out and buy you one or two things then asked me, if you please, to find out what she should acquire and, you know, what, well, shape and what size and all that sort of thing."

"If he is so concerned, I cannot see why he cannot make proper arrangements with my sister Esther" she snapped. "My clothes are at home."

Emily then checked herself.

"I am sorry Susan. It is not your fault. If I'm being allowed clothes then I cannot see why I cannot accompany Miss Jackson. She is surely a capable chaperone for me."

Emily smiled inside as she well knew Isabel would be appalled at the thought of passing any time let alone a day with her brother's "disloyal" spouse.

"It is not quite like that Mrs Jackson. The men have been told that only Miss Jackson is to be permitted out of the house."

"Men? What men?"

"Those Bailiffs your husband organised. They are here to protect us, to stop any intruders and to prevent the press or anyone forcing their way into the house. Things have become a bit scary of late. I think it is good of Mr Jackson to think of us, so very considerate indeed."

Think of us my foot thought Emily as she seethed inside. I wanted him to trust me yet it is clear he does not. The only purpose of these men is to keep me here. He did not believe my word that I would remain. Then she laughed thinking "Well as a matter of fact Mr Jackson is right. He cannot trust me!"

"Madam?" queried Susan.

"No. Susan I am not laughing at you. Now about these clothes, I certainly need to change and get out of these" gesticulating to the clothes she had had to wear since Sunday.

After giving Susan instructions about the shopping, Emily asked curiously:

"I confess I am quite surprised that my husband would favour me in this way?"

"Oh no Mrs Jackson, I cannot say that I am surprised at all. Sorry, it is not my place. However, Mr Jackson did make it known this morning that he wants you to join him and the others downstairs when he returns later on today."

"Thank you Susan, I will have my toast now."

Susan retreated from the room.

Emily stared out of the window. She had much to ponder. What had Jackson possibly planned for this evening? What if she refused to go downstairs for part of her was not inclined to merely succumb to the whims of her husband? Then there were these men in the house described by Susan as bailiffs. Emily had, she believed, summoned her family to come and rescue her whilst Jackson was out of the house. Should an attempt be made they would be met by "Jackson's guards". She felt she had led her family into a trap. There maybe fighting. People could be hurt and arrested. Emily felt very ill at ease and the fleeting peace she had encountered was, again, beyond her reach.

****

From the gap between the two hills on the near horizon the upward stream of coal smoke could clearly be spotted. The next train into Clitheroe had not much further to travel. Once again the crowd surged towards the railway station.

The station building was very modest. In normal circumstances the number of commuters from or visitors to this town hardly warranted anything more than the small ticket office and the little waiting room equipped with a small coal fire. On this very rural line the length of any train was normally three carriages. With engine and tender added to the carriages the trains extended along the platform beyond the station building. Such was the arrangement that, in the case of any northbound service, only the first carriage would be obscured from view by the station building.

The gathered host of spectators pushed against the fence and some even clambered up onto nearby walls. Hands were held over brows to admit of a clear view from the glare of the mid - morning sun. The odd individual was possessed of a telescope.

The noise of the engine got louder as the train hauled itself closer and then suddenly came into full view, billowing plumes of smoke. It drew up alongside the platform at walking pace before the metal squeal of brakes and the rush of air being forced out brought the train to a standstill. As the smoke settled over their heads the crowd stared. A couple of ladies emerged from the last coach and headed towards the station building and the exit. Doors from the first coach were heard being slammed but, of course, no one from there was visible.

You could sense the onlookers to a man, asking "Is this just another false alarm?"

Wait a minute. Another door was being opened. Jackson had waited until every other passenger for Clitheroe had alighted and chose the moment the guard had raised his flag to signal the train's departure before he emerged from the middle carriage and to light another cigar - for he knew that image was everything.

The eruption of cheering was momentous. As Jackson and his colleagues left the door of the station and headed the short distance to the Police Station, the crowd parted to allow a path through. Some patted Jackson on the back whilst others in the crowd burst into song. Their rendition of "for he's a jolly good fellow" resounded along the streets and as if "on cue" the Brass Band from Nelson struck up and provided musical backing for the crowd.

Jackson took all of this very much in his stride. It was, for him, a throwback to the days in New Zealand when he had made a "hero's return" following a skirmish with the Maoris.

Neither of the Robinsons knew exactly how to react to the mass acclaim. William tried to hide his singular embarrassment. Both brothers felt like cheats as their parts in the events that Sunday had been very minor. Yes, they had assisted Jackson but both of them knew it was Jackson the crowd were applauding. It was Jackson they had come to see.

****

Esther welcomed the Baldwins to Shawbridge. Between them, Betsy and Esther prepared tea and some scones. The scones had just been made by Esther intending that they be taken with her to Blackburn later.

As soon as they were all seated in the little sitting room, Hartley addressed the matter that was burning inside of him.

"On the day of the kidnap Emily and Betsy here struggled to resist the abduction. Is that so? It was obvious to any witness that she did not want to go?"

Betsy agreed this was true.

"Now Esther, have you seen or noticed anything in Blackburn or heard anything that would indicate Emily has changed her mind? Anything to indicate she might want to stay in Blackburn with that man?"

"Certainly not Hartley, she'd never want to stay there. I do not always know what is in Emily's thinking but I know her well enough to know she regrets that fool marriage she got herself into and how she wants nothing to do with him. Why? What makes you ask?"

Mr Baldwin pulled from his pocket the newspaper which he passed over to his sister-in-law. Esther read slowly and methodically, her face looked grim and serious before looking up and saying assertively to the others looking at her:

"Why for heavens? This is impossible. I'd say it is scandalous, a travesty and a baseless concoction. I'd contact the newspaper and demand a retraction. I'd not take "no" for an answer."

Hartley sat back. He spoke calmly.

"I did wonder about that. Yet, no, I vowed I would not speak to the press and I will only do so if I believe it to be in Emily's interests. I fear if I do say anything by way of protest they will use it to support what they have tried to imply from the start, namely, that it is us rather than Jackson who are the problem in all of this. If indeed the newspaper has made this up then action can be taken later.

If indeed Emily spoke to this Reporter, Jones or whatever his name is, I cannot believe she would not have telephoned us to intimate her change of heart. We cannot discount the possibility that it was Jackson who put her up to this and told her what to say to this Jones fellow. Your poor sister was under some duress. No. Once again ladies I fear we must keep our powder dry. I will though try to make discreet enquiry with one or two of my contacts in the world of journalism. Ones I know I can trust. One of them in particular owes me a favour."

Hartley glanced again at his fob watch.

"Just time I think for one of these delicious scones."

****

The dozen or so Reporters had all heard the word and even the two Reporters from London were in the bunch that loitered by the side door.

At precisely 10.50 am the usher, true to his word, opened the door and the newspapermen filed in.

"Not you. " and "Not you" barked the usher pointing at two men with cameras. "No photographs in Court. Only reporters allowed."

"What about me?" The usher looked down and viewed a small man wearing a cap and holding large sheets of paper.

"Excuse me, are you a reporter?"

"Well no. I'm a sketch writer" said the capped man rather sheepishly." I work for the Northern Daily Telegraph."

"You are not permitted to draw the Judges. Understand? If you do it will be contempt of Court and jail for you."

"I know the rules."

"Okay. On you go, be sharp about it. I cannot admit anyone else."

The usher shut the side door before showing the arrivals including Wagstaff's artist to their seats.

****

As they left Shawbridge, Hartley and the two sisters heard music and the sound of singing. Hartley showed disgust at this.

"I cannot understand what there is to celebrate. I mean Court is a serious business or so it should be."

When Hartley and the ladies got to within sight of the Police Court the mood of the crowd changed. From the same direction as from where Hartley had heard the cheering and singing on his way down, there now came a rising tide of jeers, heckles and taunts which he prayed Mrs Baldwin and Miss Hall did not hear.

He was shocked. Suddenly it hit home to him just how little sympathy there was for him and his family. In that instant his only concern was for the safety of his companions and so he increased his pace and took a good hold of both Esther and Betsy. The clock struck eleven as the front door of the Court was opened. The usher knew Hartley Baldwin very well. He was quick to appreciate the scene that met his eyes and with his right arm gesticulating to the crowd he kept them at bay long enough for the Baldwins and Esther to enter to the relative safety of the building.

Hartley took a seat with Betsy on one side of him and Esther on the other.

Within but a few minutes the small Court Room was packed and most of those who sought admittance had to be turned away.

There was a general hubbub amongst those sitting in the Court. All no doubt felt so lucky to have made it. To be able to witness what, without fail, would be front page in next day's newspapers. The hubbub though was quite hushed. At least, thought Hartley, there was still a modicum of reverence within the Court.

Hartley looked across the room where he spotted Colonel Robinson from Clitheroe Castle. What, he wondered, did the Colonel make of all of this? His family so steeped in service to the country and tradition yet now, here he was, about to witness two of his sons in the criminal Court.

McConnell, the prosecution Counsel instructed by Hartley Baldwin, entered the Court room. He motioned in the direction of Mr Baldwin who nodded back in acknowledgement.

It was very soon 11 30 am.

The Clerk entered and took up position in the front of the raised deck. The usher closed the internal door before proclaiming:

"Silence in Court."

The attendees stood, just as the magistrates, preceded by the Clerk, entered to take their positions looking out and down upon those assembled within the room.

Once everyone had settled, the Clerk announced:

"Call the case against Edmund Haughton Jackson, William Henry Robinson and Frederick Dixon Robinson."

There followed a silence. The attendees were gripped somewhat in anticipation. The silence was prolonged. Nothing occurred. None of the accused appeared. Mr Waugh, Defence Counsel, was not in the room.

The Clerk bent across and whispered to McConnell who then rose and faced the Court:

"Your Honours, I understand that my learned friend has only just met with those he is to represent and is, at this moment, in consultation with his clients. In the circumstances I cannot see it is of any prejudice if the Court were to grant a brief adjournment."

Mr Dewhurst glanced at the large clock and said in a clipped manner:

"Very well, we shall reconvene in fifteen minutes."

The Court all stood again and remained so until the bench had left the room. Most of the spectators had not been in a Court before. Having worked themselves up to such a pitch of interest the communal sigh at this delay was almost tangible.

Hartley left the ladies and approached McConnell.

"Is everything alright? You don't think they are concocting something through there?"

"Rest easy, Mr Baldwin. I appreciate you have a personal interest in this matter but it is really quite an open and shut case to me. Now that the warrant has been executed they will simply be paraded before the Court. You know the procedure. They will be released pending a Summons and will come back here later."

So far as McConnell was concerned it would be a formal Hearing and he would need to do very little for his fee.

Hartley briefly noticed the little man in the corner. The man appeared to be passing time doodling with pencil and paper. Mr Baldwin's gaze checked that Betsy and Esther were alright. Again he checked his fob watch this time against the time displayed on the Court clock. As he crossed back towards his seat two or three of the spectators hissed loudly. The usher moved directly over to those responsible.

"Enough of that, any further disturbance from anyone and they will be removed. Is that clear?" he bellowed. No one dared respond. No one did. A subdued hush once again settled on the Courtroom.

****

Once the Magistrates had resumed their positions the Clerk again called the case. Once more there was no sign of any of the accused or their representative.

Dewhurst tapped the bench with his fingers signifying his impatience. He was about to conclude that the accused, by not appearing, were mocking the Court when Mr Waugh strolled into the room. McConnell had a brief word with him.

The Chairman looked down his nose towards Mr Waugh.

"Do you appear for the Defendants?"

"No. I do not" responded Mr Waugh to everyone's complete surprise including Mr McConnell. He continued:

"The Defendants, as they are referred to, have attended this building rather than be arrested"

"That is but a mere quibble" said McConnell getting to his feet. "A warrant for their arrest was granted on Sunday 8th March 1891 and it is the warrant that has obliged these gentlemen to attend here today. I concede they were not arrested and taken into custody. This was an arrangement intended to spare them indignity."

Waugh continued "The purpose of this warrant, a warrant I shall have more to say about later, was to ensure the Defendants did not abscond and were produced to the Court to answer to a charge. The letter of undertaking given on behalf of the Defendants provided they would appear before this Court voluntarily to avoid the warrant having to be executed. They have duly done so and accordingly it serves no purpose and there can be no justification for any of the Defendants to be arrested now."

Before McConnell could venture to respond, Dewhurst peered over the top of his spectacles and said to him;

"Mr McConnell there is nothing before this Court other than an arrest warrant. I think there is a point here. What purpose does an execution of the warrant today serve?"

McConnell hesitated as he realised the folly of the position that was now presented to him.The warrant had no obvious force now. It mattered not whether this was or was not a ploy by Jackson's legal team, the fact that Jackson and the Robinsons were within the building and there was no actual Formal Charge to lay before the Court made the situation rather farcical. With the Court packed and with the press in attendance, this was personally embarrassing. If he did not think of something, Jackson and the others would simply have to be sent back to Blackburn.

Dewhurst prodded "Mr McConnell, are you able to address me on this point?"

McConnell grasped at the only straw available to him.

"Your Honour, I concede the point but, in the interests of expediency, I move for an adjournment of, say, half an hour. This should enable a Summons to be drawn up and served on each Defendant. I appreciate this is somewhat unusual."

Dewhurst turned to Mr Waugh. "And what would your position be Mr Waugh? If the Court was to accede to Mr McConnell's request, would the Defendants be prepared to answer any Summons today?"

The spectators sensed the importance of this moment. Mr Waugh played to the air of tension by getting to his feet slowly. There was then a pregnant pause as his eyes glanced around the Court before turning to the bench and responding:

"Most certainly, your Honour, they will."

At this a huge cheer went up in the Court Room. Dewhurst picked up his gavel and brought it firmly down upon the bench twice.

"Enough" his voice boomed out "This is a Court of Law not a venue for public entertainment. Such behaviour will not be tolerated. I will grant the prosecution motion. The Court will continue consideration of this case once Summonses have been served."

McConnell dashed off to locate the police report and the police stenographer. He would need to write out the charge in long hand to ensure it was correct and then prevail upon the stenographer to drop whatever he was doing and set out the charge on formal paper. McConnell was harassed.

This time the gallery was content to wait. To their ears they had been promised an appearance by the "Gallant Three". One man turned to another next to him and said "Tis a bit like being at the Music Hall is this 'cept there is no music! I mean we have had, as it were, the "warm up" act and soon we can enjoy the "top of the bill."

By now, Hartley Baldwin had a sense of foreboding about this day. Somehow the police or McConnell were making a hash of things. Certainly these arrangements had been made with virtually no notice.......perhaps that had been Jackson's plan.... to catch them all wrongfooted? It did seem all a storm in a teacup, a minor technical hiccup concerning the warrant. It was not as if the case had been thrown out of Court. Even so, Hartley had become unsettled. Things were not within his control. He was very much like the others there.....a spectator.

Betsy detected something of a frown on her husband's forehead.

"Is everything alright?" she asked.

Hartley's reply was rather hesitant. "Yes. Yes. I think so."

The usher proceeded to open some windows to allow air into the room. The incoming air brought with it the strains of the brass band. The crowds outside joined together in the chorus of "Molly Malone".

****

It took much longer than the optimistic assessment of half and hour for the paperwork to be completed.

McConnell, still rather stressed, checked the Summons carefully twice before signing it and passing it over to the Clerk. The charge read:

"That on 8th March 1891 outside St Mary Magdalene Church, Clitheroe in the County of Lancashire, you Edmund Haughton Jackson, William Henry Robinson and Frederick Dixon Robinson did assault Betsy Alice Maude Hall or Baldwin and inflict upon her actual bodily harm and injury."

Copies of the Summons were then made and handed to Mr Waugh for each of the Defendants.

****

There was a bristle of anticipation when the Counsel and solicitors came back into the room and resumed their positions.

The usher went round with a pole to shut the windows. The fresh air was pleasant but the "oompah" and "trills" of the band were not a welcome intrusion at this seat of justice.

The two Magistrates took to the bench once more. The Clerk now called for the third time on this day:

"Call the case against Edmund Haughton Jackson, William Henry Robinson and Frederick Dixon Robinson."

The side door was opened by the usher. The three accused entered and walked to a position in front of the bench.

This was the first time the "audience" had seen at close quarters the famous trio. Some wanted to applaud but forced their hands into pockets. Some wanted to cheer but forced their mouths to stay shut. So chastened by the earlier warning from the bench, they instead just stared with ears keenly attuned so as to miss nothing.

Mr McConnell got to his feet.

"By a quirk in these proceedings, the Summons now calls. My brief was restricted to the warrant hearing and so, regrettably, I have no instructions as regards the charge drawn from the police report. Your Honours must agree this is all unusual and accordingly I must seek an adjournment of one week"

Waugh rose "I strenuously object. The case ought to properly proceed this very morning."

A mild ripple of applause went round the Court. On this occasion Dewhurst ignored the reaction of the audience.

"The incident on Sunday is, on any view of the charge, a common assault of, with respect to the alleged victim, only minor consequence. Any delay in the course of this matter will serve only to cause further slight upon the character of the accused and, I submit, would reflect badly upon the bench."

McConnell retorted "I cannot agree. The case is indeed only one of minor significance. There can be little prejudice to anyone in the prosecution having the benefit of the adjournment sought"

McConnell had fallen into the trap set by his wily opponent. Waugh tried to seize this opportunity:

"Your Honours, my learned friend concedes the minor nature of the alleged offence. Yet in spite of the relative triviality the police saw fit to seek a warrant for the arrest of these three gentlemen." He paused to allow his emphasis on the word gentlemen to hang a little in the air. "Further the authorities pursued them across the county and laid siege for days to a house belonging to a Miss Jackson. A minor offence indeed! Has there ever been any suggestion that any of these individuals would abscond? I rather think not. Was there a basis for anyone to assume that any one of these gentlemen would fail to answer a Summons? I can detect nothing of the sort. Could it ever be contrived that any were possessed of a dangerous or vile proclivity? Absolutely not. So why? Why has all of this come to pass? With all of these indisputable facts, how was an arrest warrant so zealously sought and obtained? This has but nothing to do with a minor common assault. Is it not the case that, far from being anything to do with this case, the warrant was obtained as a device to interfere with Mr Jackson's possession of his lawful wife?"

The audience was lapping this up.

"Moreso" continued Waugh "if what I put forward is truly the case, with undue influence having been brought to bear on the authorities to obtain a warrant for purposes other than in accordance with proper process and in legitimate pursuance of a criminal matter, then the grant of the warrant was an illegal act."

Dewhurst stopped Waugh in full flow.

"Mr Waugh, as far as I am concerned you are raising matters which, although it could competently be raised elsewhere, has no bearing, so far as I can see, on the matter now before the Court. The issue of the Summons has superceded the warrant. Now had you chosen to appear earlier and your clients had been presented to me with the warrant having been executed then the competency of the warrant would have been a real and live issue before me. The matter now is whether or not the Court should accede or refuse the prosecution motion for an adjournment? As we have moved on from the warrant please address the motion."

It was evident that Dewhurst did not appreciate others "grandstanding" in his Court.

"Very well, your Honour, the Defendants each plead Not Guilty to the Charge. We are ready to proceed with this today."

McConnell looked rather aghast.

"Your Honour, the prosecution is not in a position to go ahead today. I indicated already that I have not been fully briefed for trial. I have not seen any of the witness statements. In the interests of justice, I renew the crave for an adjournment of the Hearing date."

Waugh: "I strongly object. The gentlemen I have the privilege to represent have suffered potential reputational damage by the reports thus far published relating to the incident on Sunday. The cloud resting over their characters should not be prolonged beyond this date."

Dewhurst: "Far be it for me to comment on the contents of press reports and their levels of accuracy or concoction, but such reports as have passed my gaze do not appear to me to have been particularly unfavourable to your clients?"

Waugh: "What I am submitting is that the light of the publicity, whatever its nature, is unwanted by any of the Defendants. In the case of the Defendant William Henry Robinson his practice in medicine is in considerable jeopardy by the sword of Damocles that is this assault charge. I have a further submission to make on this point?"

Dewhurst: "Proceed"

Waugh "As iterated in this Court earlier on, the charge before the Court is of the most minor in nature. There are no apparent deep or complex legal issues involved. The Complainant, Mrs Betsy Baldwin is present in the Court and presumably able to give her evidence. My understanding of the Court is that there is no other business before your Honours today and unless my Honourable friend Mr McConnell has pressing matters elsewhere, then it is expedient and I insist that the case be fully heard today."

The spectators could not restrain themselves and yielded up an enthusiastic cheer.

Dewhurst turned to McConnell: "There is a little force and quite a lot of logic in Mr Waugh's argument."

McConnell: "Your honour, I would not and do not pretend that I have other pressing commitments this day. I have though alluded to the preparation difficulties of the prosecution in rather general terms. It is now necessary for me to be specific in this regard. Those instructing me have tried to effect service of a subpoena on one very material witness to Sunday's events but have been thwarted in their attempts to do so and thus, through no fault of their own, the prosecution lacks a large piece of the jigsaw in the case against these Defendants. The prosecution has no statement from this witness. Those instructing me know where this witness is. They have sought access to the witness in question through the offices of those instructing Mr Waugh. I speak of course of Mrs Emily Jackson. This witness was right next to the Complainant when the alleged assault took place and, as such, her evidence is very material to justice in this case. By obstructing and indeed denying access to this witness the prosecution has been frustrated in presenting their case today."

Dewhurst: "How, Mr McConnell, is the situation likely to be different to that described by you should I grant your motion?"

McConnell: "With further time allowed, your Honour, I am confident that a subpoena can be served if there is sufficient opportunity between now and any adjourned Hearing."

Mr Waugh rose to speak but Dewhurst raised a hand with outward facing palm to signify to Jackson's Counsel to resume his seat.

Dewhurst: "Mr Waugh, the issue regarding the motion for adjournment has been put and has been opposed. I have grasped both sides of this argument. I do not need to hear anymore. I will confer with my colleague and resume consideration of the matter shortly."

The spectators did not react but, even so, one could detect a degree of restlessness as, yet again, all were obliged to stand as the bench left the Courtroom.

****

In her bedroom on the upper floor of West View Emily briefly pondered over what maybe going on in Clitheroe at the Court. It did not though occupy much of her thoughts. She was very much a realist in some ways. She had no knowledge of the workings of the law and of the Police Court so wondering about the proceedings and the likely outcome was but a pointless exercise. There were two matters of greatly more concern to her.

Firstly, what awful scene might transpire if her family attempted to effect a rescue in ignorance of the bodyguards, bailiffs or whoever they were that were now stationed within this house?

Secondly, in the mind of this captive, what were Jackson's plans for her? The arrangements he had made for a supplement to her meagre wardrobe denoted a motive on her husband's part that she could not quite identify. Not for a second did she believe that any garments he was soon to provide would be of the bespoke nature and quality that Emily took pride in wearing. Was this indulgence in atypical generosity just a naive attempt to wheedle a way back into her affections? If so, this simply demonstrated to Mrs Jackson how very little Haughton knew of the woman he had married. Or was there some ulterior motive behind this? Emily had been led to believe that Jackson wanted her to have the freedom to circulate within the house and yet her bedroom door remained locked. Why with these guards in position, was it necessary for her detention within the confines of this room? The more she tried to understand these signals the less sense that she could make of it all. Anyhow, what she knew deep down was that even if he could bring about in her a semblance of feelings for him, she could never ever trust this man again.

Emily thereby confirmed to herself the absolute certainty that there existed no hope of any future for her and Mr Jackson

****

Whilst the Bench was away in their private discussion, those within the Courtroom got off of the uncomfortable chairs they had been forced to remain on for so long. They would stand or move about to ease their stiff limbs.

Hartley Baldwin turned to Esther.

"Are you able to return today to Blackburn? I need to know whatever you can find out about Emily."

His sister in law responded "I should have time after this to pack my few things, have some luncheon and then get on the mid afternoon train."

"I will arrange for Hartley junior to accompany you." He then raised his hand as he detected a protest from Esther. "No. I insist."

On his other side, his wife, looking slightly concerned, spoke;

"Am I now going to have to give evidence here today?"

Realising his previous assurances may have come to grief, Hartley placed a hand on Betsy's forearm and said "I am not now very sure about what is going to happen".

"Who else is supposed to be a witness?"

"Well, with Emily not being here, it is only yourself and Dr Musson."

The usher's voice suddenly boomed out "Silence in Court. All rise."

As soon as all were seated, Dewhurst addressed everyone:

"My colleague, Mr Clarke and myself have considered most carefully the motion by Mr McConnell for an adjournment of this Hearing. We have a degree of sympathy with the position he finds himself in. Having said that, we have never before encountered a situation where the Defendants are expected to produce a witness whom they may well suspect will be disposed to give evidence against them. However, as Mr McConnell will well know when he is appearing for the Crown, it is for the prosecution not the defence to bring before the Court witnesses in support of the charge libelled.

It should be obvious also that it is not in the domain of this Court in dealing with a charge of assault to determine issues so vividly argued in the press regarding the status of Mrs Jackson within her current residence. It is quite possible that this lady is indeed being "detained" by other parties at the property in Blackburn. It is equally possible that Mrs Jackson resides where she is through a desire not to attend this Court and a wish to remain furth of Clitheroe. Both scenarios are matters of conjecture and neither can be of relevance to the Court's current considerations.

Mr McConnell, I stated the Court had a degree of sympathy with your predicament. The sympathy we have relates to your lack of a proper brief and not to your witness difficulties. There has to be an equality of preparedness on both sides. The Court acknowledges the argument put forward by Mr Waugh that the Defendants are of hitherto good behaviour and, it is perfectly fair to say, that at least two of them attract an excellent reputation locally (a nod obviously to the Robinson family!). The charge is, it is conceded, not one of much magnitude but there is inevitably the potential for reputations to be besmirched.

Mr McConnell, the decision is that the Court will adjourn the case but only until Monday of next week. The Clerk advises that a full Hearing can then proceed. In the event the prosecution are still not ready and report ongoing witness difficulties then I can be certain that, in the absence of fresh argument, no further delay in proceedings will be entertained and the power to dismiss the complaint against all of the Defendants will be exercised."

For the last time that day, the bench left the Courtroom. As they did so the mood of the spectators was upbeat and there was a mild ripple of applause. Far from being crestfallen or despondent at the lack of a full Hearing and the opportunity that would have been provided to hear from any of the "gallant trio", the statement from the bench that Jackson and his associates might be "let off" was taken as a prophecy of fact and therefore grounds to celebrate.

Celebration was not though on the mind of Hartley Baldwin as he left the Courtroom with "his ladies". Word of what had happened inside the Court was instantly communicated to the phalanx of those gathered outside and there followed much cheering. As soon though as the crowd spotted the Baldwins the mood changed and the cheering was replaced by booing and catcalls. Hartley grabbed hold of the two sisters and literally marched them as quickly as he could along the side of the building and beyond most of the gathered throng or as Mr Baldwin often referred to them as "the rabble."

****

After thanking Mr Waugh for his efforts, Jackson and his colleagues remained a while within the Court building.

"Listen to that out there." said Jackson. "It does make you feel rather good, does it not?"

"Not really" said William frankly. "We still have to go through all of this and possibly worse on Monday."

"Do not rush to such conclusions, my good doctor". Jackson had adopted a condescending tone which he was rather prone to do. "If you ask me we will not return here. Mr Sanderson, my solicitor who I have spoken to daily since last Sunday, foresaw the difficulty the prosecution has. Mrs Baldwin can say whatever she wants against all of us or any of us but it will not matter a jot. In my opinion Mr Waugh will be able to run rings round her. He is a very clever man. Dr Musson was not outside the church. All he can do is describe Mrs Baldwin's injury not how she came by such injury. Unless then I am very mistaken and have been poorly advised, without the evidence of my wife absolutely nothing can be proved. All we need to do therefore is to keep Mrs Jackson happy! Let us head back to Blackburn and there we can toast the great English Justice System."

Jackson was full of himself. He clapped his two fellow Defendants on the back.

Dixon Robinson had a rather pained expression on his face.

"What was that the judge said about two of the Defendants having a good reputation? Was it being suggested that you Mr Jackson did not merit the same regard as my brother and myself? If I were you, I would protest about that."

Jackson gave out a hearty laugh before he embraced the young man.

"Dick. Do not be silly. The judge was obviously referring to your brother and my good self. It is obvious. You are still too young to have grown a reputation-good or bad. However, mark my words when I say that so long as you stick with me you will inhabit a reputation in time that is almost as enhanced as that of myself."

William could not stomach all of this. This was indeed Jackson at his very worst. Clearly, he was using Emily as a pawn to get out of a criminal charge. It was despicable. He was so disgustingly full of himself and William so hated to see how his young brother was still taken in and mesmerised by this awful man.

"Excuse me" piped up the Doctor. "I am not coming back with you immediately. I have my own matters to attend to and wish to have sometime at Clitheroe Castle. I'm sure the two of you can manage quite well without me."

"Oh, quite well indeed" mimicked Jackson with sneering disdain. "Come on, Dick. Let's have a party tonight. Let's leave Mr Misery here."

The two companions left William in the room. He was sad to observe his brother leave robotically with Jackson and without any word to him. It was though such a relief at that moment for William to get away from both of them. William listened and heard the eruption of noise outside which was obviously the reaction of the masses to Jackson's appearance at the Court door. He himself would remain where he was for perhaps an hour. He shuddered at the notion of any accolade from the crowd. For by the time the hour had passed the mid afternoon train would have departed from Blackburn as would the crowds. They had no interest in this Clitheroe doctor and Dr William Robinson had certainly no interest in them.

****

The Soiree

The door to his office burst open which was unusual. Wagstaff looked up to find Bill, one of the senior Reporters on the Northern Daily Telegraph, standing by his desk breathing heavily. Bill was in his fifties and had earlier run up the stairs to the newspaper offices. He had been assigned to the Clitheroe case and had made it back hotfoot to his editor.

Wagstaff ruled his little empire with something of a rod of iron. Punctuality and precision were his watchwords. His reign at the Northern Daily Telegraph instilled in the staff a respect though largely a respect based upon fear.

The editor beckoned in his secretary. Wagstaff had mastered most aspects of his trade but reading another's shorthand was not an efficient use of his time. Whilst Bill recovered from his jaunt up the two flights of stairs, his notes were passed over to Miss Thorpe who proceeded to read Bill's record of the day's events in Court.

Wagstaff remained mostly impassive. However, as soon as his mind latched onto the attack by Mr Waugh and the allegation of undue pressure upon the police, his face lit up. He interrupted Miss Thorpe:

"That is our angle. An attempt to circumvent due process and we know who the finger is pointing at, do we not? It has the fingerprints of the Halls all over it."

"Sir, we cannot print that without hard facts. We might get sued and I might be taken to Court for defamation of character."

"Bill, you should know by now that where possible, we do not allow facts to get in the way of a good story. This is different though. We are only reporting what was said in Court. There is attached to that what is called qualified privilege which means we cannot be sued. We will not name anybody. We just shine a light upon who could gain from such a ploy. It will be obvious to the readers who is "in the frame" for this."

Miss Thorpe finished reading the notes.

Wagstaff: "Type them up Miss Thorpe then Bill and I will arrange the article. This is excellent stuff. What's more, with the case being back to Court next week, we do not need to fret over Tuesday's headline."

As soon as these visitors to Wagstaff's office departed, his door was opened again. There, before him, stood the fresh faced man with the cap.

"What have you got for me?" asked Wagstaff.

The man stepped forward and placed his drawing pad on the desk. He watched a little nervously as Wagstaff opened the cover and leafed through the pad. He shut the pad quickly and stood up. His hand outstretched toward the artist "You have done very well. It is exactly what I wanted."

When the artist had left the room, Wagstaff opened the pad again and turned to the drawing he had selected. He stared at it and purred in his feeling of satisfaction.

****

Also returning to Blackburn at this time was Esther accompanied by Hartley Junior. Unfortunately for them both, the early afternoon train from Clitheroe had been more than an hour late in arriving at the railway station. Rather than wait for the mid-afternoon service she had intended to get (which, no doubt would have been similarly delayed) she joined this first train after her arrival at the station only to find it was the service being used by Jackson and Dixon Robinson to convey them back to Blackburn. This was a blow. Though possessed of no fear of anyone, Esther was not at ease amongst crowds some of whom could conceivably be agents of the press. She pulled her shawl up and over her head hoping that no one would recognise her. This did not make her conspicuous as a fairly strong breeze had developed and coursed round the station building. Hartley Junior assisted her onto the step and into the carriage. Once inside they were away from the crowds. Clitheroe Station did not operate any system for platform tickets and so, apart from the railway staff, only passengers were permitted on to the rail side of the station.

This was not a busy service. Esther was happy to sit down. She had been unable to reserve a seat and hoped that by going to a compartment near the beginning of the first carriage she would avoid any passenger from further up the train walking past her compartment should he or she seek exercise during the journey. Hartley Junior offered to pull down the blinds on the corridor side of the train. Esther though believed that would seem suspicious in the middle of the afternoon and would likely attract attention to their compartment. Esther was just unsettled knowing that Jackson, Dixon Robinson, their legal team and who knows what others were on the self same train as her.

****

Once more the door of Emily's room was unlocked. Susan entered with several bags and parcels.

"Miss Jackson suggests you try some of these on. Make sure you have something for tonight that fits you."

"Susan, can you tell me what this is all about? I mean what is happening tonight?"

"I'm sure I don't know Madam. I did see that Cook is back so at least the fayre should be better!"

"But you must have some idea?"

"Best wait until Mr Jackson gets back, I reckon"

"Is there any word from him?"

"Someone called the house just after Miss Jackson and I got back from the shops. I think it was one of them reporters. She was very abrupt with whoever it was and simply informed me that her brother was on his way back."

Susan left.

Emily looked at the parcels that had been left in the corner of the bedroom. She had no interest in them. They were not her clothes.

Whatever her husband had planned she needed her strength and her wits about her. She lay down and tried to rest.

****

The door of Hartley's office was shut. The staff had witnessed his sudden arrival from the Court. Normally a polite gentleman he had made his way directly to his office without the pleasantry of a "good afternoon" to anyone. The "Do Not Disturb' Notice on his door was not displayed but even so it was obvious to all that he should not be interrupted

After fifteen minutes the door opened and Hartley asked that Mr Weeks join him whereupon the door was again closed only this time with the "Do Not Disturb" notice in place..

"It is not good my friend" said Hartley "not good at all. I fear the case against Jackson will collapse unless we can get Miss Emily out of that house."

"Why is that?" queried Mr Weeks

"I'm not happy with McConnell. He did not impress. He maybe fine dealing with mercantile contracts and banking disputes but in the cut and thrust of the criminal Court I do not believe he cuts the mustard. Yet we will never get a suitable alternative Counsel before the case is heard on Monday. I tell you that my biggest fear is not, believe it or not, Jackson getting off with this assault appalling as that would be but rather my greater worry is for my wife. Counsel for Jackson, Mr Waugh, is a bit of a cavalier type. He sails close to the wind and plays to the gallery. A sharp cookie though. He will do everything he can to run rings around Mrs Baldwin. Now my wife will tell the truth, of course she will. I fear though that with the encouragement of Jackson's supporters Waugh will make her out to be a liar. If the Court then acquits Jackson, Mrs Baldwin will believe that everyone will then view her as a liar. She could not bear that and nor could I. We need her sister to give evidence."

"But how?" said his partner.

"I really do not know. We need to find out if there is a way. I need someone to circulate around Rover Street to ask discreet questions. I need to see if there is a way to get Emily out of there."

"What about Miss Esther?"

"No, unlike my other sister in law, Esther lacks guile. She'd approach the task with a lack of objectivity."

"What about my cousin Mr Rafter? He is living in Blackburn. He does investigations for the Lancashire & Cheshire Insurance Company. I'm sure he would help out. I can call him right away. He will need a photograph of Mrs Jackson"

“Please do that. I'd be very grateful. I will find a photograph immediately.”

"Oh, one more thing. I think we should speak to some of the people who were at the Church on Sunday. We may find another witness. There is still time."

Hartley Baldwin was then left by himself. There was another matter which was troubling him. One which he decided he would not share with his partner. For Hartley Baldwin knew that, just as Mr Waugh had discovered, this pillar of Clitheroe Society and respected legal figure had indeed subjected the police to undue pressure and used his position unfairly in order to secure the arrest warrant for Jackson and the others. Yes, he had been emotionally charged at the time with his personal and protective involvement with Emily. Even so what he had done was wrong. If his actions became public it would affect the reputation of not only himself but also his business. If it came to it, he would have to divulge all of this to Weeks.

****

The train pulled into Blackburn Station. A large covered building well designed by the Railway Company's chosen Victorian Architect. This was no place for Esther to hide underneath her shawl.

Hartley Junior stood by the carriage door. Having selected to travel in the first coach, it was obvious that all of the passengers from the train's other compartments would file by on their way towards the main exit. Once Hartley Junior spied the Jackson entourage move past, they waited five further minutes before clambering down onto the concourse themselves.

They had no difficulty finding a hackney cab. "Granville Terrace" was the command to the coachman.

For Esther it had seemed a long day. She nodded to the concierge as she and Hartley Junior made their way up the stairs.

"You will stay for a cup of tea" Esther said more by way of command than any request as she crossed the threshold of the flat and headed for the kitchen.

Hartley bent down to the doormat just inside the flat.

"You have mail Aunt Esther." His hand held out the note delivered by Mags.

"My gosh." said Esther recognising immediately her sister's handwriting.

She went into the sitting room where she sat and opened the envelope with a silver letter opener. It was, of course, the briefest of notes and no sooner had she opened the envelope than she exclaimed in shock:

"No! Oh my God. No!"

"Auntie what is it?" With concern Hartley put his arms around Esther.

"It's Em. She wanted us to rescue her today when Jackson was away. It is a plea for help only I was not here. I have let her down"

She held a handkerchief to her face to wipe her tears.

"I'd best take this to my father" Hartley said removing the note from Esther's hand.

Hartley Junior remained to console his Aunt for some twenty minutes. He then left without his promised cup of tea.

****

Word regarding the Clitheroe Court had filtered through to Blackburn long before the train carrying Jackson had arrived back into town. The gossip around the streets was that Jackson had been freed, that the assault charge had been thrown out of Court. Obviously not strictly true or true by any realistic measure but this false word stirred those in that District of Blackburn and nearby to once again head towards and congregate in Rover Street.

The street vendor just got word in time. He literally threw the keys of his shop to his wife, loaded his wagon with supplies and headed with all speed to his stall. He could not miss the ready trade there for him or chance another competitor pitching up in Rover Street before him. The vendor was one of the few people present in Rover Street who had no actual interest in West View, the goings on there or the tales in the newspaper. His focus was almost entirely on the business, the extra income. Oh, he enjoyed observing the crowd and the feeling of camaraderie that there was. He also delighted if there was music for he really loved music of all sorts.

He could hear a buzz and it was getting nearer, then there was the sound of a trumpet. He could see the cluster of people heading up the hill. In the centre of the cluster marched Jackson alongside Dixon. They had elected to walk from the station. Who could say if it was a need for exercise and fresh air or to experience at close hand the adulation of the locals that dissuaded Jackson from taking a carriage as he had always done on previous occasions. The crowd outside West View duly erupted into song. Some police officers arrived just in the nick of time to ensure there was a passage for Jackson and Dixon to take to the house. Akin to a scene of a returning Roman General, Jackson stopped to salute the police officers as a sign of feigned or actual gratitude.

In an instant the pair were gone from view, the front door of the house having been opened to admit them and then closed again.

Dixon went directly to the kitchen. He was famished. Jackson went immediately to see Isabel.

"I presume all went well, brother?"

" Very much so. It went swimmingly well and how about you?"

"Well, I did as you asked. Susan and I did the shopping. Why you trouble yourself about this I do not know. Susan told me that your wife never uttered a word of thanks when given the clothes. I cannot see the point. That lady does not know the word gratitude. She should be grateful you married her. I cannot for the life of me understand her."

"Enough my dear" said Jackson as he gently hugged and squeezed his sister. "You know me, Mrs Jackson will either be grateful or she shall pay for everything for a very long time. Mark my words."

He continued:" Now. I hope you do not mind. I have invited my legal team here tonight for, how shall I put it? - a little "celebration". There will be four in total including Mrs Sanderson.They will arrive about eight o'clock. Dixon will have informed cook, so they can dine with us. The bailiffs can eat in the kitchen. There is plenty of wine."

"What about Mrs Jackson?"

"In truth my little sister, that is partly why my legal team are coming. It gives them an opportunity to see my wife. For, by observing her and engaging her in innocent conversation, they can assess the optimum way to deal with her should she ever appear in a Court as a witness."

"Is that not a bit underhand? How do you know she will leave her room?”

"Isabel, is it not the truest of expressions about all being fair in love and war? And she will leave her room. Rest assured she will" Jackson said with a glint in his eye.

He glanced at his watch. "I had best go and see the lady now."

****

It was 6 pm. The sky over Rover Street was darker than it was light. The vendor was pleased. His rush to open his stall had been well worthwhile. The initial rush for his comestibles had ebbed now but he would still hang around a bit longer. The early visitors tended to drift home before seven o'clock but thereafter people out walking their dog or those just finished the late shift at the Mill would begin to arrive. There was a clear pattern to the days and nights around this house.

"Excuse me I wonder if you can help me?"

The vendor saw the man facing him. He wore a thick coat and a hat with a large brim. Small round glasses were perched on the man's nose though strangely his eyes looked over rather than through the spectacles. The vendor did not recognise the individual. He did not seem to come from this area of the town. He allowed the man to continue.

"I'm with the Lancashire & Cheshire Insurance Company. I've been asked by my Company to report on the goings on here and any risks to the property."

The vendor gave the man an odd look. Insurance? That explained his appearance. He certainly presented as an insurance man though the business about a report was beyond the mind of the vendor to fathom.

"You know the sort of thing. What is the likliehood of disturbance or of riot? If so is the building or any part of it in danger?"

"I'd not really know about any of that. It is usually later that the crowd gets a bit boisterous. Maybe you should hang about and see for yourself."

"I might just do that. Would you happen to have some cocoa? It's getting a bit chilly."

****

Emily woke with a start. If the fact of her right shoulder being grabbed was not enough, when her eyes cleared they were met with Jackson staring down at her.

"Do you realise this is the first time I have seen you in bed?" said her husband meaningfully.

As her husband continued to lean over her, Emily recoiled further into the bedcovers uncertain as she was regarding his intentions.

The sight of his wife squirming did please Jackson. Now was not the time though to indulge himself in his sadistic vein. He moved away and proceeded:

"Emily I am disappointed. You do not appear to have looked at the clothes I got for you."

Emily had now gathered her wits again. Best play along with this she thought.

"Oh. I'm sorry. I was going to but then fell asleep. Shall I look now?"

"I need you to. I'd like you to find something to put on and to join me downstairs later."

"Why? What is happening?"

"Let's just say I'm in a good mood. We are going to have a little party this evening and I think it would do you good to be seen with your husband."

"But who will be there?"

"No one in particular - just my sister, Dick and the bailiffs who have been looking after the house. I asked the boy Michael but I haven't heard from him. If he does come, he had better not bring his dog."

"I'm not sure. It does not sound like my sort of thing."

"Come, come. You did say when we last spoke that you were prepared to try. I do not think that going downstairs later is that much to ask"

When Emily did not respond immediately, Jackson stipulated:

"I will send someone for you at 8 pm. Ensure you are ready."

Emily cringed as her husband put his arm around her back, pulled her a little into him and kissed her on the cheek.

****

Outside, the evening spectators had arrived. One enterprising resident from down the hill was very popular for he had managed, with assistance, to bring to this part of Rover Street a brazier. By calling at some nearby properties some volunteers managed to collect sufficient coal and wood to light and keep the brazier going. The heat was most welcome particularly for those who could get close.

By the vendor's stall Rafter was just finishing his cocoa when there was a bang against his shoulder such as almost made him spill the remaining contents of the cup.

“Sorry Sir, guess I must have tripped on that bag down there that someone left. Never saw it in the dark."

Conscious of his brief from Mr Weeks, Rafter proceeded to engage this young man in conversation.

"How come you find yourself in these parts?" he asked.

"I'm a journalist. I'm not supposed to be here. But you see, I spoke to Mr Jackson recently and wrote an article all about it. I've never seen him. Thought I might catch a glimpse of him. If I get the chance I'll speak to him again cos it will do my career no harm. No harm at all."

"Rafter is my name"

"I am Jones. Jack Jones."

"Well, Mr Jones. Or can I call you Jack? What exactly was Mr Jackson like when you spoke to him?"

Jones panicked. For, it was not, of course, he who had actually conversed with Jackson. It had been Marshall. He tried to head off the line of enquiry:

"Mr Jackson was very polite. Of course, the main interest here is his wife. I mean to say what is she like? What is she doing? I myself am not married. If I was though I'd not put up with that behaviour. Mind you if I was married I'd not be out here just now, would I! On a night like this I'd be cuddled up to my wife if you know what I mean"

In order not to stand out like a sore thumb and much as it pained him to indulge this Jones' chap, Rafter decided to stick by him.

"Can I buy you a coffee? Then you can tell me all the questions you'd like to ask Mrs Jackson if you had the chance to interview her."

"Oh. Yes. Oh yes." said the young reporter.

****

Isabel, as was her position in the house, sat at the head of the table. To her right sat Jackson and Dixon was on the opposite side.

The plates were empty. The wine glasses were not.

"The salmon mousse was perfect." said Jackson. "So good to have Cook back."

“I loved the pudding" said the young Robinson. "What was it?"

Jackson burst out laughing. He had been taking some wine. He looked over at his friend.

"Dick it was especially for you -Spotted Dick for Dick!"

He looked again at his pocket watch.

"Our visitors will soon be here" Jackson rose from the table. "Dick, can you see if our friends in the kitchen are finished and ask them to join me in the drawing room?"

He put down his napkin and headed away.

****

In the drawing room, Jackson checked the bottles and glasses that were laid out on the mahogany sideboard. He then went to the corner of the room and removed the dustsheet which had been hiding an item of furniture. In fact it was more than an item of furniture.There was revealed a baby grand piano. His brother had bought it in London and had it installed at West View. Isabel did not play. The instrument had not been used for a long time.

Some of the bailiffs then appeared.

"Susan, please get these men a drink. Gentleman, relax. Enjoy yourselves."

There was a knock at the door. Susan was about to interrupt the drinks service but Jackson stopped her. "No Susan. You carry on. I will get this."

Jackson strode down the hall, opened the door and greeted his friends. His solicitor, Mr Sanderson, his wife Frances and then Mr Waugh.

"Welcome to my humble residence. May I take your coats and then I will show you to the dining room."

Waugh: "Mr Jackson. I appreciate the purpose of this visit as explained to me by your solicitor. I fear it maybe unprofessional of me as your Counsel to actually engage with your wife. Irregular I would say, I understand though that Mr Sanderson has no such scruples. For my part I cannot stay very long."

Jackson escorted the visitors to the dining room. Thankfully Isabel appeared which meant that Frances Sanderson was not the only lady in the room. Jackson ensured that all present had their glasses properly charged whereupon he held up his own glass and proclaimed:

"Ladies and Gentleman, I give you the toast - To success, good fortune and to happiness".

Susan entered the gathering with some nibbles for the guests whereupon Jackson addressed the bailiff nearest him.

"My good man, could you go upstairs and inform my wife that we are ready for her?"

****

The knock at the bedroom door was quite gentle. Emily waited but nothing happened. There was no noise of the key turning. Normally any visitor, if they knocked on the door, would unlock and enter the room. The knock this time was repeated. This was curious. She knew it could not be her husband. Upon realising the caller sought her permission to come in Emily said "Yes. You can come in. The door though is locked".

After the rattle in the lock, the door opened and the stranger to Emily stood in the doorway.

"Excuse me Madam I have been asked to escort you downstairs."

"Yes. Yes. I won't be a minute."

Emily was sitting at her dressing table pretending to be sorting her hair. In truth she was doing anything to postpone the moment of having to leave her room. The bedroom had witnessed so much of her sadness, frustration and despondency and yet it had become her sanctuary. There was now a fear of crossing the threshold, of the short journey out into the world.

"Please come in and have a seat while I finish" invited Emily indicating the chair where the man should sit.

Then, very directly, Emily enquired:

"And who are you? And what are you doing in this house?"

"Mrs Jackson. I'd be lying if I said I am happy being here. I am one of the bailiffs. I am paid to be in this house. What makes me unhappy is that we are being paid to keep you in here."

"I gathered that. But, why? Why should that make you unhappy?" Again, Emily made her eyes look soft. She simply wanted to detain this man for as long as she could. Emily was not particularly interested in conversation. The man's response though was unexpected.

"Well, you see Madam. I was brought up in Clitheroe. For many years your father, the late Mr Hall, engaged me and my father to make enquiries for various legal things he was involved in. He was a great man. I became very fond of Mr Hall. He would often mention how proud he was of his daughters and spoke about you most of all. Mr Hall did not know why so many men craved having sons. He doted on you all. So, for me, you see, all this is wrong. It is not right you being kept here unless, of course, it is what you want?"

Emily now avidly embraced this conversation.

"Of course, I do not welcome all of this. I am imprisoned in this room. My husband is a brutal and uncaring man. I have no access to my family. The only thing worse would be if they put me into an asylum. Mark my words Sir I am so very unhappy here. Yet it seems I am powerless to affect my own situation."

"I can look in your face and I see the truth in what you speak."

"Do you still have family in Clitheroe?"

"Yes Madam, I have a brother who lives over the back of the town near to the waterworks. I live with my wife in one of the Mill Cottages she sort of inherited when her father died."

With the door ajar the sound of a cheer went up from downstairs reminding Emily of why this man was in her room. She had enjoyed the distraction and had enjoyed the conversation. Somehow it had given her fortitude with which to face what she anticipated would be an ordeal.

"You never told me your name"

"Birtwhistle, Madam, Jonathan Birtwhistle. Cos my father was also Jonathan though most people call me Bob. Robert is my middle name."

"I'd like to call you Robert. I think that suits you" Then she continued:

"Robert, you must now take me downstairs elsewise you and I will be in very serious trouble."

****

Hartley sat in the armchair. He was, as Esther had been, greatly disturbed by Emily's note. It was all as he knew it was. Jackson was torturing her. Not physically but torturing her soul. He thought he could swing for this man who had so disturbed and divided his family. Could he pay Jackson to go away? Hartley certainly could afford to do this. He was though getting to know his adversary. There was no certainty he would not take the money and come back later for more. Quite possibly Jackson would delight in telling Mr Baldwin to keep his money. He would laugh in Hartley's face. For much as he was convinced that Jackson had only pursued Emily for her wealth, it was becoming evident that power over people drove Jackson more than riches did. No, there had to be another way.

He put the note his son had given him into the pocket of his waistcoat. He had to keep this as it could be valuable as evidence. He did not though want to trouble his wife with this at present. Betsy had had more than enough stress that day.

Hartley Baldwin remained uneasy. Until he had a clear plan of action he could not settle.

****

At the foot of the stairs Emily turned left. The apprehension in her stomach gripped strong. She heard the noise coming from the drawing room. The laughter grew louder as she neared the door. She took a very deep breath as Robert grasped the handle to open it. As soon as he did so, Emily went cold. She could not move. Instantly the drawing room went silent and to a man and woman every head turned and stared at Emily in the doorway. So this was the creature most had heard of and read about but had never seen.

The silence seemed excruciatingly long. For the first time in years she was actually glad to see Jackson He made a show of walking across to Emily whereupon he took her hand and announced to those present:

"May I introduce you all to my wife, Mrs Emily Jackson. You see she does exist. I, for one, am so grateful for that."

There was a ripple of mild applause. Emily was simply relieved he had broken the ice.

"Emily. I'd like you to come over and meet Frances." He led his wife over to where Mrs Sanderson was seated. He made the introductions and then left her.

Emily knew she was in "enemy territory" and so when asked by Frances as to how she was keeping she responded:

"I am well thank you. The food here is acceptable"

"How do you find life in the town?"

"I cannot say. I have not ventured out yet. I do not care for all of the crowds. They alarm me. Until they go away I will simply rest and enjoy my sister-in-law's hospitality."

Emily was quite impressed with the act she was putting on. Slowly she felt a little more relaxed.

Next, Frances introduced her husband. After some pleasantries concerning the weather, Jackson's solicitor began to probe:

"I wonder where all this will end?"

"I beg your pardon" enquired Emily.

"All this toing and froing from here to Clitheroe and back, this Court and maybe that Court and who knows where?"

"Mr Sanderson I cannot say I know anything about such things. My husband does not involve me in his business affairs and, frankly, I am very pleased that he does not".

"Surely what happens is very much up to you or your family?"

"Now why would that be Mr Sanderson? Why would I, as a woman, have a say in anything? Also, I cannot be held responsible for anything my family might think or do."

"I did not mean anything by it, Mrs Jackson."

A discreet distance away, Waugh listened, observed and took note.

Emily then became less defensive.

"Your curiosity does you no favours Mr Sanderson. It is obvious to me you have no appreciation of me or my situation. I know not your connection to this household but I will not share my personal thoughts and views with anyone I met but five minutes ago."

She looked around for escape. She spotted Robert with another bailiff at the far side of the room.

"Excuse me" she said to the Sandersons as she turned and made her way across the floor. She paid no attention to nor noticed Waugh who she almost bumped into.

In her way across towards Robert she was intercepted by Jackson.

"My dear" he said this time taking her arm. Emily could detect that Jackson was starting to be affected by alcohol. This was not a good sign.

"I've just been chatting away to Dick. We were recalling the time when we were together at this bar in a small town in South Island. After the hard day that we had had we were having some beer when this local, a big big chap, sat down by the piano and played this tune. It stuck in our mind did the tune."

Jackson began to hum bits and pieces. "Think it went something like that"

"That's Libiamo, the drinking song" Emily said immediately

Of course, Jackson was well aware of his wife's long love of music and of her musical gifts. He was so pleased for she had involuntarily walked into his little trap.

"Emily. I've a favour to ask. Would you be able to play Libiamo on the piano?"

For the first time Emily noticed the baby grand piano in the corner. It had been so long since she had played an instrument of this quality. Jackson was correct. She could not resist. For Emily, the piano that evening represented a form of hideaway. If she played the piano, she did not have to speak to people. She did not have to lie or deal with awkward questions.

She actually smiled at her husband when she responded "I do not need a second invitation".

Emily moved almost unnoticed across to the piano.

Isabel beckoned to her brother. "I think we should pull the curtains as there is still quite a crowd outside there."

"Certainly not sister, this is the very time we want to be in a goldfish bowl."

****

By now the brazier was beginning to die out. The chill circulated closer around those outside West View. The vendor had retired home.

Rafter was about to take his leave from Jones who was going on about Blackburn Rovers. He was a regular attender at their football matches.

Rafter returned to the reason that he was there.

"We have seen people arrive at the house and enter it freely, have we not?"

Jones agreed.

"Would you say that there is anything unusual about this house or anything odd going on?"

Jones yawned "All very dull I'd say. So much for me getting a story."

Just then the sound of the first piano notes filtered into the evening air. Then, there was an assembly of male voices.

"Gosh" said Rafter. "They are having a party. The drinking song from La Traviata."

"They are all in that room. I can see movement."

"Jones, if we go over to that corner of the pavement and stand by that fence we shall get a better view."

"Yes" said Jones rediscovering his interest in the evening.

Before they had both got into position the Verdi had finished. It was now a song by Mendelssohn being beautifully and sensitively sung by a soprano voice. Rafter stretched his neck.

"That is amazing. In fact, it is astounding."

"What. What is it?" pressed Jones.

"It is Mrs Jackson. It is Mrs Jackson who is singing."

There was now no distraction inside or outside of West View. Only Emily's voice could be heard.

****

Those in the drawing room were wrapped up in the singing. It was as if they were all transported from their worries and cares. This applied none moreso than to Emily who had escaped into her music and carried herself far away from her awful situation. The sudden applause at the end of the Mendelssohn broke the spell and she was back in the West View drawing room. All the faces she saw were smiling back at her and clapping her. How hard to believe at that moment that they were her enemies.

"Encore" shouted a voice.

Emily stood up and rummaged in the seat for some music. She managed to find one she thought she could manage but before she was seated again, Robert was by her side.

"Excuse me, Mrs Jackson. Would it help if I played and you sang?"

The warmest of smiles graced Emily's face.

With her newfound accompanist Emily stood by the piano and sang not once, not twice but three more times. By the third song many of the guests had imbibed sufficiently well to join in the chorus.

After the final chord, Emily stood there. Her face was radiating happiness. This scene was observed by Rafter and noted by Jones.

The sense of the gathering in the house was that the party was at an end. This was confirmed by Jackson who came forward and stood next to his wife. He addressed those there:

"Thank you for joining Mrs Jackson and myself this evening. I'm sure you will agree that my wife does well on the piano. Far better than her singing I think. Those of you who need a carriage can use the telephone. Safe home my friends."

Isabel was very tired and took to her room. The bailiffs who were not on duty ....those who had been drinking too much....also left. The others detailed for the night shift remained. Mr Sanderson and Frances departed after the former assured Jackson he would speak to him the following day. Dixon had gone directly to his bedroom rather fed up as Jackson's attention had been focussed upon others all evening. Mr Waugh had gone just as the music had started.

With Jackson temporarily involved with the Sandersons, Emily turned to Robert.

"I don't know about you Robert but I really enjoyed that. If only we could do it again sometime."

"Mrs Jackson. I'm very fond of the piano." he continued "It was very wrong you know, what Mr Jackson said about your singing. He must be tone deaf. You have a very beautiful voice."

“Robert” Emily was about to continue but Jackson had returned.

"Well man." he said looking at Robert "shouldn’t you be at your post?"

"No, Sir. I'm off now. I'm not back until Saturday".

"Be off with you then. Goodnight."

Robert went in search of his coat and his scarf before leaving West View.

Jackson was now alone with his wife.

****

"That was such fun. I really enjoyed that" said Emily to Jackson as they climbed the stairs.

"I thought that you would."

She got to the door of her room. As she opened the door she said:

"I would love to do that again."

"That depends. That depends if I allow it."

The tone in Jackson's voice brought Emily back to reality.

"Excuse me?"

"If I choose to allow, it will depend upon how you behave."

Jackson took a firm hold of Emily's wrist. She could not pull free. He held her right wrist up by his shoulder before pulling her towards him. A heavy odour of beer and garlic hung on his breath as he made to force her to kiss him. As Emily squirmed and he tried to control her, a combination of his unsteadiness and one of the unopened shopping boxes caused Edmund Jackson to fall over full length across the floor.

"Get out. Get out. Have I not made it clear? I want nothing to do with you." Emily saw the door of her room remained open.

"If you do not go and go now, Mr Jackson, I will scream and wake everyone in this house."

He managed unsteadily to his feet. As he half turned to retreat from the room his eyes stared in fury at his wife who was crouching by the side of the bed.

"You are a vixen. Mark my words, I will tell the world what sort of a contemptible vixen you are."

Jackson was shaking as he spoke:

"I have given you the chance to please me and make things better. You just throw it in my face. You have no idea how to treat a man. Well, you might not regard me as your husband but you, Mrs Jackson, are and will remain very much my wife."

Then as if Jackson had suddenly sobered up, he stood completely upright.

The fury had dissipated but his face and expression were ice cold as he announced before he left:

"Come hell or come high water, you WILL obey me".

The door was slammed shut.

After ten minutes there was a fumbling sound. Her husband, having forgotten to lock the door, had clearly returned to attend to the task. It took a lot of fumbling before he was satisfied he had properly locked his wife in the room.

****

Emily remained crouched on the floor by her bed for a long time. Her new dress was getting crushed as she stayed in that uncomfortable position.

Emily did not feel hurt, upset or angry.

She felt very sad as she had been so happy earlier and Jackson had cut short her euphoria. No. She was really relieved. Had she given in to Jackson's attentions it could have made her life here easier in some respects but given her true feelings and her past, she could never have forgiven herself and her inner unhappiness would have been compounded. It was at times like this she always saw things clearly-her retrospection on the love she had had for John Anderton. For sure she had never thought or felt it was impossible for her to give her heart to another but, by the same token, that could only ever be for a man who cared even if only half as much for her as John had done. It was that love which always gave her perspective and highlighted, if any highlighting was now necessary, just how far removed in the quality of love for her were such feelings as Edmund Haughton Jackson possessed.

Slowly and silently, Emily undressed and got into bed. She did not trust anything at all about her husband. Was he still lurking about outside? If only the door was locked from the inside. She slipped out of bed. Emily put two of the clothes boxes by the door, one on top of the other. Then she removed an ornamental plate from the wall and placed it upon the top box.

Surely, if Jackson returned in the night, the crash of the tower falling would waken her?

****

The Thursday of that week was not a good day for Hartley Baldwin.

He arrived at his office sharper than was normal. On arrival he learnt his Secretary was ill and would not be at work that day.

He took the mail to his room and sifted through it. In the background he heard others arriving. Hartley was annoyed at himself. He had important work to do for his clients and yet the vision of Emily distracted him so. She was a prisoner after all. He would have to wait to see what Weeks' cousin could find out.

"Ah Weeks, come on in." he said after the former had tapped gently on the open door. Surely, he could not have news already. No, Weeks did not bring news of Hartley's sister-in- law.

Instead, Weeks produced the day's edition of The Northern Daily Telegraph.

"Have you seen this, Sir?"

"Certainly not. I would not give that publication the time of day."

"Well, I really think that, on this occasion you should. I will leave this with you". Weeks placed the paper on the bureau and left.

Hartley picked up the newspaper, shut the door and having placed the newspaper on his desk, began to read. Immediately he felt a hollow in his stomach. He knew why Weeks had brought the paper to him. The headline on the front page read:

"JACKSON WARRANT DISMISSED"

It was the sub heading that was of far more concern:

"Allegation of undue influence on the Police"

Hartley studied the article. No direct references to him. That was fine. It was reported that the police categorically deny succumbing to pressure. Yes, that is good. What is this?

"This newspaper understands from confidential sources that certain individuals who are both close to Mrs Jackson and in positions of influence conspired to obtain the warrant which was illegal. As the Court yesterday dismissed the warrant, the truth as to how it was ever obtained might never be known"

I do not like any of that thought Hartley. This again is Wagstaff 's work. Just as he thought it could not have been any worse and when he was wondering why Weeks had pressed him to read all of this, he turned over the page. He was shocked.

For directly under this article, though not a part of it, there was an obviously exaggerated caricature of Hartley Baldwin. He was depicted in the Court with a puffed out chest, huge red lips and holding a stick towards the Bench.

Whilst the drawing sported the description of "A scene from Clitheroe Police Court yesterday" and never identified the figure portrayed, to anyone who knew him this was Hartley Baldwin. Also anyone who had but a scintilla of sense could now connect the caricature with the article.

The latter was all about abuse of power and influence and now, in the drawing, the figure appears to be dictating to the Court what it should do.

Hartley sank back into his chair. Whilst again he was seething at Wagstaff, he was more anxious about his partner. He should have told Weeks about all of this yesterday. It seemed far worse to explain it all now. Yet that is exactly what Hartley had to do.

****

Susan held the breakfast tray in her left hand as she unlocked Emily's room with the other. She knocked but without waiting a response pushed the door. It would not open fully and some milk in the jug spilled over. The maid cursed under her breath. Having put the tray down on the floor outside, Susan squeezed her head around the door as best she could whereupon she spied the tower with the plate on top of it.

"My, my, what has been happening here?" she pondered to herself. She could just stretch an arm around the door. Carefully with the plate between the tips of her forefinger and thumb she was able to ease the china closer until the weight of the plate could be taken in her whole hand. Once the plate was out of the way, Susan could, with her shoulder against the door, push the boxes back and get into the room. Having picked up the tray she continued as if nothing unusual had been there.

"Well seeing cook is back. This is a real breakfast"

Susan put down the tray then walked to the window to pull open the curtains. When she turned back into the room she noticed that Mrs Jackson had not stirred. She also saw the new dress all crushed on the floor next to the bed. This was not right, definitely not right.

She approached the form lying on the bed and with a hand on the "sleeping shoulder" Susan said:

"Mrs Jackson. I've brought your breakfast Better wake up." She then gave a little shake to the shoulder. Emily remained comatose.

Susan shook a bit harder and still there was no reaction.

By now the maid was alarmed. She decided to go for help but as she reached the door she heard a moaning sound.

"Is that you, John?"

"Madam, you have been dreaming. It is me, Susan. I have your breakfast"

As Emily's eyelids parted slightly she appeared groggy. When she tried to pull herself up onto her pillow Emily coughed and coughed again.

"Please, Mrs Jackson. Are you alright?"

"Susan. Could you open the window? I need some air then hopefully I will be fine."

"Do you want me to get Mr Jackson?"

"Oh no, please do not trouble him. I will be fine."

Susan managed to unlock the little side window. She then took care to pick up the dress which she placed carefully within the wardrobe. The maid felt it was not right to lock Emily in the room seeing as how she was not well. It was though more than her job was worth to disobey Mr Jackson and so the captive was again placed under lock and key.

****

Mr Weeks stood up when Hartley Baldwin entered his office. It was most unusual for the senior partner to appear like this. The protocol had been the same for generations. If the senior partner wanted to speak to you, you were summoned to his room.

Baldwin said: "Oh sit down man. This is not a matter for standing on ceremony particularly given what I am here to tell you."

Weeks:" I gather you have seen the newspaper then?"

Baldwin: "Yes. Yes indeed. It was correct of you to draw it to my attention. It was very wrong of me not to have told you about the warrant. What I did was through personal motivation and I can only apologise to you Sir if this all rebounds on our business."

Weeks was a clever man. He could have tried to take some advantage of the situation. This was the first time he had seen Mr Baldwin look vulnerable. He had though the utmost respect for the senior partner for it was Mr Baldwin who had agreed to take him on as an Articled Clerk, had tutored him and then hired him as an employed solicitor. Indeed it was Hartley Baldwin who had recommended him to Mr Hall and persuaded Mr Hall to take him on as a partner.

"Mr Baldwin, Sir. There is no need for either of us to be despondent. We are in this business together and we will see it through together be our fortunes good or be they ill. The late Mr Hall taught us to fight hard on behalf of every client and they will repay you with their loyalty. Well, that is exactly what you have done and I firmly believe that a whiff of scandal, it is but a whiff, will not in anyway trouble the foundations of this practice."

He held out his hand which Hartley shook in acknowledgement.

****

Dixon Robinson had been up early. As breakfast was not ready, he had gone out for a walk. Now the siege had been lifted it made such a difference to be able to come and go as he pleased.

His stroll took him to a small tree lined park where he found a bench to sit on. He watched the red squirrels dart up a tree nearby. At this hour there was no sign of anyone else out and about. Dixon's mind drifted. In which direction was his life heading?

Brought up within the hallowed halls of Clitheroe Castle, Dixon's family was of traditional stock and very respected in the neighbourhood. Dixon Robinson Senior did not overly indulge his children either with favours or with time. He kept a distance from his sons but was always available should any discipline be required.

Dixon had shared a nanny with his siblings. From an early age he found the routines rather tedious. The lessons from nanny were unexciting and the games she made them play were unappealing to the young Dixon. He was a disinterested and quiet boy. He was alert enough to know that just half a foot out of line and father's hand would be summoned to ensure his obedience.

Dixon had been close to his brother William even though William was quite a bit older. However, William went off to public school and then to medical school and they drifted apart.

There had been a distinct void in Dixon's life.

For Dixon, his life changed, when, at the age of twelve, he had been sitting by the pond at the Castle idly trying to get a boat he had made out of twigs to float. Oblivious to anything around him, Dixon was startled when the voice resonated above his head:

"You must be Dick, sorry Dixon."

He had only ever been called Dixon before. The young man looked up. Standing over him was this tall man with fine features and a striking thin grey moustache.

"My name is Jackson. I have been visiting your father. He had other business to attend to so I chose to have a stroll around the grounds. And, guess what? I found you! Do you mind if I sit down?"

"No, Sir."

"In public by all means call me Sir. Between you and me just call me Jackson. It is how most grown ups refer to me."

Here was a grown up treating him like an adult.

"I see your boat there." said Jackson. "Do you ever dream of sailing on a real boat?"

"Oh yes. I do. Often"

"Well young man. If that is what you desire then that will be part of your future."

Jackson proceeded to regale Dixon junior with tales of his trips to New Zealand and to the Americas. These stories of "daring do" certainly fired the boy's imagination.

"I must take my leave of you now, Dick but all being well I will see you again."

As Dixon entered his teenage years he saw more and more of Jackson. By now Jackson was courting Miss Hall from Shawbridge. He was therefore regularly in the local area and would certainly visit if not reside at Clitheroe Castle if circumstances permitted. He would on these occasions take Dixon out for a walk. He challenged the young man's curiosity by dropping hints of something in his (Jackson's) past. Mostly the youngster picked up on such hints and dutifully enquired whereupon Jackson could impress with more impressions from his "illustrious career."

Jackson once took Dixon to an isolated spot and showed him how to use a rifle.

For the young Robinson this was just thrill after thrill. Jackson had the youth in the palm of his hand. He was idolised by Dixon. Jackson spoke to his young friend about his plans to go back to New Zealand.

"They are crying out for workers, they help you get land and get set up. It would be a rough life being a sheep farmer out there but I am game to give it a go. It is such a lovely place. The cost of passage is not too bad so long as you do not want to come back. A return passage to England is really expensive."

"Can I come with you?" asked the impressionable young man.

"I hardly think so. You are too young for all of that. Your father would never allow it.....maybe when you are older."

By 1887 Dixon was sixteen years old. Jackson having been rebuffed in love had made definite plans to leave the country. Dixon had derived confidence from his friendship with Jackson, so much so that he sought an audience with his father.

"You are telling me you want to go to the other end of the world?" asked Colonel Robinson

"So much I do Sir."

"Mr Jackson seems to me an honourable gentleman. As I see it a trip such as you are speaking of will help make a man of you which is no bad thing. How long will you be away for?"

“Mmm, it is not the intention of Mr Jackson to return."

"My son, you will be back. Of that I am certain. If you go, you go under your own steam. I will help you with your embarkation ticket but, from then on, you are on your own. It will be no holiday at my expense rest assured of that. When is all this to occur?"

"I do not know Sir. Thank you, Sir. "

Dixon could not wait to inform Jackson. By dint of fate though, Jackson did not call again at Clitheroe Castle for a number of weeks.

Things happened very quickly.

Jackson announced he intended to embark for New Zealand in November. The tickets were organised. Dixon had no qualms about leaving his family home. In his mind this is what he was born to be, an adventurer. The adventures had though started before the pair set off for foreign climes for, out of the blue, Jackson had decided to marry..

News of the wedding had been sprung upon Dickson at the door of the church. After the ceremony the wedding party retired to Dr Irving's house for a meal.

Dixon could not keep the event to himself. He was bursting to tell someone. Well, they were married now. It could not make any difference, could it? Unbeknowns to either Jackson or to Emily, Dixon went to the telephone which was in an understair cupboard at the house.

"Operator, can you put me through to Clitheroe 231 please?"

In no time at all the voice at the end of the line said "Hello, Mrs Roberts here."

"It is me, Mrs Roberts, Dixon"

"Well, you have never phoned before. Are you at the Castle?"

"No. No. I'm in Blackburn on a secret mission, so don't tell anyone. I'm just back from Emily Hall's wedding."

"Well I never. Why is it all hush hush? She's not....you know what I mean? She's not with child?"

"Oh, heavens no, nothing like that. Tell you when I get back. Remember, not a word to anyone."

He was suddenly interrupted when the noise of two combative crows resounded at the foot of a nearby oak tree. It was neither long enough nor sufficiently shrill to prevent him indulging in further reflection.

The elation as, for the first time ever, he followed Jackson onto the ocean going liner, S.S. Oroya. This was to be THE adventure.

Dixon took to it all like a duck to water. When the S.S. Oroya encountered a storm he would be on deck revelling as the salt spray covered his face. Rather than a man about the town he was a man about the ship. He would speak to the crew about the weather, about navigation and the ports they had visited. Jackson spent much of the voyage unwell and below decks. The young Mr Robinson imagined he was almost indispensable.

At the end of the long voyage the ship duly docked at Wellington on North Island. Jackson, restored to health, led the way down the gangway. At one point as he neared the pier building he turned to find Dixon standing some way behind.

"Come on Dick, have you still got your sea legs?"

"No." responded Dixon. "I was just savouring my first moment upon foreign soil."

In his dreamlike way Dixon then went through a kaleidoscope of reminiscences of his time in New Zealand before a deafening bark shook him back to the current day. His eyes were focused on this large brown Bull Mastiff standing four feet from the bench staring at him. Thoughts of New Zealand drifted from his mind.

"Chaney" was the call followed by a piercing whistle. The dog turned and enthusiastically went off the way he had obviously come from.

Now, in safety, Dixon stood up. He did not know what the time was but it must, by now, be time for breakfast.

As he ambled back his thoughts overtook him again. He did not want to be in Blackburn. Why had they had to come back? Mind you there had been the excitement of the kidnap. Yes. That was another adventure.

What would happen next? He really hoped Jackson would return to New Zealand. Whatever he did though, Dixon would be right by his side.

In better spirits than he had been in when he left, Dixon returned to West View

A Plans Occurs

Dixon passed the bailiff who had unlocked the front door and made his way along the hall.

"I have been looking for you Master Robinson".

He turned to see Isabel stridently walking up to him.

"I need you to call that brother of yours. He has to attend here right away."

"What has happened?"

"Oh, nothing really, Susan informs me that Mrs Jackson seems ill. Of course, I'd not be surprised if it is all playacting. However, we cannot take any chances. If a doctor we do not know has to see her, he may require her to go to hospital and then my brother would have lost her."

"Yes I see Miss Jackson. What does Mr Jackson think?"

"He does not think anything this morning. He has not appeared." In a disapproving tone she added "I believe any malady Edmund is suffering is entirely self- inflicted."

****

Hartley Baldwin had spent the hour since his meeting with Weeks reading and researching. Just as with most established legal practices his was equipped with all leading authorities on the law and decisions of the courts going back through the ages. He wanted to discuss his thoughts with Counsel. However, just as he thought he'd request his Secretary to place the call he remembered she was not at her work. As he sighed there was a knock on his door.

"Enter".

This time it was Weeks coming into his office. Baldwin stood up.

"Mr Baldwin. I think you should be seated."

"Why, what is it?" said Hartley in a worried tone.

"It is hard to make sense of it. I have just had a long conversation with Rafter. You know, my cousin."

"He has news?" Hartley had gone from worry to sounding rather excited.

"He certainly has. He tells me that there is nothing obvious from outside West View to suggest that any form of siege is in place. People were seen to enter and leave the house quite freely last night."

Any word yet? Any sign of our Emily?"

"Well, you see that is just it. My cousin witnessed what was clearly a party at the house. It was in full swing and Jackson was obviously holding court." Weeks cleared his throat before carrying on.

"Then for most of the evening Miss Hall, sorry, Mrs Jackson was entertaining the company by playing the piano and singing. Outside the spectators joined in. Rafter remained on watch until the party disgorged. Your sister-in-law was left in the room with Jackson. She was smiling and almost laughing. She looked happy."

There was a silence. Hartley was trying to assimilate what he had just heard.

Weeks continued.

"I'm afraid I believe Rafter. He is a good man and a thoroughly sound bloke. He would not speak as he did if he was in any way uncertain of his facts."

Hartley was obviously deflated.

"Thank you, Weeks. I will have to have regard to what you have said."

As Weeks left the room, Hartley, ever conscious of courtesy and manners added

"Please convey my gratitude to your cousin. Make sure that any costs he has incurred are promptly settled."

Once more Hartley found himself enclosed within his room. He had to believe what he had been told. Yet what of the note sent by Emily to Esther? Perhaps, since that note had been penned, she had succumbed again to Jackson's charms? Disheartening and unsatisfactory as this news was, Mr Baldwin had to wrestle with himself to curb his eagerness to speak with Counsel. The new facts did not justify the intended approach.

****

Marshall checked over the advertisements and notices for the next day's publication. He took particular care to ensure that there were no errors in the draft print. An advertiser paid good money and if a word was misspelt or a highlight overlooked then the business maybe lost to another newspaper.

There was the Bourneville layout. That was in order. Dash it. They had misspelt Lozenge as Losense in the notice for the sore throat remedy. As he moved onto the Lost & Found notices Marshall interrupted his concentration, got up and walked to the ante room. There was no one there so he proceeded to the print shop.

"Where is Jones?" shouted Marshall. The foreman shouted back "Not turned up."

Not the first time thought Marshall. Sometimes wonder if that lad wants a job or not. He returned to the tedious task of proof reading.

****

Esther, as usual, sat in the window chair. After seeing the note the previous day she resolved that, apart from the hours of sleep, she had to remain in the chair all of the time. She daren't risk letting Emily down again.

There had though been little, if anything, of note for her to witness. She had seen Dixon Robinson enter the house. She had seen a woman at a downstairs window. It had not been Emily so she assumed the person to have been Jackson's sister.

There was but one policeman who she could see.

The vendor once more had just opened his stall.

It was beyond Esther's understanding all of this. Why would anyone want to hang about in the street day after day after day? What were they expecting to occur? It was all so ridiculous. Why could they not simply release her sister? Emily was the innocent swept up in all this storm provoked by the attention seeking, greedy and selfish Edmund Haughton Jackson. Esther made herself all hot and bothered.

How long would she need to be dormant here in Blackburn? Of course, she would remain for as long as it took to set free her sister. Yet she longed to be back at Shawbridge with the family who understood her. She pictured her family and wondered how they were doing. Esther had trusted the Smiths on Canal Street to tend her family, her flock of turkeys. Renowned were Esther's turkeys. There was a pair she had entered for the National Show at the Crystal Palace. Surely, she would be free from Blackburn duty by the time of the show in June? If not then Betsy would have to take over the vigil here. There is no way Esther would miss the exhibition in London.

****

William was not happy about the call from his brother. The doctor had been feeling much more himself since he extricated himself from the others after the Court. Now he had the feeling he was being dragged back into Jackson's tortured world and he did not like it.

It was only the word that Mrs Jackson was not well that made up William's mind to go. He rearranged the morning Consultations and hastened to the railway station.

****

"There you are. What time do you think this is to turn up for your work?" stated an unhappy Marshall as he saw Jones come through the print room door.

"I have a good mind to dispense with your services. In fact, can you give me any good reason why I should not do so?" he was now staring at Jones.

The young reporter pulled from his bag a large notepad and, without saying a word, held it up for Marshall.

In the mood he was in Marshall snatched the notepad, opened the cover and started to read. As he did so his humour seemed to improve. He sat down and finished reading.

"And precisely how, Mr Jones, did you get all this? Have folk been spinning you a yarn?"

"No. It is the truth Mr Marshall. You see I was there last night. I was in the crowd until very late. There was this insurance man. Least that is what he said he was. He wanted to find out what was going on. He went to the side of the house and I went with him. We both saw her. We both saw Mrs Jackson singing and smiling away."

"How do you know it was Mrs Jackson?"

"The insurance man told me it was?"

"Who was this insurance man?"

"Oh I can't remember his name. Was it Raffles? No. I cannot recall."

Jones could tell that his boss was unconvinced.

"When everyone left, the lady was with Mr Jackson - just the two of them. I'm certain it was Mrs Jackson."

"I'm very tempted to run with it Jones. I will make further inquiries. If it holds up then you have indeed done very well."

When Jones left, Marshall phoned one of his allies in a competing paper. After some small talk, he asked "have you anything new on the Rover Street affair?"

"No. We are running a bit more about the family background, just trying to keep the story going until the Court on Monday."

Marshall was satisfied there was no gossip about the party, the singing and Mr Jackson's obvious reconciliation with Mrs Jackson. In other words Jones had indeed brought him a scoop. There was, of course, one way for this story to be confirmed. Yes. That is what he would do.

****

It was mid morning by the time Jackson stirred. A good wash, a shave and he felt as right as rain. He felt good in himself. The vision of the incident the previous night did not unsettle him for rather than dwell upon Emily's rejection of his advances he preferred the image of the fear in her eyes as he had tried to approach her. All he really had to address this day was the promised call from his solicitor.

Jackson left his room. As he passed through the dining room he encountered Dixon. The young man smiled.

"What is the plan for today?" asked Dixon.

"The plan? Dick, I have no particular need of you today so you may do exactly as you please." dismissed Jackson.

At this point Isabel approached from the direction of the kitchen.

"Edmund, a word please?" Jackson knew his sister very well. She was not pleased. He looked at Dixon who sighed and left the siblings alone together.

"What exactly did you do last night?" Isabel asked as soon as Dixon was out of earshot.

"I do not understand"

"Well, when I left you and Emily together she appeared to be radiant happy and well. So when Susan told me she could hardly wake your wife this morning and that Mrs Jackson appeared very unwell I had to believe you did something to her? As you were obviously too hungover to trouble I had to force myself to see your wife which I did. She did not speak. At times her breathing was very bad. She was groaning. I ordered Master Robinson to get his brother here immediately."

"What is this about William?"

It was obvious that either Jackson's head had not yet cleared as well as he had thought it had or that this was merely a tactic to delay answering her main question."

"The woman needs a doctor. I thought we cannot allow her access to a stranger."

"Yes. Yes. I see Isabel. You are quite right. You have done well."

"So, brother what did you do to her?"

"Sister, I did nothing to her. I reckon the party was just too much for her. She was not herself going up the stairs so I simply ensured she got safely to her room."

"I hope for your sake that you are right. For, there has been more than enough scandal in this family of late."

****

In the upstairs bedroom, Emily felt pain all over her body. One minute she was curled up under the blankets for warmth and the next she became so hot she'd throw off the blankets to try and get cool again.

For once the windows of her room were open and yet she lacked the strength or the balance to steer herself to the window where she could possibly attract Esther's attention if indeed her sister was still across the street.

Her state of illness seemed to magnify her desolation. When she had been fit her world had seemed hopeless, now it felt worse than hopeless.

Even in her fevered mind the question still hurled itself round and round in her head "What, oh God, have I done to deserve all of this?"

****

William's cab dropped him a short distance from West View. The crowd still made it awkward to get close to the property. Dr Robinson eased his way towards the front door of the house and was but a few yards from the steps when there was a scream.

"Oi you. You owe me money."

William turned rather perplexed.

"Don't pretend. I did as you wanted and now you have to pay me."

The crowd laughed in amusement. Some wise crack whistled and appealing again to the crowd's sense of humour shouted across " don't matter if you are posh or you ain't posh, all us men have to pay for our pleasure."

William became all very embarassed as he faced Mags.

"You promised to pay but then you scarpered."

The Doctor did not want to hang about and argue with the girl. He just wanted away. William could not even remember how much he had agreed to pay for the delivery of Emily's note.

How did he even know the note had been delivered? He thrust his hand in his pocket, grabbed some loose change and forced it into Mags' open palm.

Mags looked at the overpayment in her hand.

“Thank you kindly, Sir. An absolute pleasure doing business with you."

The crowd let off another loud burst of laughter.

William banged upon the front door praying it would open very soon. One of the duty bailiffs recognised the good Doctor and let him in without a fuss.

****

Jackson had had two cups of coffee but his physical disposition did not yet admit of any food. He was in the study when the telephone rang.

"Mr Jackson?"

"Who is that?"

'Marshall of the Herald here we spoke the other day."

"I told you then I was not making any further statement to the press."

"Now, Mr Jackson, I did what you said last time. I do not call on my own behalf but rather on behalf of Jones. You know the young journalist."

"I have not forgotten, man. Tell me what this is all about or I will hang up."

"Well young Jones has come to me with a story. One that I think is excellent news but nonetheless I'd welcome some verification from you."

"Go on."

"His article, suggests that there was a lot of socialising at West View, and that Mrs Jackson entertained your guests and was seen to be entirely relaxed and indeed the appearance of a wife completely reconciled with her husband. So far as I know no other paper has this story."

Now this was even better than Jackson had hoped for when he had, the evening before, forbidden his sister to close the curtains. Jackson was very pleasantly surprised to find such an ally in the young reporter or "journalist" as Marshall insisted upon referring to him as.

"Mr Marshall, I could not have expressed the position with my wife more accurately than expressed by Mr Jones. Please congratulate him on his endeavours. And once more I trust you will give him due credit."

"Of course, Mr Jackson. If you do not mind I have one or two follow up questions...........Mr Jackson?..........."Jackson had ended the conversation.

Jackson could but wait. Mr Sanderson was a busy man. He will call when he is free.

****

Susan ushered William into Emily's room. The patient was hardly visible beyond the boundaries of the blankets.

"Please leave me. I'll call if I need you."

The doctor pulled back the upper blankets and felt Emily's pulse. He then put his hand upon her brow at which point the patient stirred.

"Mrs Jackson. It is Doctor Robinson. William. You have a fever. I need you to tell me if you have any pain."

Emily half opened her eyes. As she saw the kindly face of the doctor she tried to smile.

"Doctor I ache all over. I am so very tired."

"I recommend you have plenty of water to drink. No food other than soup. I will see the pharmacologist and get some pills for this."

"What is it? Is it serious?"

"Oh, it is certainly not pleasant. If I am right though it is the same bug I came across in Clitheroe last month. You should feel better tomorrow and be right as rain the day after."

"I do not want to see anyone."

"I will try and make sure you are not disturbed, Madam."

****

Meanwhile, downstairs the long awaited phone call from Mr Sanderson was underway.

"Thank you for last evening Mr Jackson. It was indeed insightful to have been able to see Mrs Jackson. I do not mind saying that she was nothing as I might have imagined following your previous description of her. She was very entertaining"

"Well, that was last night. The bird is locked up in her cage, again."

"As a friend Mr Jackson I understand but, as your solicitor, I must advise you to review the arrangements at West View. The longer you keep your wife under lock and key the more likely her family will be to take drastic action - be such action legal or illegal."

"Sanderson, I don't understand. You have always led me to believe the actions I have taken in respect of Mrs Jackson are actions the law entitles me to take."

"Yes, Mr Jackson. You have not done anything the law does not permit. Circumstances can change though. Sooner or later Mrs Jackson will see her solicitor and will see her family. By all I hear and read you have the overwhelming sympathy and support of the public. Should it get out or if your wife chooses to publicise the conditions as they have been with you, then public sentiment is fickle and could well turn against you."

"I cannot just let her go. Is that what you suggest?"

"No. I know that last night I saw a woman who did not come across as anxious. She was not handcuffed so far as I could see. What I am saying, again as your friend, is why must you keep her in an upstairs room? At least allow her the freedom of the house. Give her less scope to later complain or cause trouble for you."

"I cannot do much just now Sanderson. Even were I to take your advice and I am not saying that I will, I cannot at this point in time. I am told my wife is ill today so I imagine she will have to stay in her room."

Sanderson had wondered and did again now wonder about the sort of man he was representing. A husband who gets a Court order to get his wife back, takes the law into his own hands and gets her back and is lauded as a romantic in sections of the press and yet, he says, he is told his wife is ill. Has he never checked her himself? Sanderson remembered he was this man's solicitor and not his conscience:

"If I were you I'd get a doctor to look at Mrs Jackson."

"The doctor is with her now. I organised it first thing." lied Jackson who then continued:

"Yes, Dr Robinson came from Clitheroe as soon as I told him."

"You mean the Doctor Robinson who was in the dock in Clitheroe yesterday?"

"The very same."

"No. Mr Jackson that is not good enough. Now I do not know Dr Robinson but if, heaven forbid, there is something seriously wrong with Mrs Jackson that this doctor fails to notice, he is so very closely associated with you Sir that it may be perceived by many as a conspiracy. Indeed it might be suggested you deliberately deprived the woman of independent medical advice. For your own sake I urge you to have her seen by a Blackburn doctor."

"It sounds all rather exaggerated to me. I'd almost think you were deliberately trying to get me worried."

"Mr Jackson perhaps the more pressing matter relates to your next Court appearance at Clitheroe on Monday."

The rest of the conversation related to Monday's Hearing. Sanderson noted all he could from Jackson regarding his sister-in-law Betsy which could be of use to Mr Waugh in his cross examination of the victim of the crime.

****

William met his brother in the drawing room.

"Are you back off up north?" asked Dixon.

William peered out of the window, his eyes scanning both this way and that.

"I need to get to the pharmacy but want to make certain that that infernal paper girl is not about."

"Oh dear brother, I have no idea what this girl has done to you but most unlike you to be so flustered. You are usually so calm and collected."

"Be quiet Dixon. I do not have the time to bandy words with you.'

No sign of Mags. William made his way to the front door.

Jackson came from the study.

"Where is your brother?"

"He just left" Dixon said in a rather offhand manner.

"What did he say regarding Mrs Jackson?"

"Nothing"

"Did you not ask? snapped Jackson.

"Guess it slipped my mind."

Dixon knew well he was irritating Jackson. He did not mind. He was bored with all this Mrs Jackson stuff. Dixon had witnessed exactly how Jackson could treat others so, he reckoned, he could try to play the same game.

****

Word soon spread around the street of the witnessed jollities at West View the previous evening. As a result, the numbers who flocked to the street that morning were even greater than before.

The man with the bugle who had been present on the first day of the siege was back. There was certainly a musical "flavour" to the gathering this Thursday as, of all things, a hurdygurdy had been brought and set up just outside number 4 Rover Street.

The vendor, of course, was present. By this time he had built up a regular clientele to serve. The vendor's wife though was greatly displeased. She was tired and her mood seemed to swing from disenchantment to rage. She could accept being conscripted into the shop in an emergency. For example, if the vendor was sick. However, the Rover Street situation had gone on now for days. The shop was a good but not spectacular business and, without any children, provided a comfortable albeit simple standard of living. The vendor's wife was accustomed to being at home, entertaining a friend to a cup of tea with a small tipple besides, calling on a neighbour to catch up on local gossip and to strolling past and looking into the windows of shops. The early rise and daily trek to the shop and being confined therein for the daylight hours was not pleasurable and she ensured the vendor knew this. He was immune to her hostile carping and was making money as he knew the Rover Street affair would not last that much longer so he simply had to make the most of it.

****

When William re-entered West View, his way to the stairs was blocked by the figure of Jackson.

"Doctor Robinson. Would you be so good as to provide me with a report upon my wife's state of wellbeing?"

"Of course, Mr Jackson" William was a little out of breath and was still uncomfortable conversing with Jackson. "The lady has had a bad bout of fever. She has a high temperature but I believe that so long as she has rest and plenty of water she will be much better by evening time. She can have no food other than soup. I have just bought these pills for her. Mrs Jackson must have two of these every four hours. Oh, I do not recommend that the patient sees anyone in her room. She needs complete peace and quiet."

"Thank you, Doctor. I will take those" said Jackson holding out his hand to receive the pill box.

"But Sir, I said, the lady should not be disturbed."

"Doctor, your business here is finished. You may post your bill to this address. Now, good day to you." Jackson, having thus dismissed William, turned on his heel and headed towards his study.

Jackson's suspicions had been raised. William's emphasis upon his wife being left alone suggested to him a plot. A plot between Mrs Jackson and the doctor? Surely not. What could they possibly conspire about? Yet, thinking back, Jackson recalled the words of concern from William, the sympathy he had expressed at times for Emily. It had been the doctor who had been entrusted to deliver food to Mrs Jackson's room where he had, on occasions, dwelt longer than appeared necessary. Jackson could not work it out. He only knew he could not again allow Dr Robinson back into the house. Now he felt he had to keep an even closer eye upon his wife

****

It was lunchtime at Prospect House. Charnock had set the table. Betsy waited. As the hall clock chimed the half hour past noon she saw Hartley senior and Hartley junior walk together up the front path.

The three of them were seated around the table each enjoying a bowl of fine healthy vegetable broth and freshly baked bread.. The vegetables were from the garden at Prospect House.

Betsy asked "Any word of what we are doing about Emily?"

Hartley replaced his spoon into the bowl and fiddled with the silver initialled napkin ring.

"It does not augur very well my dear. I really do not see what I can do. After what was relayed to me today, it maybe folly for us to make any move."

A look of concern invaded Betsy's eyes. She waited patiently for her husband to explain.

"I have very reliable information that there was a party at Jackson's house last night. Your sister was seen smiling and enjoying herself to the full. Why she was even seen walking upstairs at the end of the evening with that husband of hers. How can I think of taking any legal steps? I have to prove she is being held in that house against her will. I'll be honest with you Betsy it does not look good."

"But how do we know? She could have been put up to it? She could have been threatened?"

"That is just it. Supposition and more supposition. No proof."

"Excuse me sir" interjected Hartley junior. "I could go down again and see what I can find out?"

"That would be good" said Betsy before Hartley banged the napkin ring on the table and declared:

"No. It is too dangerous for any of us to go near that house. The place seems to be crawling with reporters. We can find out no more than anyone else walking in Rover Street, I have my own sources. For now, the Baldwins had best not be seen to be abroad in Rover Street. It is unfortunate that we have no spy from within the house."

At that Mr Baldwin Senior arose from the table- a sign to his son.

They made their way back to the office.

****

Jackson entered Emily's room.

Still suspicious of what his wife might be planning, he went immediately to shut the bedroom windows. The noise of the windows caused Emily to stir.

"The doctor tells me you should be better by tonight."

He walked to the bedside cabinet and put down the pillbox. "You must take two every four hours. Do you understand?"

Emily nodded in the affirmative rather than speak.

Jackson made no mention of the incident in her room after the party. It was as if it was inconsequential to him as, indeed, it was.

"I want you to get better Emily. You need to get out of this room."

Emily was certainly not well but she could not believe her ears were affected by the infection. Did she really hear what Jackson had just said?

Jackson was worried about the situation between her and William. He could not, for the moment, do anything to engender further fury and venom from his wife. The lecture that Sanderson had given him had begun to seep into his consciousness.The solicitor had been correct. For so long as the bailiffs did their job the security of the house could not be breached. It could work quite well with Emily remaining a fish but in a larger bowl. Jackson thought it a clever tactic for he would appear to be both kind and generous and yet Emily would not guess that his desire to punish her was just as strong now as it had been when she had first refused his request to assume the relations of a normal married couple.

"It was good for you to be able to circulate last night. So, I am now quite content for you to go downstairs and play the piano, read or whatever you want to do. Please though try not to annoy my sister-it is after all her house."

Emily murmured "Am I allowed to go out?"

"Not yet my dear, not quite yet. Let us see how the new arrangement works."

Emily whispered through lack of strength "Whatever you want." Her eyes then closed.

****

Jackson raced downstairs. "Where is McAllister?" he asked one of the bailiffs.

In a few minutes the heavily built head bailiff appeared. "You wanted me Mr Jackson? I hope that nothing is wrong."

"There will be something very wrong if there is any slip up. From now on there are changes to the arrangements. I need an assurance that the changes will be imparted to all of your men including those who are off duty. There must be no slip ups."

"I understand."

"Firstly, the doctor who was here today, Dr Robinson, is not to be admitted to this house again."

"Understood."

"Also, I am permitting Mrs Jackson to have the freedom of the house."

"Pardon me for asking, but does that mean she will be playing the piano again?"

"That is entirely a matter for her, McAllister. Anyway, you are well aware that your primary duty to me is to ensure that no one enters this property to remove my wife. It is though equally the case that Mrs Jackson is not to be permitted to leave the house. My wife can be conniving and I worry, I confess, that she could get round one or more of your men by giving them some hard luck story, I don't know. Whatever she says will be lies, remember that. It is on your head McAllister. If she gets out it is you personally who is responsible to me. If any of your men , by oversight or deliberate act, facilitate her escape then it will be a breach of our contract and I will not hesitate to seek substantial damages."

"There will be no cause given for such. I can guarantee that."

"I hope so" said Jackson as he walked away.

Something was up thought McAllister. In his prior dealings with Mr Jackson he had found him very cool, confident and collected. The man he had just then conversed with was obviously unsettled. He would almost say rattled by something. He had never encountered Jackson like this. Certainly, it was not McAllister's position to question the relationship between a husband and a wife. Having though observed Mrs Jackson the previous evening, he found what people had been saying about her hard to credit. McAllister was something of a music afficionado and had been impressed by Emily's singing. Even so, there could be a perfectly good reason for Jackson keeping his wife indoors. McAllister had his orders and to disobey these orders would result in him never being hired for any security work ever again.

****

By evening time Emily had perked up just as William had anticipated. Her temperature felt more normal which she ascribed to the pills. She was fed up with soup.

She could hear the hubbub of the crowd still outside. Also reaching her ears was the sound of horses going along a nearby cobbled street. Every so often a section of the crowd would break into song and it was almost as if the crowd, having witnessed the house party the previous night, was now trying to provide the entertainment themselves.

Emily was not unsteady now. She managed to get to the bedroom door where she turned the handle and found that the door was indeed no longer locked. She shut the door quickly. Jackson had given her freedom yet she was too reticent to leave her room. Let's suppose I do go down there, thought Emily. What will I find? Miss Jackson who detests me and wishes I was not here or that stupid young acolyte of my husband. I will never forgive him that phone call he made from Blackburn on my wedding day. I may encounter the bailiffs who I do not want to converse with. And then there is my husband himself. If he could be normal for a while I do think I could pass the time of the evening with him. He cannot though be normal. He usually wants to control me or embarrass me. If he drinks he becomes aggressive. There is no point. Were he to leave the house, I would maybe be able to play the piano.

Emily gave up this course of thought.

"No, no, no. It is no use" she screamed to herself. "I'm still a prisoner. I am indeed a bird who cannot fly. I do not belong in this cage. I need to get home. Will I ever be allowed to see my sisters again? Will I ever be able to revisit John's grave?" Emily had, by now, worked herself up into quite a state.

As she lay back and let her tears run onto her pillow the sound of the hurdy gurdy pierced into Emily's conscience. The crowd took up the tune "Home Sweet Home" - for the captive in her bedroom this was cruelty beyond measure.

****

The citizens of both Clitheroe and of Blackburn woke on the Friday morning to some very inclement weather. The wind had picked up and the rain which had begun as light became very heavy.

Outside West View, Rover Street was, for once, deserted. The torrential downpour proved that there were indeed limits to the interest of the public in the ongoings at that address. The vendor's stall was closed. The vendor's wife may therefore have the rest she certainly believed was due to her.

From the bedroom window Emily looked out safe in the knowledge that there was no one about out there to stare at her. The dark clouds and general gloom reflected on her mood. She could not find any grain for optimism as she gazed through the window without looking. Suddenly her eye caught a movement. Automatically she tensed to retire further into the room. Just in time she registered that the movement she had seen was Esther frantically waving from the flat across the road. Emily then enjoined with her sister by waving just as keenly in return. Emily's initial joy though was short lived. To see her sister but be unable to properly communicate or speak with her just made Emily upset. She continued to wave but at the same time tried to discreetly wipe her tears with a handkerchief.

She was still there waving when Jackson strode into the room. He made directly for his wife and before she realised he had taken her by the shoulders and turned her around. Not aggressively but in a controlled manner. Emily did her best to recover her composure as her husband said:

"My dear, you look better than you did yesterday. Indeed much much better. May I suggest you get dressed and then join me downstairs for breakfast?"

This caught Emily rather off guard. As had happened before with Jackson when she was not able to countenance an argument with him, she just agreed.

"I will return for you in fifteen minutes."

Under her breath after he left Emily cursed and cursed. Why had she agreed to this? Well, perhaps it would be alright. At least she would be accompanied downstairs which was far better than facing it by herself.

****

Hartley Baldwin and his son were swept along the road by the wind and each fought manfully to control their umbrellas as they walked to the office. It was not that far from Prospect House to the office and Hartley Baldwin had always made a point of walking between the two places. This was not for health reasons. No. He had learned from Mr Hall that by making the daily journey on foot you were seen. You became known. People who may swither before formally contacting the office for a Consultation may well take an opportunity to converse with you in the street. Yes. Some very useful and profitable business had been picked up by way of the walk to and from the office.

Hartley Senior said "Good morning" to his Secretary who was once more at her desk.

"The mail is in your tray, Sir."

"Thank you."

Not long after, Hartley was in his chair slitting envelopes with his silver letter opener. His son entered

"Sir, perhaps you should see this. After what you were speaking about yesterday at lunch, it does appear after all to be true."

Hartley saw that his son was holding the Manchester Herald. He more or less knew what to expect in that paper. Left to himself he may have questioned if there was any point in even reading it. Out of deference to his son's obvious consideration he took the paper in his hand and with a heavy heart found the article by Jack Jones on the inside page.

He read the full description of the joyous party and the opinion of the reporter that both Mr Jackson and his wife looked happy with each other. It was when he saw a quotation from Jackson that was printed that Hartley refused to read anymore. He briskly closed the paper, folded it and handed it back.

"It is not as I would have wanted things to be. Your Aunt Emily has her own mind. I have advised her more than once what I believe is best for her. I have done all I can."

Hartley wanted to shut off his current train of thought and distract himself with his work. He looked up at his son.

"Young man, do you not have work to get on with? I do not pay you to just stand there!"

****

As she descended the stairs with Jackson, Emily had her senses about her. She did not like the touch of Jackson's hand on the back of her waist but was powerless to shrug off his hand without it causing a fuss. She looked to her right and noticed two men by the front door.

Emily was led by her husband to the small dining room. He pulled out a chair for her to sit on before sitting opposite her. Within minutes Jackson stood when his sister entered. Emily remained seated with her eyes fixed on the table.

"Good morning sister, I trust you slept well."

"I did, thank you, until that rain started battering against my window."

Susan entered with a tray. Three bowls of prunes were deposited on the placemats.

"Is Master Robinson not joining us?" enquired Isabel.

Jackson replied "I suggested he eat in the kitchen. Frankly he is starting to irritate me. Anyhow he always does as I ask."

"Such a shame that others do not do so" said Isabel.

Emily knew well this comment was a dig at her. She remained calm. The prunes were finished in silence.

Susan then removed the bowls before bringing to the diners a steaming dish of kedgeree which was immediately served onto plates.

"Have you heard from Raynsford?" asked Isabel.

"No. I have not, have you?"

"No."

The rest of the meal was effectively spent in silence only occasionally being punctuated with small snippets of conversation between the siblings at the table. At no time did either Jackson or Isabel seek to engage Emily in any conversation. To all intents and purposes she was ignored. It was almost as if they wanted her there for show but did not really want her there at all.

At the end of the breakfast Emily did not forget her manners. For as she stood up from her chair she glanced towards her husband and said "Thank you for breakfast. It was very nice."

Emily felt like saying that whilst the food was fine the company was dreadful. She remained though restrained.

"I will go back to my room now. After yesterday I do need to take rest.If you will excuse me?"

"Of course, my dear, I will help you upstairs."

"No, thank you. There is no need. I will summon you if I need you."

Emily returned along the hall towards the stairs. She was conscious of the "guards" staring at her as she went. It made her feel uncomfortable.

As soon as Emily was out of sight Isabel sniped at Jackson.

"At times you make me cringe. All this "my dear" business. "I will help you upstairs". What is all that about brother?" Isabel continued: "It is obvious to me you do not care a jot for that woman. What was the point in her coming down for breakfast? You never spoke one word to her. She made it clear she had nothing to say to you and that she did not want to be here. Her whole presence in my house upsets me, after all she and her family have done to you. You know what Edmund I reckon it is time that you were honest with her, honest with me and of course honest with yourself"

"I'm sorry Izzy. It is just the way I am". Jackson rarely used his childhood pet name for his sister.

As Isabel herself left the dining room she muttered "I do not understand you."

****

Jackson remained at the table for sometime. It was true he thought. He did not feel his normal self. He started to take stock. He had just fallen out with his sister and she had sounded serious. His charms were not working on his wife. Dixon appeared disenchanted with him. He had banished Dr Robinson. It looked like everyone was deserting him. For a moment he felt vulnerable. Only for a moment though. He metaphorically stood on that fleeting moment of weakness. No. He did not need any of these people. When friends and followers had previously deserted him he had always found more to replace them. Jackson was his own man. Why he could indulge himself in more adventures. A return to New Zealand perhaps? If only there was not the perennial issue of money. His resources were very low. He then realised that was the cause of him not being his usual self. The one fear he had had for a long time was running out of money. His brother had agreed to sponsor the abduction adventure but he knew Raynsford would not indulge him for much longer.

This period of introspection made Jackson feel better. So long as he could bury his secret fear by pretending it did not exist then he could still ingratiate anyone with his charm.

****

When the interruption came, Hartley was engrossed in studying the title deeds of an estate near Preston owned by a member of the House of Lords. Mr Baldwin's client had been shooting on this estate for some five years. Now the noble Lord had ordered him to stay off the estate. Hartley held a magnifying glass close to the deed plan. He was trying to follow the boundary line when the knock on the door sounded.

"Not now" said Hartley.

"Excuse me, Sir" said the secretary as her head appeared round the door.

"It is not a good moment."

"I understand. But the man says it is very important."

"What man?"

"He won't give me a name."

"Well, I'm not seeing him."

"He asked for you by name."

"It does not matter. He can make an appointment to see me. Tell him he can book the appointment under a false name if it makes him feel better!!"

"I did suggest he make an appointment but the man said he can only see you now as he has to get back to Blackburn."

The word Blackburn made Hartley suspicious. Was this a reporter? He could not be doing with that.

"Did he not say why he has to see me?"

He mentioned something about the old Mill Cottages.

By now Hartley's attention was far removed from the boundary of the landed gentleman's property. He sighed, folded up the plan, stood over his chair and said to the Secretary:

"Well. I might as well see your mystery man"

****

When his Secretary next opened the door she was followed by a man Hartley thought he recognised yet could not place.

"Please sit down, Sir" invited Hartley pointing to the chair by his desk. "Now what is this about Mill Cottages?"

"Please forgive me Mr Baldwin. I am not here about Mill Cottages for that is only where I stay. I just thought if I told you the real reason for my visit you might refuse to see me. I am here about Mrs Jackson. My name is Birtwhistle."

Hartley looked very carefully and almost suspiciously at his visitor.

"Birtwhistle? The name is certainly familiar to me. Anyhow, with the greatest respect, Mr Birtwhistle, if you are who you say you are and live at Mill Cottages, what could you possibly tell me about my sister-in-law that I do not already know?" He continued to study the man sitting opposite to him.

"Mr Baldwin. I used to carry out work here for old Mr Hall. That is maybe how you heard of my name. Well that is how I first met Emily. Sorry, I mean Miss Hall. The family were very good to me back then so

I simply could not believe what I have been reading and hearing lately about the lady. Well, I now know that none of it is true. Even so, I reckoned it is not my place to interfere until that was this morning. When I read that article in the Herald I just realised I could not simply sit back and say nothing."

"My man, slow down. I do not understand. You say you know the stories are untrue but exactly how do you know this?"

Robert then explained to Hartley how he had been part of McAllister's team hired for security at West View, how he had encountered Emily and that Jackson had more or less blackmailed her into attending the party everyone was speaking about. Emily had confided just how unhappy she was and how she longed to be back with her family. Jackson kept her locked in a room and was, according to Robert, a nasty piece of work.

From having been so despondent these last days Hartley was now again motivated and determined to meet the challenge.

"Mr Birtwhistle. I am indebted to you for coming to see me today. What you have told me is invaluable. Tell me. Would you be prepared to give evidence?"

"Sir, I would do almost anything to help you get your sister-in-law back but alas I cannot give evidence. I have my wife to support. Were it known I had provided evidence, let alone were I to give evidence in a Court of law, then I would have no job and little chance of getting another one."

"No. No, of course, I understand." Hartley did understand. "I will sort it all out Mr Birtwhistle and, when I do, I will make sure Emily knows of the help you have been to her and your visit today."

"Thank you. There is no need though. I will tell Mrs Jackson myself."

"What? You are going back there?"

"Yes. I am back on duty tomorrow morning. I confess it feels all rather strange. I am being paid to keep Mrs Jackson in the house and yet I feel I am part of a conspiracy to get her out. If you have any message for your sister-in-law you can let me know. I will be at 2 Mill Cottages. I leave for Blackburn at five thirty in the morning."

As Robert got up to leave, Hartley also stood up and walked across with outstretched hand. His handshake with Robert was enthusiastic.

As soon as Robert had left Hartley went immediately to Weeks' office.

"Are you having difficulty with the Estate Plan, Sir? Need a hand with it?"

"Estate Plan? Oh fiddlesticks to that. No. It is Emily. Mrs Jackson. My whole time now is devoted to getting her home" He then summarised all that Birtwhistle had said.

He then issued instructions to Weeks.

"Please phone the Clerk of the Queen's Bench directly and organise a Hearing for Monday morning. Next, I'm calling the Inner Temple to find out the best Counsel available."

Hartley then proceeded smartly along the corridor to his son's room.

"Hartley, I need you to leave immediately. You must go to Blackburn. Get hold of your Aunt Esther and tell her she is needed back here."

Hartley junior had inherited his father's knack of knowing when to ask questions and when not to. He would have loved to know what had happened and why everything was suddenly urgent. He knew though that this was not the moment for questions. If he left right away he should just catch the lunchtime train.

****

Betsy Alice Maud

Esther Anne Maud

THE DAILY GRAPHIC

An Illustrated Newspaper.

No. 371.—Vol. V. [Registered as a Newspaper.] LONDON, THURSDAY, MARCH 12, 1891. [Price One Penny.

The Weather.

"VERY COLD."

The following forecasts for to-day were issued from the Meteorological Office at 8.30 last evening.

District.		Forecasts.
[illegible]		Northerly or north-easterly winds, light or moderate; very cold, slight snow showers, bright intervals.
[illegible]		Varying light northerly winds; fair and very cold at first; possibly slight snow later, and tending to fog.
[illegible]		Same as Nos. 4 to 5.
[illegible]		North-easterly to easterly winds, cold; fair as a whole.
[illegible]		Wind becoming south-easterly or southerly; fair and less cold than of late, unsettled subsequently.
[illegible]		Same as No. 7.
[illegible]		Easterly winds, freshening; some snow.

Warnings.—None issued.

Remarks.

As the depression in the east disappears, quite steady weather is likely to occur over England. The new depression in the south-west can scarcely advance quickly, but it would do so at all.

LATEST READINGS BY NEGRETTI & ZAMBRA'S INSTRUMENTS.

Barometer (corrected for temperature and reduced to sea level), [illegible]. Thermometer, 28. Wind, S.S.E. [illegible] as recorded by the Jordan recorder, two hours [illegible].

HIGH WATER AT LONDON BRIDGE.

To-day ... Morning, 2h. [illegible]m. ...... Afternoon, 3h. 31m.
To-Morrow, Morning, 3h. 51m. ...... Afternoon, 4h. 12m.

THE SNOWSTORM.

TRAFFIC PARTIALLY RESUMED.

ACCIDENT TO A LIGHTSHIP.

DEATHS FROM FROST.

Telegraphic communication with those districts in the south and west which had been isolated on Monday night having been resumed, instances of the discomforts and disasters of the recent gale continue to come in. The Miserable Monday of 1891 has indeed fully earned a place in meteorological annals but little less prominent than that of the Terrible Tuesday of ten years previous. Like the whirlwind of 1881, that of last Monday and Tuesday was felt most severely in the south, its centre moving apparently up the Channel, and its circumference sweeping the southern counties of England and the northern coast of the Continent. Penzance, Weymouth, Ventnor, and other health resorts which pride themselves on the mildness of their winter climate, felt the rigours of the icy blast more keenly than the places further north. It is reassuring to learn from the report issued last night by the Meteorological Office that the complex depressions of the past few days are passing completely away from our neighbourhood, and are being succeeded by a general rise of the barometer, decreasing northerly winds, falling temperature, but, in other respects, improving weather. Snow showers are still reported in many parts of England, but in the west and north-west the sky has cleared, and in the south of Ireland the wind is veering somewhat, with a rise of the thermometer. Over France, westerly and south-westerly winds are reported, and at Rochefort the wind (which at 2 p.m. was north-westerly) has backed to south-west. At 6 p.m. yesterday the temperature was—Highest: 52deg. at Biarritz and Brest, 46deg. at Rochefort, and 40deg. at Valencia; Lowest: 7deg. to 20deg. at the Scandinavian stations, 24deg. to 30deg. at the Scotch stations, 26deg. to 30deg. over England. Hard frost prevailed last night over the inland parts of our northern counties and in central Ireland. The weather was fine over the northern, north-western, and western parts of the kingdom; less fair in the east, where snow showers were still reported, but with bright intervals. The snow last night was again heavy over our southern counties, and much rain fell in the northern parts of France. In London, yesterday, thousands of men were employed in clearing away the snow, some of which was carted away and thrown into the Thames, while in other cases it was flushed into the sewers by means of the hose. Numbers of seagulls were to be seen in the Thames between London and Kew. At Battersea Waterworks, which are situated by the side of the river, a large flock assembled during the morning. The boisterous weather on the Essex and Kentish coasts has, it is supposed, driven the birds so far inland.

ON THE RAILWAY.

The Duke of Edinburgh is still detained in Taunton, as no trains can get through to Plymouth. He visited the places of interest in the town yesterday under the

(Continued on page 3.)

THE ABDUCTION OF A WIFE: THE SEIZURE AND DETENTION OF MRS. JACKSON BY HER HUSBAND. (See page 3.)

LAW REPORT.

COURT OF APPEAL.

(Before the LORD CHANCELLOR, the MASTER OF THE ROLLS, and Lord Justice FRY.)

BOILER EXPLOSIONS.—The case of the Queen v. The Commissioners under the Boiler Explosions Act, 1882, was an appeal from an order of Justices Cave and Charles, discharging a rule nisi for a prohibition to be directed to the Commissioners for the purpose of preventing them proceeding with an inquiry into the cause of a fatal explosion of certain steam pipes, which occurred in a coal mine, in Durham, belonging to the Tyne Coal Company (Limited). In the Act the Commissioners are empowered to inquire into the causes of any explosions of "any closed vessel used for generating steam." For convenience' sake, the steam used for working a steam engine in the mine in question was generated in a steam boiler on the surface of the ground, and the steam was conducted through some hundreds of feet of piping to a steam chest in the mine, whence it was conveyed to the engine. The explosion occurred at the lower end of the pipe in the mine, and the question was whether the portion of the pipe came within the definition of a closed vessel used for generating steam, and if not whether the Commissioners had power to inquire into the cause of the explosion. The Court below were of opinion that the pipes were part of the closed vessel, and that the Commissioners had power to inquire into the cause of the explosion.—The Tyne Coal Company, Limited, appealed.—Their lordships affirmed the decision of the Court below, being of opinion that the object of the Act was that inquiries should be held in the case of all steam explosions, and that the pipes constituted a part of the closed vessel.—The appeal was therefore dismissed with costs.

CHANCERY DIVISION.

(Before Mr. Justice ROMER.)

WERTHEIMER v. COHEN.—The plaintiff in this case sought against the defendant, Mr. Cohen (the publisher of the *Financial News*), an account of the profits made in connection with a certain speculative adventure under an agreement in writing, whereby the plaintiff was to have two-thirds of the cash or shares realised by the defendant. The plaintiff's case was that the defendant had accounted to him up to a certain date and point, but not fully. The defence was that the plaintiff had not fulfilled one of the conditions precedent with regard to the advance, and that the defendant had accounted fully. It appeared that in January, 1887, defendant applied to the plaintiff to advance money for the purchase of a property in which he and others were speculating, but did not give particulars of the property, which now turned out to be a mining property known as the Kea Farm. Upon application the plaintiff paid the defendant £500, and agreed to advance a further £1,000. The plaintiff's case was that the £1,000 was not required, while the defendant alleged that application was made for it, and that Mr. Wertheimer failed to advance it.—Mr. Neville, Q.C., M.P., appeared for the plaintiff.—Mr. Haldane, Q.C., for the defendant, said that if his instructions were correct he was so confident that the defendant had accounted fully that he would submit to an account being taken, and abandon the other defences.—Mr. Justice Romer thereupon made an order for an account to be taken of all the cash, shares, and other considerations received by the defendant in respect of the profits accruing to him in respect of the speculation in the agreement referred to.

THE ABDUCTION OF A WIFE: SKETCHES AT CLITHEROE POLICE-COURT DURING THE HEARING OF THE CHARGE OF ASSAULT.

The curious romance at Clitheroe has reached to the police-court. The charge against the husband, who has abducted his wife, and his friends, Mr. W. H. Robinson and Dr. Dixon Robinson, is one of assaulting Mrs. Jackson's sister, Mrs. Baldwin. The hearing has been adjourned. The defendants were cheered by the crowd that escorted them to the Court.

HONOURING THE NEW ASSOCIATE OF THE ROYAL ACADEMY AT THE GLASGOW ART CLUB: MR. DAVID MURRAY, A.R.A., REPLYING TO THE TOAST OF THE EVENING.

The annual house dinner of the Glasgow Art Club has been made the occasion of congratulating Mr. David Murray, one of the original members of the Club, on his election as an Associate of the Royal Academy. The health of the new Associate was proposed by Mr. Francis Powell, President of the club, who made humorous reference to his first meeting with Mr. Murray on the shores of Loch Sunart. Other honours recently conferred on members of the club formed the subject of a toast proposed by Mr. James Bell, and replied to by Mr. James Guthrie, whose pictures were the chief of the Scotch work which commanded admiration at the Munich exhibition last year. The toast of the Glasgow Art Club was proposed by Professor McKendrick; that of the guests being responded to by Mr. W. D. McKay, of Edinburgh.

QUEEN'S BENCH DIVISION.

(Before Mr. Justice GRANTHAM and a Common Jury.)

"A DANGEROUS PERSON."—The case of Harris v. Opperman was an action brought by Mr. H. G. Harris, a solicitor's managing clerk, against Mr. H. J. Opperman, who had been co-trustee with the plaintiff under a marriage settlement, to recover damages for alleged slander. The defendant denied having used the words complained of, and pleaded that the words he did use were true. The slander was alleged to have been uttered by the defendant to a solicitor, and to have been in these terms: "Be very careful of him, as he is a very dangerous person, and has received £150 from the trust, and has fraudulently kept it, and for doing that has been kicked out of his situation." Mr. Kemp said there was no foundation whatever for the allegation of fraudulent dealing with the trust fund. The plaintiff did borrow £150 from the settlor, which he had been unable to repay, but that was not part of, and had nothing to do with, the trust funds.—The solicitor to whom the slander was said to have been spoken did not remember the exact terms used, but admitted that the representations of the defendant made him distrustful of the plaintiff. The defendant himself denied that he made use of the word "fraudulently," and the statement he sought to justify was that the plaintiff had received the money and not paid it back. The defendant also denied having said the plaintiff was kicked out of his situation, stating that what he did say was that he himself had kicked the plaintiff out of his (defendant's) office.—The jury found a verdict for the defendant, and his lordship gave judgment accordingly, with costs.—Mr. Leonard: Will your lordship grant a stay?—The Judge: I admire your courage. (Laughter.)

CENTRAL CRIMINAL COURT.

(Before the RECORDER.)

STEALING POSTAL ORDERS.—Percy Bent, eighteen, labourer, was indicted for stealing three postal orders, the property of the Postmaster-General.—On the evening of the 19th ult., the prisoner entered a post-office on Twickenham-common, and asked for some postal orders, and also for some postage stamps. The post-mistress produced the postal orders, and while she was getting the stamps the prisoner suddenly snatched the postal orders from her hand, and ran away. Information of the robbery was circulated to the neighbouring post-offices, and the following day, upon the prisoner attempting to negotiate the stolen orders at a post-office in Sudbury, he was arrested.—In defence, the prisoner urged that he was the dupe of other persons.—The jury found the prisoner guilty.—Mr. Richards informed the Court that for some time past a gang of persons had carried out an impudent method of robbery at various suburban post-offices by this method of "snatching," or else by "ringing the changes."—Prisoner was sentenced to twelve months' hard labour.

STEALING A CASK OF WHISKY.—Francis Gosin, twenty-six, labourer, was indicted for stealing a cask of whisky, value £14, the property of John Stuart.—The prosecutor is the proprietor of the Clachan, Newgate-street. On the 3rd ult. prisoner was observed wheeling, on a barrow, a cask of whisky from the premises of the prosecutor. The prisoner was followed, and upon being stopped he stated that he had been engaged by two men to remove the cask. He failed, however, to give any further information.—The jury found the prisoner guilty, and he was sentenced to six months' hard labour.

(Before Mr. Justice HAWKINS.)

THE HOUNSLOW MURDER.—Alfred James Bartlett, thirty-five, wheelwright, was indicted for the wilful murder of Rosina Bartlett.—Mr. Mathews, in stating the facts of the case, said the circumstances under which the charge was made were of an extremely painful character. The prisoner was a respectable, hard-working, and industrious man, who followed the occupation of a wheelwright, and had been in one situation for many years. Unfortunately, some ten years ago, the accused had a fall. Since that time he had been subject to epileptic fits, and had of late acted in a very strange manner. At the time of the occurrence the prisoner, his wife, and his daughter (the deceased), aged five months, were residing at Hounslow. On the night of the 18th ult. the prisoner returned home and went to bed at about seven o'clock in the evening. His wife left home for a few minutes upon some domestic errand, leaving the child and the prisoner alone in the house. Upon her return the prisoner made a communication to her, and in consequence the police were sent for, and in the presence of the police officer the prisoner said, "I have murdered my baby." The child was found lying on the bed, having apparently died from suffocation. The prisoner went quietly to the station, and in reply to the charge, he told the officer that he "killed his baby with a brace."—A doctor, of Hounslow, spoke to attending the prisoner, who, he stated, was subject to fits. He had often complained of pains in the head and sleeplessness.—Other medical evidence was given, and then for the defence it was submitted that death was due to natural causes.—The jury found the prisoner guilty, but that he was of unsound mind at the time the act was committed.—His lordship made the usual order for the prisoner's detention.

THE CAT.—George Chandler, Herbert Hyde, and John Causton were indicted for a highway robbery with violence. Hyde and Causton pleaded guilty.—The prosecutor, Edward Fisher, resides in Eagle-place, Mile-end, and about eleven o'clock on the night of the 1st ult. he was in the Whitechapel-road. He was set upon by the prisoners, who were well known to the police. They knocked him down, and, having very roughly assaulted him, they robbed him of three shillings. The police came up, and Hyde and Causton violently assaulted Constable Elliott.—The Common Serjeant sentenced Chandler to twelve months' hard labour, and Causton, who was described by the police as a cowardly ruffian, to eighteen months'; Hyde was sentenced to twelve months' hard labour, and both Causton and Hyde, in addition, were each ordered twenty strokes with the cat. Both these prisoners had been previously convicted.

THE ATMOSPHERE OF THE COURT.—Mr. Avory complained before the Recorder of the atmosphere of the court, stating that the ventilating machinery, instead of pumping in pure air, appeared to be filling the place with sewer gas, or some equally poisonous kind of vapour. The Recorder directed that the matter should be inquired into.

PART TWO

Emily's Story

From 1891 until her death, the name of Emily Jackson was known to most of England. Her name had featured in every newspaper whether local or national. Her name was in articles in the press in both New York and in New Zealand and yet such fame, such notoriety, was the very last thing this lady would have wished for.

Emily Emma Maude Hall was born on 10th February 1845. She was born into a typically Victorian family which held high moral principles, were regular church goers and who firmly believed in discipline.

Emily's two older sisters were different in nature. The eldest Miss Hall was Betsy Alice Maude Hall. She was a talkative and sociable girl and young woman. The middle sibling Esther Ann Maude Hall grew into a dogmatic, outspoken and independent individual. In comparison to the others, Emily was a quiet but thoughtful child who very much kept her thoughts to herself. Though her personality was so very different to her sisters she was, nonetheless, close to both Betsy and Esther throughout her life.

Emily's upbringing was traditional and secure. She did not enjoy particularly good health being afflicted with bouts of rheumatic fever. Emily discovered a passion for music and, as a child, spent hours playing the piano. She would certainly come out of her shell given an opportunity to play for the family.

The three sisters were brought up at Shawbridge a solid and spacious property in Clitheroe. They were materially well provided for.

Very much the head of the household was Henry Hall. The girls' father conducted a legal practice from Duck Street in the town and was much respected in local circles and beyond. Henry Hall was elected Mayor of Clitheroe on four occasions and he viewed the position as a great honour and indeed a mark of his position in society.

Mr Hall ensured that his three daughters were "educated" in the values of the age such as deference to elders, obedience and the observance of Christian principles. Behind these stern teachings though Mr Hall cherished his children. He was well aware of the dangers he perceived in society at large and the motivations of jealousy and greed that were so easily prevalent when you entertained or encouraged the company of persons less well off than he was. He would therefore ensure that he knew exactly what any of the girls were up to in order to, as he saw it, protect them from the evils abroad. His position in the town meant it was relatively simple for him to make enquiries regarding any of the Miss Halls without raising suspicions. At the time Clitheroe had a population of barely ten thousand or so and if any of them had wanted to, it would have been very difficult for any of his daughters to operate in secret from their father.

As the girls grew up, the vetting of any suitors for his daughters became instinctive. It has to be remembered that the feelings of any of Henry's children were very secondary and would be simply dismissed if Mr Hall determined that any particular suitor did not "fit the bill".

Betsy, being the oldest child, was the first Miss Hall to encounter the rather brusque rejection of male admirers by her father. She would not be consulted as any gentleman in question would be summoned to see Mr Hall and after a meeting of no more than ten minutes the gentleman would depart and Betsy would not see him again. She would thus be upset on many an occasion.

It did though all work out for Betsy. For, in time, she attracted the attention of a young solicitor in the Duck Street Practice. This was Hartley Baldwin. Upon Hartley Baldwin being assumed a partner in Mr Hall's practice he became engaged and then married to Betsy.

Esther did not cause her father to fret. She did not overtly show any sign of interest in romance. Should any man appear to have amorous designs he would often be thrown into retreat by Esther's cutting tongue and manifest rejection of friendship let alone anything more. This Miss Hall was more wrapped up in her poultry breeding and looking after her turkeys than interactions with people she neither knew nor wanted to know.

This left young Emily. She was possessed of romantic dreams but for her they were just dreams. Emily was content that they remain as dreams for she was basically very shy and also rather in awe of her father. Within family life, her music, reading and the church the youngest Miss Hall was quite happy with her life. It was comfortable so why should she upset such a life and cause unhappiness.

Emily would accompany her sisters to local social events such as fetes or go to picnics organised by the family. At these gatherings Emily tended to watch the others who were there. She would be perfectly polite and would converse well if anyone engaged with her but she would not encourage or be overly friendly or interested.

The stars did align for Emily for when, the son of the former Vicar at St Mary Magdalene Church in Clitheroe disclosed an interest in her, she soon fell in love. This was John Edward Anderton.

By sheer coincidence, John Anderton was, like her father and her brother-in-law, a solicitor.

Emily was excited but nervous. She would see John at Church and in passing at some local soirees but finding time together proved very difficult. Emily would always have to explain to Esther or her father where she was going. She did not want to lie but equally did not want to risk upsetting her father.

The moments she did manage to snatch with John were the happiest moments she, in her young life, had known.

John Anderton was perfectly respectable. His connections with the Church and with the law would, one may imagine, have recommended him to Emily's father. Indeed, this suitor had personal resources and could well provide for Emily.

However, just as fate had brought this happiness to Emily's door, so fate turned against her and cruelly took it all away.

The first upset for Emily came on the Sunday when John got a message to her at the Church service to meet her on Back Lane that afternoon. Esther was too busy cleaning out her turkey shed to be concerned and Emily did not need to say anything, as she first brushed her hair and then skipped off to meet John.

John was waiting for her. There was no one else around so she put her arm in his as they walked out into the country away from both the Church and the town.

For his part John found it so very difficult. Beside him was the woman he loved and she was radiating joy as she smiled and looked up and into his face with her soft eyes. Yet inside the weight of what he had to tell simply grew heavier with each step forward that he took.

When he could bear it no longer, he took hold of Emily by the shoulders and turned her around. She could then see the seriousness in his eyes.

"What is it John? I can tell something has happened."

"I need you to be strong Emma" said Anderton using the name that no one else called her. "I had to see the doctor yesterday about this cough I have had."

Emily then looked even more concerned.

"Well. It seems I have tuberculosis. I may not have very long to live."

John then held her in his arms in an embrace and in a silence that spoke more than any words.

John then continued:

"I am so sorry Emma. I had so wanted to spend the rest of my life with you. Though I never said and we never spoke of it you must know I would have married you."

Emily suddenly pulled herself together and then said impulsively "We can still get married. We will get married."

The two of them parted just as the now distant clock struck 3 o'clock.

As she half walked and half ran back to Shawbridge Emily's head was bursting. The dreadful news of John's health tore at her and yet the joyful thought of marriage and not having to hide anymore kept her buoyant.

****

Back at the house, Esther looked several times at her sister. She knew something had happened. She did not ask and Emily did not tell her anything. All in good time thought Esther.

****

After 7 o'clock Henry Hall could always be found in his study where he would be dealing with Council work or tying up some unfinished office business.

The gentle knock, the slow opening of the study door revealed Emily entering the room. Mr Hall knew this must be serious. His daughters never entered his sanctuary and certainly Emily would be the very last he would have expected to do so. He laid his pen on the desk. Anticipating some dreadful news from her he gave her a reassuring paternal hug.

The last thing he expected to hear from this child was of a marriage proposal. As accorded with his legal training though, Henry listened patiently to Emily. He was irked from the start by the fact that he himself had been singularly unaware of her infatuation with Anderton. His humour did not improve when he learnt from her that it was effectively Emily who had proposed the marriage to Anderton. The final straw came upon learning of Anderton's diagnosis.

He interrupted his daughter.

"It is no use. I cannot possibly agree to this. The man cannot support you when he is dead."

"But father, we love each other." Emily beseeched now in tears.

"What can you know about love? It is pure infatuation in my book. You are motivated by sympathy for his illness. That is all. I shall pay Mr Anderton a visit tomorrow."

"No father, do not do that."

"Enough. I have said what has to be said and what must be. The subject is closed. You have to give up on this man for he cannot bring you happiness."

****

True to his word, Henry Hall called on John Anderton the following day. John could not but agree with Emily's father that the marriage Emily so craved was pointless. He agreed to put distance between himself and Emily. The two men shook hands."

For weeks, Emily was grief stricken. John did not return her messages. He was not attending the Church. She knew her father had sent him away from her. Slowly and gradually over months, normal life returned to Emily. The simple life with Esther and her turkeys.

Emily, though wistful regarding her parting from John, would not allow herself to dwell on it or wallow in any feeling of self pity. She became quite content with the peace she found in reading, the beauty of the countryside she beheld on her regular walks and the escapism she would find in the piano. Yes, there was ingrained in her a deep seated grievance at Mr Hall's ruthlessness and lack of any obvious empathy for this daughter's feelings but she refused to become a rebel within the family. She lived with this grievance but she would not allow it to become manifest in any of her conversations or dealings with her father.

****

Jackson's Story

Captain Jackson of the Royal Navy shared something in common with Henry Hall. His marriage produced three children, only in his case they were two sons and a daughter.

The Jackson history was predominantly one of proud military service and Captain Jackson epitomised the lineage. What of his two sons? Could they fall into line as it were?

The older son, Raynsford, decided to go into commerce and, following a good education, became a cotton manufacturer in Blackburn. He was not though disinterested in military matters. Raynsford devoted much of his spare time to developing a new form of Artillery Defence and made such an impression that he was made an Honorary Colonel of the Lancashire Regiment.

In 1842 Raynsford's life was turned upside down when he became temporarily homeless. For in Preston that year, some three thousand cotton workers elected to strike for a fair day's pay. The dispute was bitter. Raynsford was vocal in his support for the Cotton Masters against the workers and this led directly to a small group of the strikers setting fire to Raynsford's house and razing it to the ground. The incident shone a spotlight on the town of Blackburn which was in uproar at what the press described as the "sacking of Mr Jackson's house".

Raynsford was though fortunate in that the Cotton Masters, in acknowledgement of his support of them, gathered together the sum of £10,000 which they gifted to Mr Jackson.

Raynsford could not face living and working any longer in Lancashire. He used the donated funds to start a new life for himself in London.

The daughter of Colonel Jackson was Isabel. Isabel grew up to be fiercely loyal to not only Captain Jackson but her brothers also. Anything that was said by way of criticism of the Jacksons she would almost perceive as a call to battle. She would be the first to rush to defend the family honour.

Perhaps this closeness to her family was, in a way, conditioned by Isabel's personal situation, she was unmarried and with no obvious prospects. Following the death of Captain Jackson his estate, which could be described as not overly substantial, passed to his sons.The house where she stayed at West View, 2 Rover Street, Blackburn was provided for her by Raynsford. Accordingly, this Jackson daughter had every motivation to support, protect and maintain the unity of the family.

So, what of the third sibling?

Edmund Haughton Jackson was born in 1840. As a child he was not particularly striking or special. He laboured somewhat when it came to academic studies but excelled at running and at sports. Young Edmund left school with a record that would at best be described as distinctly average. A couple of years later with still no clear picture as to what he wanted to do with his life, Edmund, having heard tales about various British Colonies, decided he would travel abroad.

His travels saw him arrive first in Australia and then in New Zealand in 1857. At the time the Maori Wars were ongoing. From about 1845 until 1874 there were a series of wars between the colonial settlers and the native population. No sooner it seemed that one truce was signed in one part of the islands than armed conflict broke out somewhere else. The government was enlisting volunteers. The groups of volunteer fighters were known as Irregulars. In modern parlance the Irregulars maybe akin to a band of guerillas where standard rules of battle do not apply and yet camaraderie amongst the group is immense.

Whether hearing tales of these Irregulars in a bar near Watanui one night triggered the "call to arms" inherent in his family or not, the following day Jackson went and enlisted at the nearby Government Office.

Jackson was an excellent shot and following the first skirmish involving his small band, he discovered a taste for this life. As the accomplishments of his troop grew, the men looked to Jackson for leadership. Though there were no official ranks in the Irregulars, Jackson became known as and was called Captain Jackson. Standing this was the same rank that Edmund's father had held at the end of his career this "Irregular" Jackson felt very proud of himself in achieving this at his young age.

When the next truce was signed with the Maoris, Jackson's troop was ordered by the Government to disband.

There was a first flush of success as Jackson told of his adventures to an eager audience whether at his work, in a bar or wherever. In a short time most would have heard the tales before and wanted then to look ahead and to beyond the wars.

He was working at The New Zealand Post Office and even earned a promotion. Jackson again became tired with the lack of direction and the sameness of one day into the next left him both bored and unsettled. He felt the same as he had done back in England.

Through his position within the Post Office word came to him of war having broken out in America. Surely there was a need for fighting men over there?

Captain Jackson duly found his place taking part in several battles between 1861 and 1865. When the civil war ended he drifted briefly down to South America where there were various indigenous disputes ongoing.

In his early thirties Captain Jackson returned to England. He returned a different man than the one who had left over ten years previously. He had cultivated a thin moustache which, no doubt partly due to the humidity and heat in Brazil, had turned prematurely grey. Jackson's exposure to foreign climes had given his complexion a tanned colour. The rigours of the mercenary life gave him a rugged appearance and he could accurately be described as "a fine figure of a man".

Now his manner was confident. Jackson regarded himself as a born leader.

Upon setting foot again on a British shore Edmund went directly to Raynsford whose house was at Sydenham in London.

There the elder brother immediately noticed the changes in Edmund.

"Edmund, my brother, you are most welcome here."

"I do not use that name anymore." said the younger Jackson. "Those in my troop called me Haughton and that is how I wish now to be known"

"Well, whatever. What do you intend to do with yourself now?"

"In the course of my travels I encountered a lot of important people, Government people. I have a list of contacts. I believe a number of rewarding opportunities will come my way."

Jackson went out most days supposedly to speak to his "contacts". In reality he'd spend most of these days strolling about London. Jackson would get the occasional job but, as these tended to be fairly menial in nature, he would never mention them to his brother. These positions never lasted very long. It was not that Jackson was averse to hard labour, he most certainly was not and was in fact a good worker. It was those who gave him orders that he could not deal with. For, in his mind, he was a leader and could not tolerate being spoken to in such a manner and would simply walk out.

As the months and indeed years passed Jackson got used to his London life. The free accommodation at Sydenham, fleeting spells of employment and occasional dalliances with women in the city kept him occupied.

It was not Jackson who tired of all of this but rather his brother. Raynsford had several times to assist Haughton financially since he had returned and he was happy to do so until he realised that the younger Jackson was just "playing", making no effort either to settle down or do a proper day's work. Why, Raynsford had even lined up a job for his brother with a friend who operated a brewery only to be met with:

"Thank you brother but no I cannot take that position. I have an interview next week for something more significant."

In the end, Raynsford managed to prevail upon Haughton to leave Sydenham. As Raynsford put it to his brother:

"There is no obvious reason for you to linger further in London. I believe that there is considerable industrial expansion taking place in Manchester and thereabouts. There will be prospects for you there. In any event our sister needs assistance with roof repairs and decoration at West View. You must go and assist her."

Jackson could not refuse. The cry to family loyalty was as strong to Jackson as it was to the other two. Little did Jackson realise that he would, before very long, be seeking help for himself from both his brother and his sister.

****

The Picnic

Henry Hall died in 1875. His estate fell to be divided equally among his three daughters. The firm of Henry Hall & Baldwin which had commenced in 1841 was now in the control of Hartley Baldwin.

Having been in business with and being related to the late Henry Hall, Hartley Baldwin was intimately aware of how Betsy had been brought up and her father's protective attitude to all of his daughters. Hartley Baldwin took on the responsibility of the legal practice and, as the only male with a connection to the Hall family, it seemed natural to Hartley to take on the mantle of protector over them. This was, to his mind, even more important now that Esther & Emily enjoyed their paternal legacy. If he was honest though, Hartley had to admit his prime concern would be Emily. With respect to Esther, Emily's looks made her more likely to become snared by some inappropriate and unscrupulous man. After all the trouble with Anderton, yes, Hartley, just like Mr Hall, had to be possessed of hawk eyes so far as his younger sister-in-law was concerned.

Colonel Arthur Robinson was Steward of the Honour of Clitheroe and was based at Clitheroe Castle where his youngest son Dixon also stayed. In view of their station in the County the Robinsons were well known and generally would be invited to any grand gathering or event in the neighbourhood.

Arthur Robinson was another with a military background and, although he had served in the army, he had come across Captain Jackson at some Joint Service meetings and had remained in contact with him after they had respectively left the armed forces. It was through this connection and at the suggestion of his sister that led Edmund Jackson to first visit Clitheroe Castle. Quite apart from his father's connection, there could conceivably be benefit to Jackson in forming an acquaintance with the esteemed title holder of Clitheroe.

It was on his initial visit to the Castle that Jackson came across and introduced himself to Dixon Robinson. Of course, Jackson was confident enough to present the correct impression to Colonel Robinson who, for his part, was happy to exchange military tales with his visitor. For, time had moved on for Colonel Robinson and it was not often these days to find a younger man interested in regimental stories. In short Jackson endeared himself to the older man who made Jackson promise to return to see him.

Jackson proceeded to find excuses to make regular visits to Clitheroe Castle. He still hoped that Arthur Robinson, with his connections, could find him a position that brought with it a respectable income. Yet the Colonel appeared to always defer such an enquiry.

"You need not worry. Something will come up for you soon. Now, did I tell you Edmund of when the regiment was posted to South Africa?"

That Jackson persevered with his visits probably had something to do with young Dixon more than the progressively tedious recounting of army life by the Colonel. At times Clitheroe Castle was something of a refuge. Now away from the attractions enjoyed by him in London, Jackson found life in the north not exactly as comfortable. Isabel was always on at him to do this about the house or do that. Unlike at the Sydenham property, Isabel would make it clear to her brother that she expected him to contribute financially to the running costs of West View and further displeasure he derived from the climate. So far as the wind and the damp conditions were concerned, he was hardy enough alright but, in comparison to the milder temperatures in London, it was simply uninspiring.

However, the young Robinson always managed to boost Jackson's ego by the innocent enthusiasm he displayed for anything Jackson told him. To pass time with the young lad also put off the hour he would have to return to Blackburn.

****

After the death of their father, Esther and Emily continued to stay together at Shawbridge.

They kept to simple routines. After Church on Sunday they would repare to Prospect House for luncheon before strolling home together in the mid afternoon. Emily would find time most days to play the upright piano whilst Esther would busy herself in the kitchen preparing food for the two of them and feed for her turkeys.

By and large the sisters had few, if any, visitors. Apart from Betsy who made a point of joining them for afternoon tea on a Tuesday, Esther and Emily lived very much by themselves.

The Halls did not mix in the highest of County Society with the great landowners of the time. They did though have a clear social circle of respected business people and church goers. In the course of any year there would be the usual circuit of dinner parties, whist drives, fetes and other such functions to attend.

In early summer of 1881 the two sisters were sitting at Shawbridge one afternoon. The weather outside was grey and inclement. Esther turned to Emily and said:

"You know Em. I think it is our turn to organise something for the summer."

"You are right it was the Vicar's wife who arranged the tea and flower afternoon last year and old Mr Kitchen's daughters organised the Easter Parade."

"What shall we do?"

"Let us do something very simple. Let's make it a picnic."

"Yes. Betsy and I can manage all the food and sandwiches if you Em can sort out the invitations. All we need to do is to find a suitable date and a suitable place."

They looked out the window and then said in unison "and some sunny weather" before laughing together.

****

Emily had chosen where the summer afternoon picnic would be.

The small village of Sawley occupied a position on a bend in the River Ribble and the grassed bank provided ample room for the picnic party.

When the day arrived the invitees gathered and then relaxed on blankets spread on the ground. Nearby were hampers of fruit and sandwiches along with wine and cakes. Esther & Emily's prayers had been answered in that the sun shone brilliantly, glinting as it caught the ripples of water on the river.

Many referred to Esther & Emily as The Hall girls even although at this picnic they were respectively aged 37 and 36 years old.

The usual people attended. There was the Vicar with his wife, Mr Kitchen with his daughters and also Betsy Baldwin and her widowed friend Agatha. There was a group of young mothers from the church with their children of different ages. At an event like this the menfolk, if they could be so described, tended to allow the ladies to indulge in "womens' talk" and therefore they tended to turn up later.

There was more than enough food and wine left when, after an hour or so, the men began to appear. Colonel Robinson arrived and, after shaking hands with the Vicar, headed for a glass having already opened a bottle of his favourite Malmsey. It was some fifteen minutes later when Dixon appeared in the company of a stranger.

Now the picnic group was a perfectly hospitable bunch but there were rules to occasions such as this. One only attended if invited and so there was a hush and some quizzical looks between some of the group. Most though presumed that the 12 year old Dixon was unfamiliar with the etiquette and therefore they could blame neither him nor the stranger.

The soldier of fortune moved effortlessly amongst the picnickers in the full knowledge that many were staring at him. He was the perfect gentleman as he engaged courteously with this person before moving onto the next.

General contemporary accounts of Emily at this time presented her as an attractive woman and a woman of many qualities, gentle in many things, kindly, yielding, impulsive and confiding. Photographs show Emily to have a slim lithe figure and striking blue eyes.

Jackson's eye fell approvingly upon Emily at the party. On this occasion he appreciated her from afar. Being aware of Emily's eyes gazing at him, Jackson did not feel the need to converse with her here. For, he was in no hurry. He could take his time.

On his return to Clitheroe Castle, Haughton persuaded Dixon to walk with him rather than accompany the Colonel in a carriage. Quite apart from the prospect of engaging with the Colonel after his several glasses of Malmsey, Jackson wanted to speak to his young friend.

"Dick, the two ladies your father spoke to, the ones who were packing up as we left. Who are they?"

"They are the Halls from Shawbridge. Very well off I would say. You see their father died last year and he was a solicitor."

"So there was no male inheritor?"

"No, just the three ladies."

"Three?"

"Yes. Their sister lives in the big house called Prospect House. She is married."

"I see. And of the two at Shawbridge neither has married?"

"Not that I have heard of"

"Excellent. That is indeed most excellent" mused Jackson.

"What is excellent?" enquired Dixon

"The picnic...... what else?"

Jackson's strategy towards Emily was methodical. Well planned. For unlike the rushed passionate dalliances experienced in London this was so very different. Was he in love? Was it a realisation that, at 41 years old he should settle down? Whether it was either of these or neither the fact that Emily was of independent means was a most persuasive factor for Jackson.

Haughton now spent even more time around Clitheroe. He managed to use Dixon to find out, if he could, where there were to be soirees or local dances at which the Halls would likely or definitely be in attendance. Then he would somehow manage to orchestrate an invitation for himself, or, just as he had done at the picnic he would simply turn up.

Progressively, he became known to the regulars in this social circle including Emily and eventually he warranted his own invitation!

Having gained her acceptance as one of the group, Haughton then began to pay her more personal attention. When dancing, he would utter a little whispered flattery, the intimate way he would help her on with her coat or a feigned sigh when they parted.

For her part Emily did not find Jackson unattractive. She enjoyed the growing friendship but, according to her several confidences to others, it was at no time anything more than a friendship and never did she encourage Haughton to read more into the friendship than there ever was.

Courtship

For Emily it was, if anything, a tonic to have the companionship of a dashing stranger. Indeed, for so long that is exactly what Jackson was. He revealed very little of himself and Emily had but a bare interest in Jackson's life. He was a man to be seen with at social events and a distraction from spending most of her time with her sister.

Of course, Emily was flattered by compliments from this stranger but she did not and could not allow Jackson into her heart. She simply would not let go of John. There was room there for no one else.

Haughton was dogged in his pursuit of Miss Hall. If he made any move to become physically intimate such overture was repelled and when he made any reference to a future together Emily would become cool towards him. Haughton proposed marriage and Emily declined to accept. None of this seemed to deter Jackson in the slightest.

For those outwith Jackson's family, one enigma was how this man supported himself. He had no obvious occupation yet he gave the appearance by his manner and his dress that he must be comfortably well off. Emily presumed he was of independent means. In conversation with her Jackson did not regale her with historic tales of mercenary adventures for they were employed to impress men and certain women of which he knew Emily was not one. The conversation he ensured focused upon Emily, her background and her needs.There was therefore more than a veneer of interest which Emily, during this time, believed to be genuine.

Over such a period of time therefore Jackson amassed a lot of knowledge. The strengths and weaknesses of Emily's character, the importance to her of attending church, the strong veil of protection that seemed to be placed over her by her brother-in-law. He also detected a fierce respect in Emily for her late father which curiously appeared laced with a degree of resentment. He did not press her to explain.

There were two subjects Haughton would not raise with Emily.

Firstly, he did not make any enquiry nor allude in any way to her financial situation. Any disclosed interest on his part could prove fatal to his plans. Secondly, though he was not uncurious about any former liaisons of this lady who was in her late thirties it was far beyond what was socially or morally acceptable to enquire of .

Dixon had been able to inform him of Emily's perceived financial standing following her father's decease. On the other subject he could only inform Haughton of a rumour that had circulated several years ago that Emily had been involved with a male party but that it had come to nought. Accordingly, Jackson was not made familiar of any detail of Emily's previous love interests let alone the identity of the particular amour.

At a fairly early stage Jackson did speak to Emily about his thoughts on going back again to New Zealand. He imparted that this colony was desperate for British emigrants to live there and build up the country. There were advertisements in the papers. He told her his wish was to buy land out there, build a big house and become a sheep farmer.

To Emily's family and others attending these social events, Jackson and Emily appeared to have a relaxed friendship. There were to any observer no signs of intimacy between the two of them and, so far as Emily's sisters were concerned who were her only confidants, Emily rarely if ever referred to Mr Jackson in her idle or other conversations. There therefore seemed nothing for her family or indeed Hartley Baldwin to be concerned about.

Despite the personal rebuffs and the lack of any progress with Emily, Jackson was nonetheless unshaken in his confidence that Emily would come around and eventually agree to become his wife. The only time Haughton became a little anxious about his "romantic" plan was in August and September of 1885. For although in these months there was both a Country Fayre and a reception at the Civic Hall in Clitheroe at which he would have expected to see Emily she was at neither event. He wrote two notes over this period yet got no response. In desperation he asked Dixon Robinson to call at Shawbridge under some pretext whereupon it was reported back to him that Emily was well and was spending much time these days in Manchester.

Jackson was perplexed. Emily was a little quiet bird in his cage. His Emily did not have adventures. He did not like not knowing what Emily was up to.

****

It was the second week in August when Emily again became both disturbed and distracted.

Around the middle of the day in question the brass knocker on the front door of Shawbridge sounded. When Esther made her way to the door she found there a boy. He was holding a note.

The boy said "I've to deliver this to Miss Emily Hall"

"I will take it for her" snapped Esther as her hand made to grab the note from the caller. He was though too quick for Esther and withdrew his outstretched hand.

"No, Madam. Pardon but my instructions were very clear that I have to deliver this in person to Miss Emily Hall."

The caller waited at the door as Esther huffed, shook her head and went into the house to find Emily.

Emily was curious. She greeted the stranger with a pleasant smile, took the note, thanked the boy and shut the door behind her. Only then did she look at what she had been passed. She froze to the spot upon seeing the handwriting on the envelope was that of John Anderton. Her suppressed feelings started to well up. Yet what could this note bring? Instead of rejoining her sister in the little sitting room, Emily went upstairs to her bedroom.

Esther, sitting back in her chair downstairs got that self same feeling she had had the day Emily had returned from her walk along Back Lane all those years ago now.

As she lay on her bed the first thing Emily noticed was that the note was very short.

"My Dearest Emma,

Forgive me for writing after such a long time.

I have very little time left now.

I often dream of how we were and what could have been, yet, just as you should not weep I do not. It is far better for me to have had the short time I had with you than to have lived longer and to have not known you.

Do not cry, be happy. I love you even now, John"

Emily lay in her bed staring up at the ceiling. John had opened the well and so, in spite of his words, she just let the tears freely flow. Yet through her tears, Emily saw appearing a picture. It would complete everything for her. She began to see how it could work.

****

Esther never asked her sister about the note.

Despite the overwhelming impatience she felt to put her plan into action, Emily had the resolve to allow two weeks to pass. She had to distance the trigger which would set off her plan from the arrival of the note. Then, just when she thought the time was right, she engaged with Esther over breakfast.

"Esther, do you recall how, some years ago, father wanted me to go to a music tutor in Manchester?"

"No. Emily, I have no recollection of that. Why was that?"

"Well, he thought, at the time, it would cheer me up."

"Oh. It was back then was it?" said Esther recalling her sister's withdrawn and sad times.

"Well anyway I've decided that if that is what our father thought I should do then it is what I'm going to do now. I will contact the Professor."

Emily then wrote two letters and posted each of them. One was to Professor Rougerie, the tutor in Manchester. In this note she set out how it had been the sincere wish of her late father that she benefit from both piano and vocal coaching from him and that if he could accommodate her she would willingly settle the fee for a block of lessons in advance.

The other letter she wrote was to John.

****

The Professor, in response, informed Emily that, although unfortunately, he was not familiar at all with the late Henry Hall or his wishes he could indeed make room for her with his regular pupils.

Vocal lessons were in the mornings and piano in the afternoon. He provided details of his rates of charge.

Before the Professor could change his mind, Emily had organised and sent him a bank draft to cover the fees for the entire month of September.

****

The first Monday in September arrived. Emily had to leave very early to catch the first train out of Clitheroe Station for Manchester. She then arrived at Professor Rougerie's residence at about 8 45 am in time for the vocal tuition to commence at 9 am.

The vocal lesson ended at 11 am. She then addressed the Professor.

"That was excellent. I really enjoyed that."

"Well my lady. You have the basis of a very good voice but there is definitely scope for improvement. I believe I can assist you. I look forward to this afternoon to gauge how you get on with the ivories."

"Ah. Well. I've been thinking of that. I might have been slightly impetuous when I wrote to you. I did not appreciate the gap of three hours between the singing and the afternoon classes. I really do not think I can usefully put in this time. Therefore, I'd like to keep to the morning classes and perhaps see you about the piano another month if that is alright?"

She saw a quizzical look on the Professor's face.

"Oh. Do not worry. I'm not asking you to repay me the afternoon fees."

The grin from Professor Rougerie clearly conveyed that Emily had succeeded in convincing him that she was just a fanciful frivolous lady and she was perfectly happy for him to believe that was so.

Freed from the tuition studio after 11 am, she made her way promptly to the station where she boarded a train for Clitheroe yet although the destination on her ticket was indeed Clitheroe she alighted from the train at Whalley which was the last stop before Clitheroe. From the station there it was but a ten minute walk to Parson's Cottage where the ailing John was living out his final weeks.

The note she had written to John before embarking on her plan read:

"Dearest John,

My heart was indeed warmed by your thoughtful note. It would be very wrong of me to pretend I never shed any tears when I learned from you that your time on this earth was now so limited.

I cannot and do not dwell upon what might have been between us. If you will excuse me saying so, I have a lifetime ahead to indulge in such sad ridden joy.

For now, I have but one need, one obsession driving me. That is to spend some of the time remaining to you with you. I will try to understand if you may prefer me not to see you when you are so ill.

I have a plan. All being well I will be able to visit you soon. I just cannot say exactly when it will be. In an afternoon I think.

I am driven by my love for you. I pray we can find just a moment to be by ourselves.

If you cannot or do not want to see me then do not answer the door when I call.

All my love

Your Emma"

John Anderton was, notwithstanding his progressive illness, still able to organise his household. He told his nurse to leave him to sleep of an afternoon and to return to his house at supper time. He made it known to his own relatives that, to maintain his little strength, he needed complete rest in an afternoon and that they should not call on him except in mornings or evenings. He did not know if or when Emily would manage to visit him.

John had spent four afternoons by himself at the cottage in Whalley. At least he knew his dictates to nurse and family seemed to work in that he was not disturbed.

That first lunchtime when Emily saw the wooden fence and gate and the garden blooms of the cottage getting nearer with each step she took, she became very tense. Emily was excited, but nervous. Would

John want to see her? Had she been fooling herself with her imaginings? If there was anyone there at the cottage, how would she possibly explain her visit? One deep breath as she opened the gate which creaked a little on a rusty hinge. Her heart fluttered as she saw immediately that the door was half open - a sign of welcome? When she was level with the threshold she spoke very softly:

"Hello"

From inside the house she heard in response the ring of a little handbell. She walked in and through to find a couch in front of the fire made up like a bed and there, propped up on a mountain of pillows, was John. Much thinner in frame and face than when she had last seen him but still very much John. She rushed over, she could not stop herself. Just in time she did stop and then stuttered:

"John. I. I forgot. Is it alright to......to hug you?"

"Yes. Yes. If you do not then I will certainly hug you!"

Apart from one occasion, each weekday afternoon saw the two of them together. Of course John was very weak and could not talk for very long at any one time. Emily felt it was just meant to be that she was there to nurse him as best as she could.

The afternoon she could not call upon John was when John's sister insisted upon visiting him. She refused to take "no" for an answer. This meant Emily had to pass the time in Manchester in order to arrive back at Shawbridge at her normal time. She enjoyed herself buying one or two little things for John.

****

At Shawbridge the initial interest of both Emily's sisters in the music lessons and Professor Rougerie waned. They could not but notice how chirpier Emily was and assumed her joy was all connected to her music. Emily tried hard not to feel bad about deluding her family. She did though shiver a bit inside when one day Esther quipped to her:

"I do hope it's a case of money well spent on this man in Manchester. Can't be wasting money at our stage in life."

****

Of course, the month passed all too soon for Emily. John was such a kind and caring person. He never asked anything of her. He was selfless in that he was always at pains to say he did not want to get her into trouble over him and how he would understand if, for whatever reason, she could not call.

****

Macassar Box

E M Hall
1875.

When the last day of the month arrived neither Emily nor John were sad. They were each openly energised by the time they agreed they had "stolen from fate" and Emily was sincere and earnest when she told John she would do all she could to engineer another visit in the weeks to come.

****

After ten days back at Shawbridge Emily decided to write another note to John. So much had been said yet she always found more words she wanted him to hear. She did not finish this note by the time she was summoned to Sunday lunch at Prospect House. Before going downstairs she slid the unfinished note into her little box. The box had been a gift from John ten years previously. It was made of Macassar ebony. The box was used for scent, toiletries and jewelry and had been inscribed "E.E.M.Hall 1875". The note slid easily behind the mirror where it would not easily be discovered by any prying eyes.

The family luncheon tended to involve the three sisters talking much amongst each other although it was Betsy who did most of the talking. Esther would tend to join in only when something was said that she disagreed with or held a strong opinion about. Normally Emily would be the most taciturn though during and since her journeys to Manchester she was noticeably more engaged with the others than normal. Hartley would sit at the top of the table. He enjoyed feeling "host" to his family although he tended not to say that much himself. Hartley Junior was rarely an attendee at these ritual gatherings on a Sunday preferring the company of others of his own generation.

Towards the end of luncheon on this particular day, the telephone at Prospect House rang. Charnock came in:

"Mr Baldwin, Sir, it is Master Hartley on the phone for you."

Hartley was not amused. His son well knew that his father would not welcome an interruption to the family gathering.

"Excuse me ladies." He rose from the table and left the room.

When Hartley returned and entered the dining room his expression was very sombre. He looked down at the three sisters still seated at the table but his eyes looked directly at Emily.

"I'm afraid my son has brought sad news. He has just received word that John Anderton passed away this very morning."

Esther also now looked at Emily. Never one to indulge in sentiment or emotion, Esther took her younger sister in her arms and held her tight.

"I am so sorry my little one."

It was as if Esther had known everything all along.

****

Emily felt she had been widowed so young yet she still felt the glow of that month she had had with John and decided that gloomy was not a state which became her well. She would indulge what she described to herself as her "happy sad" feelings by going for solitary walks along Back Lane, by visiting John's grave and by occasionally taking out her unfinished letter and reading it over. She would not add to it as, for her, the letter was just a reflection of her time with John in that it was and remained "unfinished."

****

"That's a note arrived for you." said Esther one morning. "If you ask me it's from that Jackson person. He has been asking after you."

Emily pocketed the small envelope. She was not of a mind or disposition to open the correspondence.

The next morning when Emily came downstairs her sister was once more in the hall.

"You must be the most popular person in the town Em. There's more mail for you today. It's over there" Esther said pointing to the table by the coat stand.

Emily's hackles rose as she imagined this was Jackson becoming a huge pest but when she looked at the envelope on the table she noticed the name and address had been typed. Emily was not accustomed to receiving such official looking correspondence. Under the eagle eye of Esther she carefully slit open the envelope and started reading. It was from a solicitors' firm she had never heard of and it read:

"Dear Miss Hall,

The Late John Edward Anderton

We were charged by the deceased John Edward Anderton of Parson's Cottage, Whalley with the duty of administering his estate in terms of his Last Will and Testament.

We can advise that under the Will, Mr Anderton made you his sole beneficiary and quite apart from the pecuniary provisions you will inherit the Patron of the Living in respect of St Mary Magdalene's Church in Clitheroe.

The sums falling due to you are quite substantial and we would welcome a meeting with you, at your convenience, when we can explain more fully the investments and how they can be transferred to you and best utilised by you.

When contacting us, please ask for our Mr Benyon.

We must explain the delay in notifying you of the foregoing. It is the case that the deceased's living relatives tried to object to the provisions of the Will alleging that there had been undue influence upon the late Mr Anderton on account of his terminal illness. Certainly, we do not wish to visit upon you any upset, but take the view that frankness in such matters is essential.

You may though rest assured that, as the Will was made the day following Mr Anderton's diagnosis, when he would have been relatively unaffected by his terminal condition, it is deemed there was no factual or legal basis on which to seriously dispute the Will.

You can possibly understand the suspicions of the deceased's family standing the fact that none of them claim to have had any knowledge of you prior to the reading of the Will.

We look forward to being of assistance to you.

Yours truly etc"

Emily stared and stared at the letter. There was attached a copy of John's Will. It was indeed dated the day following her walk with him along Back Lane. Indeed the Will had been signed the very day that

Henry Hall had prevailed upon John to discontinue the relationship. She was dumbstruck.

****

At the start of November 1885 another note arrived at Shawbridge.

"I do not know what you think you are doing Em but you cannot ignore Jackson forever. You know I do not care for him but it is your doing. Our father always said that "manners are everything". Well, manners dictate that you must respond to these notes."

Emily had a wry grin to herself. To listen to Esther, of all people, lecturing on the subject of manners was really very very amusing. She did tacitly acknowledge she was being discourteous to her friend Haughton. After all he had been dogged and loyal in his friendship and she had effectively cast him off without notice.

She went to the small study, sat at the desk opened the notepad and began to write. Twice she started and almost immediately crushed the paper she had been using. No sooner had she commenced writing when it struck her how different it all was. In writing to John or reading his letter she had been so full of feeling and had been overflowing in her pen. Before she commenced her third attempt, she gave herself a strict talking to.

"Emily. Get a control of yourself. This letter has to be written out of a sense of what is decent and proper. This has nothing whatever to do with John. You cannot live in fear of writing."

She composed herself and embarked on her note:

"Dear Haughton,

I can but apologise to you for my failure to communicate with you sooner. It has not been nor is it my intention to display rudeness towards you, or, for that matter to anyone else. Indeed, I am touched by what I'm advised is your concern for my welfare.

Whilst I do not feel obliged in my position to offer explanation for my silence, I believe it only fair that I do so.

I have not been struck by any malady indeed, quite the contrary. I have been particularly well. Much of these past weeks were taken up with lessons. Yes, I have been going back to school! Seriously, every day for a month I was in Manchester where I had singing lessons. Such a joy for me although I'm hardly a songbird and whether I can justify the cost of the lessons is not really for me to say. Anyway, with this commitment in Manchester and little time to catch up with family and friends, I hope that you will understand.

I see that the Countryman's Ball is to be held at Clitheroe Castle on 15th prox. I know not if it is your intention to attend but I shall certainly be there.

I hope you are well.

If our paths do not cross next month, I wish you a Happy Christmas and a prosperous NewYear"

Best wishes

Emily Hall"

She put the letter into an envelope before she changed her mind. No. She did not reconsider sending this note. She had though agonised about being a bit more forthcoming to Haughton. Yes, she had deceived her family about seeing John but lying, or not being open, was something she hated. Could she not just inform Jackson that she had been busy following the death of a close friend? But then he would no doubt expect to hear more about this "close friend". As Emily saw it, she would just get tied in knots. For as long as she cherished her moments with John, they were secret and special. They held magic for her. If she was to tell anyone, she feared that the magic would be gone. The letter had to be sent before she changed her mind.

****

Whilst no one knew of Emily's intimacy with John Anderton quite a few people learnt of her good fortune in inheriting his estate. His sisters and other nearest relatives ensured there was no secret about that. Needless to say, there were scurrilous rumours circulated by them as to precisely how Miss Hall had prevailed upon the dear departed John to part with his assets. Thankfully none of the gossip concerning this reached Emily's ears. However, the same could not be said in respect of Dixon Robinson.

****

Having ensured that an invitation was extended to him by the Robinsons, Jackson arrived at Clitheroe Castle the day prior to the Ball. Thankfully Colonel Robinson was up to his eyes with the preparations and whilst effusive in his welcome to Jackson was too committed to the tasks to engage his visitor in the usual conversations.

This was the first occasion in a long time that Jackson had met his young friend. He gave him a bear hug and then slapped him on the back:

"How the devil are you my good man? Any shooting?"

Dixon beamed at the return of his friend.

"Can we maybe go shooting tomorrow? Just the two of us?"

"Don't see why not. What time does this Ball start? I'm afraid I did not really read the invitation."

"People are supposed on arrive at 6 o'clock for a drinks reception followed by a four course meal. Then everyone goes to the ballroom."

"Now why is it called the Countryman's Ball?"

"Well, there are a number of toasts. My father announces the prizewinners and makes presentations. You know the sort of thing? Point to Point champion, best home made wine, horse and trap winner, rifle champion and all that stuff. The dance is mostly country dancing."

Jackson mused to himself. Not exactly my scene. Even so he was not uncomfortable in the Castle surrounds and, of course, he knew exactly why he was there. His conversation then turned to his quarry.

"Well Dick, are we to have the pleasure tomorrow night of the Hall sisters?"

"Not all of them."

Jackson was suddenly alarmed. If Emily was not turning up, why was he there?

"The middle one has called off."

Relieved, Jackson asked:

"Is she unwell?"

"No. I believe it is a turkey that is ill rather than Esther Hall"

Before Jackson could continue with his enquiry, Dixon changed the subject.

"Have you done anymore about New Zealand?"

"No." clipped Jackson "I'm not really thinking that far ahead at the moment.

"Can we not go soon? There's nothing really happening here. I'm sure my father would let me come with you."

"Dick, you are still too young" said Jackson firmly but not wanting to upset the young man unduly. "Now what else has been going on in Clitheroe?"

Dixon leaned over across the arm of his chair and spoke in a confidential tone:

"There is something concerning the young Miss Hall. Miss Emily. She has, it seems, come into a lot of wealth."

"I know that. Everyone knows she got her share of Mr Hall's estate." said Jackson dismissively.

"No. No, I do not mean that. Listen, they say there was a local man who gave his fortune to her when he died. His family got not a penny. I heard she seduced him to get his money."

"Well that's one thing, Dick. She can do that to me, but there's nothing for her to get when I die!"

Jackson laughed and gave the impression that what he had just been told was frivolous. Inside though, he was analysing this news. For one thing he had never suspected, was that Emily was a money grabber or that she would trade favours for such gain. What if he was therefore to boost his assets in her eyes? He could weave a tale for sure and he did detect there was a fondness for him. No. He could not really take the risk. If his pretend wealth was unpicked he would be exposed as a fraud.

Jackson resolved that covering up his financial embarrassment was one thing but inventing non existent resources was not a very clever thing to do.

****

The next evening the carriages pulled up at regular intervals in the forecourt of Clitheroe Castle as the invited guests alighted for the Countryman's Ball. In good time Esther's coachman arrived, dismounted from the seat and proceeded to assist Betsy and her sister from the step to the ground.

Once inside they were met by the sound of avid conversation amongst those already there. Even though everyone knew each other and encountered the others reasonably frequently, the surroundings of the Castle and everyone in formal dress seemed to encourage loud greetings to be exchanged.

Jackson had slipped into the banqueting hall. From a brief reconnoitre he noticed to his displeasure that his place name was next to Colonel Robinson at the head of one table and, to the left was Mrs Madge Leverhulme an organiser of the town Salvation Army and, if he had heard correctly, something of a religious zealot. This was not good.

The Castle had had to hire in additional staff for the function. At the end of the room Jackson spied someone topping up a crystal decanter from a small barrel of brandy. In his best "officer" sounding tone Jackson, having approached, said to the man with the brandy:

"I believe there has been a serious lapse in the table plan. The place I was assured of has not been given to me."

"Sir, with respect, the plan I was given was followed to the letter. Perhaps you should take it up with the regular staff?"

Jackson walked authoritatively over to the other end of the table where he picked up one place name and proceeded to hand it over to the footman.

"Here, please ensure that this is swapped for my place name."

"But?" queried the man before he felt the cold metal in his palm along with the card. The sight of a crown was sufficient for the man to smother his protest and continue with the decanter.

Upon leaving the banqueting room, Jackson immediately espied Emily. He thought "very nice" as he admired her blue dress which would harmonise with her blue eyes. His gaze swept around the reception hall. No obvious sign of Emily's brother-in-law, that was something of a relief. The hawk eyes of either Hartley or Esther he had been aware of at other functions and he was convinced that such observation made Emily more self conscious. If it proved to be that only Betsy was her chaperone then this evening could yet be a success. For he had noticed again during other gatherings that Betsy was easily distracted and drawn into conversation by anyone she knew.

Mr Jackson did his usual. He would pay Emily scant, if any, attention at the start of an evening. He would, despite her being his quarry, make a point on circulating and giving the appearance of being very interested in what others had to say. The exception to this ploy would be the Colonel who, for different reasons, he would also try to avoid.

The gong sounded and the visitors slowly filed into the banqueting hall. The men would stand at their places until the ladies had located their positions and taken their seats.

Jackson was one of the last to enter. Of course, he did not need to enquire about his table placing. He made his way directly and, sure enough, the place next to Emily was free and "E Haughton Jackson" was displayed on the card that was there.

"Well, am I not very fortunate Miss Hall? I could not have planned this better myself."

During the meal itself, Jackson displayed impeccably good manners. He asked after her family, he showed interest in her travels to Manchester and he even enquired about Esther's sick turkey! For her part Emily responded with politeness and as manners dictated she respond in a similar vein:

" What, may I enquire, have you been up to since we last met?"

"This and that. Isabel said she needs a man about the house and that man is me!"

"What about your young friend?"

"Dixon? If I say he is as young as ever, would that be unkind? He keeps on about New Zealand but he is hardly man enough."

"So, you are still planning upon going?"

"Most certainly, land there is reasonably priced. I can purchase a plot and build a house and a future."

At this point the Colonel got to his feet, rang a bell and quiet descended on the assembly. There followed a rather dry address and then the various awards were presented. During the address Jackson whispered to Emily:

"Excuse me I need to take some air." Though very rude and contrary to etiquette Haughton half rose, crouched and slipped out of the room.

The dinner concluded with the traditional toast to "The Countryman" whereupon the men were directed to the Smokers Lounge with the Ladies being invited to retire to the Library. Emily waited for her sister before leaving the banqueting hall. They then strolled, arm in arm, as any combination of The Hall girls tended to do until, half way along the hall, Betsy parted and went in the direction of the powder room.

Emily continued on her own before stopping to look at a large portrait on the wall to her left. As she was about to continue her journey to the Library she heard:

"Psssst. Over here."

The words led her round a corner where standing behind a plant pot was Jackson. He held out in his left hand a flower he had obviously picked from the Castle grounds:

"This is for you my Emily. I only left the dinner in order to get you this."

Emily giggled "Don't be silly. I do not believe you. You would say that to any woman who had come this way!"

Haughton held out his hand. "Let us go for a stroll outside"

"Romeo, it is December. It is cold outside. It is definitely not Juliette weather. Anyway, my sister would panic if she could not find me." She pulled away her hand.

"That is just it, Emily. It appears I can never see you on your own."

She turned and said teasingly. "Patience is an excellent virtue my good man" before disappearing into the library.

As he pulled out a cigar in readiness to join the men, Jackson, not unaffected by Emily's playfulness, thought that if what he had been told by Dick the previous day was true he could begin to understand how this mystery man had been "enticed" into parting with his estate.

The rest of the Ball was uneventful. Jackson decided not to demonstrate his ignorance of country dancing though when this was followed by traditional music he was able to take Emily to the floor on two occasions. Emily was certainly in good spirits for she even dared Haughton to dance the last waltz with Madge Leverhulme!!

****

Pre Nuptial

Whilst Emily could never have been described as an extrovert, there was always within her a streak of childish devilment, a playfulness which would, now and then, come to the fore.

She enjoyed the Countryman's Ball and in the course of the succeeding days as she sat with her sister at Shawbridge she reflected on all that had happened. She thought of Jackson and believed him to be a rash but handsome fellow. He was able to amuse her and she enjoyed their badinage. For Emily, it was a harmless friendship and whilst Jackson's designs on her were patently obvious she always felt that she was in control. She was not swayed by the silly emotions of younger women. Emily was, she believed, able to accept Haughton's attentions yet remain distant from them. How odd she thought. Now Emily did not want to consciously encourage this man and yet Jackson's complaint that they never had time together was, she confessed to herself, perfectly justified.

To consort with Jackson in the form of anything that appeared to the world to be a courtship would bring the scrutiny of family attention and stress that she did not want. She could well picture in her mind the interrogation that Hartley Baldwin would put Jackson through and all for what? Just a friendship? Any confrontation between Jackson and her brother-in-law would not, she believe, augur well. No one would be happy. Not herself, not Jackson and not her family.

Once more Emily found herself scheming.

"Give a penny for them" Esther interrupted her sister's musings.

"Oh, nothing important."

****

"Dear Haughton,

I happen to have business at Copster Green on the 20th and the matter in hand would, I think, benefit from your experienced advice.

I would not contemplate dragging you all the way over here and, for personal reasons, I think it optimum that we are not seen together in this town. I will explain if you will allow me to.

Should you be free and able to attend on me, I expect to be at Langho around noon.

My kind regards

Emily"

****

Jackson read this note. The intrigue appealed to him. He had no insight into Emily's mysterious business but did conclude that Emily was reaching out beyond the gaze of her family protectors. This was very encouraging indeed.

On the due date, Haughton's train from Blackburn arrived at Langho Station at 11 22 am. The service in the other direction did not get in from Clitheroe until 12.06 pm. He bought a newspaper and sat on a platform seat. He read about a defeat suffered by the Italians at the hands of the Abyssinians. The pulse of his "Irregular" blood started beating. Jackson continued to browse. He spotted a notice that he had read before. It was the call for emigrants to the colonies of Australia and New Zealand. Once more Haughton questioned exactly what he was doing sitting on a Lancastrian Railway platform when the world out there was waiting for him. The increasing noise of the approaching steam engine told him exactly why he was there.

Only two persons alighted from the southbound train. The first to appear was a tall gaunt man carrying a box shaped case. Then just as this man shut the carriage door behind him, a door further down swung open and Emily stepped onto the platform. She was wearing a casual blue dress and sported, as always, a matching bonnet.

Before Emily spotted him, Haughton folded his newspaper, put it under his arm and headed round the station building to approach her from behind.

Emily could not see Haughton. Suddenly she thought her scheming and effort to have been a waste of time. She had been so certain that Jackson would "take the bait". She was just starting to say "Emily it serves you right for playing these games" and "when is the next train back to Clitheroe' when the voice from behind her startled her:

"You really meet the oddest of people in the oddest of places"

Emily turned, smiled and said:

"Looking at you I think you are quite correct!"

"Well, what is this business you wanted me for?"

"Let's find a seat."

Once they had found a platform bench where the building sheltered them from the prevailing breeze Emily proceeded to explain:

"I hope you will not be angry. I sort of misled you."

Jackson raised his eyebrows

"You see there is no business at Copster Green. It is just that you said when last we met you regretted we could never be by ourselves and so I just thought of this on the spur of the moment. Is it silly?"

"But why the cloak and dagger stuff?"

"Haughton, that is a bit harder to explain. You see it started with my father. You may have heard that I do not keep very good health. Whether because of this or because I was the youngest, my father tried to protect me from the world. If he reckoned anyone was a bad influence upon me he would ensure that that person stayed away from me. It is still the same to this day only my sisters and Mr Baldwin assume the duties of my protector."

"So you think I am a bad influence on you. Is that what you are saying?"

"Haughton, please do not jump down my throat. That is uncalled for."

"I am sorry. It is just that what you say is so foreign to me. It is not right. I mean I do not pry regarding your age but I think I am safe to suggest that you should, by now, be free from such family strictures."

"In this situation Haughton it is my doing, it is my fault if you like. You see I do want to be free by which I mean free to relax and not fret over any consequences of amity. You are, I feel, a good friend. I would not want to risk losing your friendship over any misconception on the part of my family. I am very close to my sisters. I do not want to be in a position where I have to choose between on the one hand a good friend and family on the other. I'm sorry again. You will not understand."

"Emily. I will try to. Honestly, I will. But what does it mean for us?"

"Haughton, you do not need to look quite so serious. We can still see each other as we have been doing this last while in the social circle but maybe we can also have some little times like this, by ourselves. For my part though, I must be careful and I must trust you to allow any assignations like this to remain secret?"

"If it means I can share more time with you then secrecy is a price I willingly pay."

This is how Jackson and Emily embarked on a number of clandestine meetings over the next eighteen months or so. The vast majority of their encounters took place at railway stations between Clitheroe and Blackburn. Once in the summer months Emily took with her a small basket of food and they risked having a mini picnic in a field about a ten minute walk from Daisyfield Station. On another occasion Haughton persuaded Emily to go all the way to Blackburn where he treated her to luncheon. Emily was though too much on edge. There were so many people on the pavement and it would just take one person who knew her directly or by association with Mr Baldwin and there could be trouble.

For his part, Jackson did find Emily an enigma. She was happy to be in his company. She laughed and appeared very relaxed and yet if he tried to steer the conversation to any future together or to anything romantic she either tensed up or laughed as if his train of thought was simply too ridiculous. He slowly became frustrated with her and yet there was for him something magnetic about the whole involvement. He did, in time, become conscious of the fact that Emily would always refuse to see him at Whalley. She told him it was too close to Clitheroe and too risky. Haughton was not convinced. She never imparted that it was because that station had been her stop when going to Parsons Cottage.

****

Emily was indeed quite content with the course of her life at this time. She had her life at Shawbridge with her sister, would take herself off from time to time to be by herself and there were the regular social events. In addition now there were her secret meetings with Haughton.

In September 1887 Haughton had, for the second time, proposed marriage to Emily and she hastily declined yet again. After this rejection Jackson resolved that this cat and mouse game had to reach its end. If he as the cat could not trap or catch the "Emily mouse" then he must venture to pastures new.

A short time afterwards it was the second anniversary of John's death. Emily was affected again by a shroud of sadness. She felt lost and low.

On 27th October 1887 the next clandestine meeting of this odd couple took place at Wilpshire Station. It was six years since Emily had first met Jackson. He had asked for this meeting specifically to inform her that his plans were sealed and was arranging to withdraw the funds necessary for the passage to New Zealand. Young Dixon Robinson was now 18 years old and they would be setting off together.

This news hit Emily hard. Her feelings of loss at this time were only tempered by the presence of Haughton. He had always managed to distract her from her inner self and yet now she was presented with him disappearing far away and for a long time or forever.

At this point Jackson, conscious of the silence and detecting Emily's sadness, looked into her eyes and said:

'You have refused me more than once before, but, if you would agree to marry me it would mean everything to me."

Emily was getting confused within herself. First the blow that Haughton was to be leaving her and then the unexpected further proposal.

"What means have you of maintaining a wife?"

"I have enough money to keep myself but not enough for a wife."

Without thinking very much Emily responded:

"If we become engaged, you must come over to Clitheroe and meet my family and friends."

“It would absolutely delight me to do so"

****

Emily returned to Clitheroe feeling euphoric. She would not tell her family of the engagement. She was very unsure about Jackson and Emily prayed his motives were honourable. She considered how the family had, to her mind, deprived her of happiness with John Anderton. In this new circumstance, should she be that concerned about the hurt that may now be felt by her family at her latest very sudden decision?

Before the weekend Emily sent a note to Haughton via Dixon asking the former to join her at Prospect House for 3pm.

Mr Jackson attended on time with young Mr Robinson by his side. As the fiance of the young Miss Hall, Jackson no doubt expected a warm and almost regal welcome. If that is what Haughton anticipated then he was to be very very disappointed.

Charnock opened the front door whereupon the visitors were informed that Mrs Baldwin refused to see them, Esther Hall was upstairs recuperating from her roast beef dinner and Mr Hartley Baldwin was settling down in the sitting room for an afternoon nap.

Emily appeared and soon learned to her embarrassment that none of her family was willing to meet her fiance. This was the very disapproval she had feared. She had not broken the news of her engagement but, somehow, she just knew they had found out.

The fact that all knew through Dixon Robinson of the plan to go to New Zealand Emily believed had made a bad impression on her family and hardly encouraged a favourable reception of her betrothal to Mr Jackson.

She took Haughton to one side. She had wanted Dixon Robinson to go away but, as usual, he lacked the perception to know when to make himself scarce.

So Emily whispered to Jackson so that only he could hear:

"If we are getting married our future should be here and not in New Zealand. As your fiancee I beg you to reconsider your foolhardy venture."

In a cutting tone that, in the future would become familiar to Emily, Haughton responded:

"We have been over this before. You were aware of the plan before we got engaged. You cannot just change your mind on a whim. Not when I have invested so much for so long in the plan. Anyhow it would be grossly unfair to Dick to call it off now."

Emily was staggered. "You tell me your friend is more important than me? This is not the way things should be."

She composed herself before looking at him without feeling and saying:

"I am sorry. I cannot marry you" whereupon, she turned away and ran upstairs.

****

There was a further meeting between Jackson and Emily shortly afterwards. This was at Clitheroe Castle. Relations between the two of them worsened.

"Emily, you must reconsider. I have made all the arrangements to go. The passage money is paid. Clothing and other necessities have been purchased."

"Very well, our engagement is at an end."

As she stood to leave, both Jackson and Dixon who had, of course, been in attendance, set about Emily accusing her of duplicity and falseness to her undertaking. She was subjected to a degree of rudeness beyond which a lady of that time should not have been.

The following day a note arrived from Dixon Robinson seeking forgiveness for his outburst and trying to excuse what he had said on the basis that she had tried to ruin his chances of going abroad.

Over the next two days there was silence. No communication from either Jackson or his young friend.

On Tuesday 1st November 1887 a letter arrived from Jackson. The note could be described as piteous. The letter set out how miserable he felt.

"Did you want to break my heart? How can I go to New Zealand and never see you again? I love you so much."

****

The Wedding

Emily was strangely affected by the letter. She detected the words to be a genuine cry from the heart. She could not, and indeed would not, risk seeking counsel from her sister. Yet what should she do? It was pointless writing another letter. She had to make up her own mind - to ignore this note or to act upon it?

Emily impulsively chose to act.The very next day she hastened by train to Blackburn and there hired a carriage to take her to Rover Street. Westview, the home of Haughton's sister, where she expected to find Mr Jackson.

As Emily's visit was unexpected, Susan, the maid, had her wait just inside the door. After a short while, Isabel appeared. She invited Emily in. Isabel was welcoming enough but Emily felt her stare had a cool edge and that she was examining the visitor very closely.

"My brother never mentioned you were coming."

"No. It is, in a way, a surprise. I thought I would call on chance."

Isabel did not pretend she was entirely convinced by this explanation.

"I will inform Edmund that you are here."

The next time the door of the room opened Jackson entered. In his face he seemed upset. In a dramatic gesture, Jackson went down on one knee, took her hand and sought her forgiveness for his ill behaviour. Emily was moved by this and, just as Isabel came into the room again, Miss Hall agreed to renew her engagement.

Isabel was surprised whilst Jackson was delighted and almost overcome as he embraced his fiancee.

Things then accelerated very quickly.

On 3rd November 1887 Jackson insisted upon meeting Emily in Clitheroe. As Emily had a prior commitment to go to nearby Chatburn to visit friends who lived there, the couple walked together. As they headed to Chatburn, Jackson, feeling more than ever that Emily was firmly in his grasp, told her how he wanted to marry before he left for New Zealand with Dixon Robinson. Emily did not respond.

At the house of Emily's friends, Mr Jackson behaved to those there with exemplary decorum. He knew precisely how to make a good impression. He was confident enough in this impression to tell these people he had never seen before of his engagement to Emily, his commitment to emigrating to New Zealand and his burning desire to get married before he left. Those sat around showed a smiling interest. This good looking man with such charm and manners conveyed a picture of such a fine romance.

Haughton begged the company to employ their powers of persuasion on Emily to yield to his desire for marriage. He glanced coyly towards Emily. As those there sat around the table having tea and cake, Jackson proceeded to extol the virtues and good fortunes of moving to New Zealand. He drew a rough sketch of the large house he intended to build for Emily. Emily much later recounted how Jackson "gave the most glowing account of his prospects warming all the women present to the idea."

Jackson further went on to impress that he had many friends in New Zealand and that there was a ready made society for him and Emily. He claimed to have letters of introduction to persons of consequence in the country and mentioned by name in this regard (no doubt conscious of his fiancee's devotions) the Bishop of Auckland.

Everyone was very enthused about Emily's future life as it had been laid out before them.

By this stage, even Emily felt enamoured about the whole idea. Sensing his improved situation, Haughton suddenly proposed:

"What about getting married this Saturday? St Paul's Church in Blackburn would be fine for me. What do you say?"

The others in the room retired whereupon Jackson spoke tenderly to Emily. He asked that she come out to New Zealand once he and Dixon were settled and had found a place to live and they could then build their own home.

Emily was overwhelmed. She listened intently to Haughton's plans but, as she listened, the realities of the situation brought more doubts to her consciousness. In New Zealand she would only know her husband and

Dixon Robinson and no one else. She would be entirely at their mercy. She sought some reassurance. With tears she looked into Haughton's eyes and said:

"Please be good and kind to me."

Taking her hands in his, Jackson promised to treat her so, eternally.

Emily consented to the marriage.

Jackson set off hotfoot back to Blackburn leaving Emily with her friends. His long long pursuit of Emily as his wife and possibly his benefactor had succeeded.

Within a very short time a telegram arrived at the Chatburn house. It was from Jackson and it read:

"Please supply me with your full name and date of birth in order that I might make the necessary arrangements for Saturday."

****

Jackson was "fully charged" with all that had to be done within a matter of hours. He had to secure a Marriage Licence from the Registrar but, given his circumstances whereby he had to leave the country within days, he did not see this as a problem. Though buoyed by Emily's recent positivity, could he rely upon her this time to keep her word? She had already called off their engagement once. Then there were the Baldwins. He had to marry before they interfered or caused any trouble. There was nothing any of them could do after he and his bride were legally married. Of course, Jackson told his own family and close friends.

Isabel told her brother "Well, so long as she is good to you and you are happy both of you will have my blessing."

Raynsford told him "This is a surprise. I'm amazed anyone will have you! Make sure you bring her down with you next week."

Then there was Dixon Robinson. He had to be able to trust his young friend. Haughton had therefore to make a special trip to Clitheroe Castle the day before the wedding. Dixon was in the throes of clearing and storing his possessions to ensure their safety whilst he was abroad. He was surprised at Jackson's unexpected appearance at the castle.

"I have a task for you my young man" said Jackson.

"Yes." replied Dixon keenly.

"This is a highly confidential matter and I must rely upon you to maintain the utmost secrecy. In New Zealand I will need to be able to trust you. Accordingly, should you let me down in this current matter it would bode very badly for our life in New Zealand."

Jackson stopped to make sure the impact of what he had just said had hit home to Dixon. He then continued:

"I appreciate you have much to do before our departure but, even so, I need you to absent yourself from Clitheroe tomorrow. You have to be at the Railway Station by 9 o'clock. There you must wait. It may be for an hour but possibly less. On the platform you will meet a lady and you will accompany her to Blackburn. You must stay with her and do not leave her side until you meet me."

Dixon was very taken with this cloak and dagger mission. He never questioned why or to where his escort duties would lead. He did though enquire:

"But who is this woman?"

"You will find out Dick. Unless there's a convention of the Women's Institute taking place, there are not likely to be many women about to board the train for Blackburn at that time. Just ask any lady if she is heading off to meet with me and then simply stay with her."

Jackson had to be certain that Emily would not change her mind and would actually "get to the church on time." Yet he could not really trust Dixon by saying he was to meet Emily and that she was going to her own wedding ceremony. He did not believe his young friend could keep such a secret.

The same day as Jackson was at Clitheroe Castle, Emily was at Shawbridge. A note had been delivered to her confirming the time of the wedding and that she should go firstly to Isabel's house.

Emily's apprehension multiplied as the hours wore by. She was excited at the prospect of marriage and knew she was committed now to the course of wedlock. She could not let Haughton down again. She had given her word. Yet the day of reckoning with her family would come. Then, the risk was that her family would cut her off leaving her life and fate inextricably linked to that of Jackson. Emily well knew the risks she was running. This could transpire to be the very best or indeed the very worst decision she had ever made in her life.

She lay in her bed that night, restless and uncomfortable. Her mind was too exhausted to think any rational thought. It was not a good night at all. In some ways it was a long night and yet in other ways it seemed no time at all before the daylight rays poked through the bedroom curtains heralding a new day. Not though just any day. This was Emily's wedding day.

****

Thankfully in some ways for Emily, when she went downstairs Esther was gone. She noticed her sister's galoshes were absent from their place behind the back door. The evidence pointed to a turkey emergency of some sort for that was certainly one of the very few things which would prevail on Esther to abandon her breakfast.

Yes, this was good for Emily. She was spared having to look her sibling in the eye with guilt in hers about not disclosing what she was about to go away and do.

To avoid undue or any suspicion, Emily donned no finery at all in her preparations to depart the house. Oh, Miss Hall was smart enough for she was too proud to be seen in public wearing anything that could be described as dowdy let alone anything that was not clean.Yet the clothes she sported for her wedding would be classed as her normal attire and from the same wardrobe as she would have used had she been popping round to see a neighbour or when she visited Prospect House.

Emily's inner guilt made her believe that everyone in the street was watching her. Unusually, as she walked to the Railway Station she kept her head down. She wanted to avoid eye contact with anyone she knew for that was, she thought, the best way to avoid any awkward questions or questions that would give rise to any lie on her part.

At the ticket office she asked for a return to Blackburn.

"Madam, are you wanting a day, a weekend or an open return?"

Emily thought. It would not be a day return for this was her wedding she was going to. She did not know what Jackson's plans were going to be. She took the safest option:

"An open return, please"

When she took her ticket she placed it inside her reticule alongside a note she had written the previous day with some degree of difficulty. It was a note to Esther. She could not simply not turn up at Shawbridge that night. The note was a summary confession to Esther about her marriage. She would not tempt fate by sending it before she had actually married, but would ensure the terms were telegraphed to Shawbridge before any panic regarding her disappearance set in.

With her reticule and her small but very fashionable parasol, Emily walked onto the platform. The time was 9 35 am.

****

From his seat on the platform Dixon, adopting the role in his head of an international spy, had been pretending to read a newspaper opened wide in front of his face but in reality peering around the side of the sheet to keep an eye on all arrivals onto the platform. The 18 year old Dixon did give himself some credit for a degree of deductive powers of his own. Before Emily appeared, he had observed a hunched up and very elderly woman walking with the aid of a stick. He could not imagine that Jackson had any business with her. Next, he saw two young girls. They had both been to Clitheroe Castle a couple of times and he had spoken to them. He knew that most Saturdays these two friends left Clitheroe to go to Manchester where they found romantic interest in the young men of that city. The Blackburn train was due in 7 minutes. To ensure he did Jackson's bidding Dixon would soon have to approach the old lady with the sticks and the young joy seekers just to make sure they were not intent upon meeting Jackson.

Dixon started to become rather nervous. Precisely how does he proposition the old woman without causing offence? And what about the young ladies? I mean he knew their morals were questionable but to openly suggest they had an assignation with a man they possibly did not know or, if they did, who was thirty or more years their senior would result in his risking one or more insults or a slap across his face.

He was shaking with apprehension just when Emily came into his view. Immediately for Dixon it all made sense. Of course, it would be Emily who was going to see Mr Jackson. He was unaware that Jackson had patched up his differences with her. Maybe they had not sorted out their problems and Jackson was luring her into his trap. Relieved he had not to address any of the other women on the platform and full of motivation to carry out the task instructed by Jackson, Dixon rose from his seat and walked over to Emily.

"Good morning, Miss Hall. I think it is probably your good self that I am intended to meet?"

"I beg your pardon" said Emily who was not only taken aback to see Robinson on the platform but also totally confused by his address to her.

"I mean. You are having a rendezvous with Mr Jackson today are you not?"

"Well, as a matter of fact I am" Emily said hesitatingly trying to work out how much the young man knew.

"I was detailed by Mr Jackson to escort you though, in truth, he never said exactly where I am supposed to escort you to."

Emily did not know whether to be flattered that Haughton had provided this escort or perceive this as an affront to her freedom, her independence.

"I guess you will simply have to follow me then."

The seats in Emily's carriage were all taken. Dixon Robinson, akin to her guard, had therefore to stand at the end of the coach from where he could keep an eye on his charge.

As the train steamed through the rural countryside Emily stared out of the window. The views of this railway line had become so familiar to her this last year or more, stopping off at the stations where she had mischievously met Haughton. She tried to quash the voice inside her which was saying "Yes. You thought it was all such fun, all the hiding in stations and little chats and laughs that seemed very innocent. Well, my lady, perhaps you see now where all that has led you to. How serious all has become." The voice was like a warning but she could not listen to it. It was far too late. The dye had been too well cast.

Upon leaving Blackburn Station followed by Dixon, she hailed a carriage. Dixon heard her say to the driver "West View, Granville Terrace" and recognised this as where Jackson stayed. Yet why would Jackson want him to be with Miss Emily? Dixon was still none the wiser as to what this day was all about. It did not seem that Miss Emily was about to enlighten him. All this changed once the carriage pulled up at Isabel Jackson's house. For, whilst Dixon was left to pay the driver, Emily went directly up the steps to the front door. She knocked several times on the door but got no answer.

Emily began to panic. Had she misunderstood the message? Had she got the time wrong?

"Is something wrong?" enquired Dixon as he joined Emily on the steps.

"Quick, Master Robinson. Get that carriage back"

The carriage had just completed a turning manouevre and was about to accelerate back into the town. Dixon charged out into the middle of Granville Terrace waving his arms frantically. The carriage managed to stop and the two of them boarded once more.

"Where are we going?" asked Dixon.

"St Paul's Church"

"St Paul's Church, driver." shouted Dixon. As he turned to Emily she said:

"You might as well know Master Robinson, Mr Jackson and I are getting married."

****

Emily stepped out of the carriage and stared upwards at St Paul's Church towering above her, a large Gothic building. A shiver ran down Emily's spine. If she had ever pictured her marriage it would never have been like this. No family. No friends. No female confidante be it bridesmaid or lady-in-waiting, simply no one. She felt very alone as she walked slowly along the path to the church door. Even Dixon was no longer visible.

At the church door Isabel was waiting. She smiled before accompanying Emily down the church aisle. Each of the bride's footsteps echoed on the stone floor. There were a few attendees but none that were familiar to Emily. She banished the thought that she was walking to the guillotine but, even so, at this moment Emily felt joyless. The church was soulless.

The service was brief, being performed by the Vicar, Benjamin Thompson. The official witnesses were recorded as Doctor William Irving, Isabel (declaring her full name - Isabella Louise Le Sage Jackson) and Dixon Robinson.

****

Following the ceremony the wedding party adjourned to Dr Irving's house. Dr Irving was a friend of Jackson of many years standing. At the Doctor's house the party enjoyed a glass of wine before adjourning thereafter to West View where Isabel had arranged for a meal to be served.

During the meal the party appeared in excellent spirits though the conversation largely excluded the bride who, rather than traditionally being the focus of attention at any wedding, was almost overlooked as if simply an extra to the cast of Jackson's cronies.

Then, on one occasion, when she engaged one of the guests in conversation she was interrupted by her husband who asked in a voice for all to hear:

"Emily. Where are your h's?"

Emily was horrified and in no small measure made to feel insignificant. It was an affront. In that one moment she saw Haughton had transformed from a romantic suitor to a demanding husband. Any lingering exuberance for her day was expunged.

The guests departed West View at around 4 pm. Jackson organised for Emily and himself to visit other friends nearby before they returned to Isabel's house. At this point Haughton asked a rather weird question of his brand new bride. He said to her:

"Well, Mrs Jackson where do you intend to spend this night?"

Emily's mind was assailed. She was furious that a husband would pose such a question of her on their wedding but also Emily was hugely relieved to perceive a way out of this so dreadful a day.

"Take me home and leave me there." Emily said with force.

Jackson looked at Emily, expressionless and without comment, as she put on her bonnet and got ready to depart.

"We may just catch the 6pm train" were Jackson's first words to his wife.

"We will do no such thing. I will return to Clitheroe by carriage".

The journey back was made in silence.

Emily knew that she could not now withold the news from her family particularly as she was in the company of her husband. Her dilemma, given how she felt, was whether to come right out with the news or leave it to Jackson to make one of his bold announcements. The latter found a degree of favour with her as then perhaps most of her relatives' disdain would fall on Mr Jackson rather than her.

When she walked into Shawbridge she knew immediately something was not right. For instead of being met by Esther, the figure of Hartley Baldwin waited for her in the sitting room.

"What is it?" enquired Emily rather meekly

"Esther is very very upset and I must say I am none too pleased either. We are your family. Yet, without a bye or leave, you run off and get married."

The onslaught from her brother-in-law brought back to Emily how her father had "laid down the law" with her and John. Suddenly she forgot her dreadful day at the hands of Jackson and became rather emboldened.

"Mr Baldwin, with respect, this approach is precisely why it would have been inappropriate for me to confide in my family. No one ever seems to consider my happiness."

"Emily, do not misconstrue my motives. I desire only your happiness. I just pray you will not regret what you have done today."

The repressed feelings of spite were released as Emily again spoke forcefully to Hartley:

"If I was to do it all over again I would do the same."

On witnessing what he perceived as his wife standing up for him, Jackson entered the conversation with a degree of caution:

"What exactly is your objection to me?"

Baldwin: "You have no business or occupation."

"I have enough to keep myself in bread and butter."

Emily: "Mr Baldwin, I want a settlement of my property to be prepared."

This was the true reason for Hartley's care and concern. For to give away any of her precious resources to a person who he was convinced was a man of straw was a great folly. Yet Emily was of sound mind and he knew that were she to insist she would have to get her own way.

"Perhaps it would be best if you got someone uninvolved in the family to do it?"

"No Mr Baldwin, I insist that you prepare the settlement in the proper and usual way."

It was as if Emily was trying to get her own back on all the years of hurt she partially attributed to her father and now her brother-in-law.

Jackson said: "Oh, I certainly agree with that. I am leaving for London tomorrow before sailing on the 9th or 10th of this month. The settlement must be ready for then."

Jackson turned on his heel and having asked Hartley Baldwin to take care of Emily, the two men shook hands whereupon Mr Jackson departed for Blackburn..

Emily could not face her sister that evening. She had had a harrowing day all things taken into consideration. She had expended so much nervous exhaustion that all she could do was collapse on her bed. Too tired to feel or to think, she did not even undress.

****

In the morning Esther waiting at the breakfast table. When Emily joined her Esther took control of what could have been an otherwise awkward situation.

"Em, you know I was very hurt and upset yesterday and you also know why. I could not come down last night because, pardon me, I did not want to lay my eyes upon THAT man for fear of what I might have done or said. But that was yesterday. Today is today. You have laid your bed as they say. Just so as you know, whatever happens I will always be here for you."

Emily got up and reached over the table to hug her sister and to have a little sob upon her shoulder.

"How? How did you know? I had prepared a telegram to send to you but when I found out I was coming back here I did not trouble the telegraph office to send it."

"Oh, it was that other pal of yours, Dixon Robinson. He called his friend at the Post Office around lunchtime with the news and it was then all round the town within a couple of hours."

"I see." said Emily calmly though seething inside at the young Robinson and his loose tongue. "Believe me Esther I would not have wanted you or anyone dear to me to find out that way."

"What happens now?"

"Well" said Emily "I think it my duty to go and bid farewell to Haughton before he goes south."

This struck a dull note with Esther. Her sister, not yet married for a day, viewed seeing her husband off as "a duty". Esther was indeed troubled by this.

Emily rushed off. The journey was now familiar to her, with the train to Blackburn and the carriage to West View. This though was not the journey she had expected. There was a breakdown on the railway and several hours delay before she managed to find a carriage to convey her to Blackburn. Emily did not arrive until almost dusk.

West View was a bustle of people and activity. Last minute packing involved a large number of trunks and bags. Dixon Robinson, whom Emily now despised given her sister's disclosure, appeared to be in charge of the comings and goings. The two travellers were laughing and joking about their trip to the three or four friends in attendance. Again, Emily was largely ignored.

Jackson and Dixon left the house about 8 pm. Her farewell to Haughton had taken place in the dining room in the presence of Jackson's sister.

Emily returned by carriage to Clitheroe that night. In her mind there was something very far wrong. Once she had conquered her pre-marital nerves just before the service and been prepared against all her forebodings to make a go of the marriage and strive to be happy but since the exchange of her marriage vows she had spent no period of time alone with her husband. Jackson had displayed no vestige of interest in being with her. He used to complain about the absence of time together yet now it was as if this was the very last thing he wanted.

Emily felt very unloved on that journey home .She had vowed to love, to cherish and to obey a man who had embarked upon a trip to the farthest point in the world from her with no certainty if or when she would ever see him again.

The clouds in Emily's world had become very, very dark.

****

Apart

In travelling south Jackson was obviously little inclined to enjoy a honeymoon however short it would have been. Instead he went to Sydenham to stay with his brother Raynsford and his wife.

The atmosphere at Shawbridge was awkward. Emily preferred not to raise the subject of her situation and became rather withdrawn. Her family wanted to try and understand how the marriage had come about but as Hartley had witnessed how hurt she had appeared when she had called with Jackson, he thought that he should let time wash under the bridge before any attempt be made to get to the bottom of it. He strongly urged both Betsy and Esther to leave matters be for the moment. It would indeed be far better to see if Emily chose to confide in either of her sisters rather than that they try in a way to interrogate her.

Betsy endeavoured to pour oil over troubled waters and wrote to Jackson in the following terms:

"Clitheroe

8th November 1887

Dear Mr Jackson

Emily was much distressed by the events of last evening and I agree they ought to have been much different.

I promised Emily I would write to explain that bygones should be bygones and that should, in the course of time, you return to these shores you will not find us wanting in welcome.

Believe me to remain

Sincerely yours

B A M Baldwin"

This provoked the following response:

'Ashurst West Hill, Sydenham

9th November 1887

My dear Mrs Baldwin

I thank you very much for your letter. It is a great pleasure to me and very kind. Do not fret anymore about Saturday for we are very happy- at least I am. I feel it is very hard to go away now but I think it is for the best. No doubt we shall return someday and have a good look at you all.

Take care of Emily for me and believe me,

Ever your affectionate brother in law

Edmund Haughton Jackson

PS I hope your sister Esther will write to me.

Jackson wanted to be reconciled with the whole family.

There was one matter outstanding that had to be completed before Jackson set sail - the Settlement from Emily. Jackson need not have fretted though. Hartley Baldwin had done as Emily had bid him. Mr Baldwin dispatched his partner, Mr Weeks, to Sydenham with the Settlement for Jackson to sign.

When Mr Weeks arrived at the home of Raynsford Jackson, he was taken into the study where Haughton was already seated. Haughton acted nonchalantly despite the importance to him of his wife's Settlement.

Haughton picked up a quill and dipped it into the inkpot. He held the quill at an angle.

"Just put the deed on the table and show me where I sign."

Weeks pulled the document out of the satchel he was carrying and as he unfolded it and put it down said:

"Mr Jackson it is only correct that you read this deed before you sign."

"There is no need. I'm aware of what is in this and anyway, it is of no real consequence to someone in my position."

Once the deed was signed, Weeks was sent away back north with little courtesy from his host and, given the length of his journey, no offer of rest or refreshment.

On 10th November 1887, Jackson and Dixon Robinson were aboard the S.S.Oroya when it embarked from London Docks on the long voyage to New Zealand.

During the period immediately before and following the departure Jackson was exuberant. He revelled in writing to his wife and wrote in great detail and in such affectionate terms. Before leaving London he suggested to Emily that the Queen Victoria Jubilee celebrations were actually for their marriage. When upon the ocean wave he went on at length to describe the comfortable and spacious accommodation on board, how excellent the catering was and much much more. He would post a letter to his wife at each port the Oroya stopped at. His letters always started "My darling little wife" and ended "I remain my darling little wife, your ever loving husband, Haughton."

Haughton showered Emily with letters. They arrived for her from London, Plymouth, Naples, Port Said, Sydney and eventually Auckland.

Emily had a spring in her step. With anticipation she awaited each letter and in her head she imagined each of the places her husband had called at. She found the letters interesting and even romantic. For her part, she would always write back to Jackson sending a letter to wherever the Oroya was next scheduled to find port. Emily's letters were keen and eager and expressed her desire that it would not be too long before she could join him.

At Clitheroe, Emily's family expressed grave concern. Not regarding the matter of the marriage - for though disquieted by how it had all happened - they were accepting of the situation. No. Both Betsy and Hartley Baldwin told Emily they believed it reckless beyond measure for her to contemplate going to New Zealand. With a history of serious rheumatic fever they reckoned it would be hard for her to survive the voyage. Also, what would occur if something happened to her husband and what then would she do out there all alone and not knowing anyone?

Emily at once focused upon reality. She saw the risk to herself. She had only become enthusiastic to the notion of travel by Haughton's letters. He had made it all sound so attractive. His letters were charming and yet he had been so uncaring on her wedding day. Instantly she recalled how cold and unloved she had felt then. What would she do in New Zealand if that was how her husband made her feel? She realised she had been rash in some of what she had said in her letters thus far.

Emily finally resolved "If Haughton loves me, he will return to me."

And so she picked up her writing paper once more.

"My own dearest Haughton,

I would so dearly wish that you were home here with me and that we could have a little house of our own.

The family is quite reconciled about everything to do with the marriage except my coming to New Zealand. This they will not hear of and, darling, I want you NOT to buy land or begin to build a house. Really, Haughton dear, to tell you the honest truth, I don't see how I can, well, come out. All my property is here and I am so frequently required to sign papers and documents that I think it would be better for both our sakes if we settle down in the south of England. Darling, just think of it seriously and, remember, you are not fit for hard work. I am sure the south of England will do just as well for you Haughton, when I am always with you to look after you. I don't know what Dixon will think or say of my suggesting your coming home, but I really mean it Haughton dear. It is so nice to feel at peace with my people. They are getting so nicely reconciled and tears are nearly over and their sleep is returning. It was a terrible shock to everyone.

Your own loving wife

Emily

P.S. Be sure you do not go and buy any land. I am writing today to Isabel"

****

Correspondence

This last letter awaited Jackson when he disembarked at Auckland. Dixon Robinson later described his friend as visibly shocked at the contents of the letter. As soon as they were settled in their lodgings, Jackson set about penning a response to his wife. He only started writing once he had reconciled the dilemma within himself. On the one hand this New Zealand project was his independence and represented the control he needed to have over his life. On the other Emily offered him financial security and a continuation of his life which had largely been one of decorative idleness. Yet it was truly outrageous that he was being summoned home before his bags were even unpacked.

He tried to compose himself before he wrote:

"My darling little wife,

I do so want to be at rest with you. So darling we give up New Zealand but cannot go home without means and that is a hundred pounds and a little more. As soon as I get it, we will take our passage and be home as soon as possible.

Darling I could not leave Dixon behind. It would kill him. You know darling, it was through him that we are together and that I am so happy.

When I get home, we can settle what is to be done. What Dixon and I should like would be a little farm near a town anywhere you like and, if it can be managed, a little place for my sister, Isabel, nearby where Dixon could stay with her.

The money has only to be placed to E Haughton Jackson, Bank of New Zealand.

I remain, my darling little wife, your ever loving husband

Haughton"

****

Emily was becoming progressively disenchanted with her situation. Within Clitheroe her private life had become the subject of gossip. Upon learning about her marriage as a consequence of Dixon Robinson's indiscreet telephone call on the wedding day, some locals then brought to mind seeing Emily and Jackson at their clandestine meetings at railway stations. The busybodies in the town indulged in much speculation and moreso in view of the fact that, not once since the apparent marriage, had Emily been seen in the company of her husband.

These circles in Clitheroe Society were desperate for information. A few would comment in Esther's presence and enquire of her as to the current living arrangements at Shawbridge. These people should though have known better. If their enquiries were not stunted by Miss Hall's glowering expression they were left in no doubt by being told bluntly and very much to the point to mind their own business.

Esther, though aware her sister would be disturbed by it, felt she had to inform of how people were gossiping about her. She could not have her sister going around the town unaware that certain persons would be whispering behind her back. Also Emily could better be prepared for any questions that might be posed to her whilst waiting for service in a shop or the Post Office.

Emily throughout her life had been a very private person. Her thoughts and her business belonged to no one other than herself. Just as she had no interest of any sort in speaking of others she was indignant that her life should not become the currency of coffee shops.

She could see no way of curtailing the gossip which was fuelling the idle tongues. Were she to make any sort of statement to anyone the chances were that it would just serve to fan more flames. No. There were two hopes that Emily tried to cling to. One was that Haughton would soon return and, once settled, those wicked minds would turn away and leave her in peace. The other hope was that it would soon become stale news and that the chatterers would alight upon something fresh to "scandalise" over.

When the letter from Auckland arrived, Emily became excited. This was the response she had been holding out for. Yes she was nervous for, if Jackson simply refused to return to her, all would be almost lost. The romantic in her persuaded Emily that the letter would be the overture to a happy reconciliation.

Sitting opposite her sister in one of the armchairs, Esther saw Emily's expression suddenly change as she read Jackson's letter. The colour drained from her face and Emily looked in a state of motionless shock. The hand holding the letter fell onto her lap. Esther rose and removed the letter and meeting no objection from her little sister started to read the note herself.

Never one to beat about the bush Esther decried the terms of the letter:

"Why should you have to send money? I thought Mr Jackson was intent upon buying land so surely he has the funds for his passage? You are expected to pay for Master Robinson. The man has a bloody cheek. What does this tell you about this man you have gone and married that......you are to provide a house for his sister? I have never before heard the like of it. You know you cannot entertain this. The man is a snake. You must inform Mr Baldwin of this for, if you do not do so, then I most certainly will."

Emily burst into tears. This was, if anything, worse than had Jackson simply insisted upon staying in New Zealand. She could almost understand the attraction to him of the plans he had laid. Then she could still have persuaded herself that Haughton loved her despite staying abroad. It was now so clear that he cared not a jot about her and certainly cared more about her wealth than her own wellbeing.

Esther held out her arms but Emily gathered herself and, albeit rather unconvincingly said,

"No. I am alright. I will be alright. Do not worry."

****

Another letter arrived for Emily a few days later. This note was penned by Haughton's sister.

"Dear Emily

I am very angry with you for not telling me before writing to him to come home.

His big cases are on the way back.......unopened.

Ever yours sincerely

I W Jackson"

Two weeks later another note from Blackburn arrived at Shawbridge:

"6th April 1888

My dear Emily,

What do you fear about writing to me or coming to see me? I think there is no one more to be envied than you.

When did you send him the money?"

Ever yours sincerely,

I W Jackson"

Emily became very irked. Why should she be ordered about by her sister-in-law? The note joined the other one on the mantelpiece. Within days a third note from Isabel arrived:

"10th April 1888

My dear Emily,

If you have not sent the money, say so. I am most uneasy about Haughton.

Most sincerely yours

I W Jackson"

Emily had had more than enough of this and immediately responded:

"Shawbridge

11th April 1888

Dear Miss Jackson,

As money appears to be your only thought, I beg once and for all to tell you that I intend to be the sole master of it, and henceforth I wish to be troubled with no further letters.

Yours truly

Emily Jackson"

As part of her contemplations, Emily had enquired of her brother-in-law about the cost of a passage from New Zealand to England. Having looked into it Hartley duly reported to Emily and the information further undermined any lingering trust she had in her husband. It was perfectly possible to hire a standard cabin for such a passage at a cost of £40 and such a cabin could accommodate two persons. So why had Haughton asked her for more than twice the passage charge? Was Haughton to be a lover or a leech?

Emily was now the reverse of how she had been following Jackson's departure. She was no longer possessed of romantic notions let alone romantic dreams. In point of fact she now felt a dread at the spectre of her husband's return. Even so, as with so many of the Victorian generation, Emily was conscious of a sense of duty. She could be vilified were she to be seen to have abandoned Jackson in New Zealand when it was clearly within her power and her means to bring him back.

She wrote a brief cold note to Jackson:

"Shawbridge

15th April 1888

Dear Mr Jackson,

I have this day transferred to your Account the sum of £50.

I am assured that this will cover not only your passage to England but also allow for any necessary acquisitions en voyage.

Mr Dixon Robinson is, despite the construction you may place upon our situation, not my responsibility.

Yours truly

Emily Jackson"

Emily wrote a longer letter to Jackson the following day, 16th April 1888. Before Jackson received this he had written a veritable stream of letters to his wife. Three arrived within days of each other during the first week in May 1888. His letters were all long and loving in their terms. They conveyed a man in good spirits. They were humorous.. He wrote recounting their days of courting and to boating trips on the River Ribble and all the things he would soon experience with her once more. Then by a letter of 7th May 1888 he proclaimed that both he and Dixon would arrive back on 16th or 17th July 1888.

The tone of the correspondence altered upon Jackson's receipt of Emily's letter of 16th April 1888.

This letter started with Emily stating she would not listen to pleas on behalf of Dixon Robinson. That man was old enough now to look after himself. She barely hid her disdain for Robinson for it was he, of course, who had caused all the grief between Emily and her family the previous November.

Emily then set out her next grievance:

"You remember the day we became engaged? Well, everything we spoke of has been repeated to me. Only the two of us being there, I fear it is you who have told all. I thought you had more common sense and respect for me. Several other things I could mention if space allowed. Now I don't expect this sort of thing to go on and I won't have it. I must add that everything you have told me not to repeat from your letters, I find currently talked about in Clitheroe and Blackburn almost before I hear the news myself. I cannot understand this sort of thing and have never been accustomed to it."

She continued:

"About meeting you, I shall not come south at all. Go to your own people in London and if you will write to me from there, I will let you know when to come to me.

About the partnership in farming, you know as well as I do that farming anywhere, let alone in England, requires capital. If you go for it, you must make yourself responsible for it, for I shall advance you no money whatever. Dixon, of course, must go home. Who more likely than his own folk to look after him? Not you, for when we have a house, I do not intend anyone to live with us.

You ask me if I have picked any place in my mind where we shall live. I must say I have my own ideas, but you know it is customary for a man, however limited his means, to find a house for his wife. Therefore you and all your well-to-do people cannot expect me to do this, though Miss Jackson has dared to write and ask me if I have sent you out the passage money. I must tell you that I have told my people everything and shall set by their advice, in which I concur.

They consider, and I do, that I am grossly insulted and never heard of such a monstrous thing in their lives for any lady to be thus attacked by a comparative stranger. Miss Jackson keeps annoying me about nothing but money and I have been compelled to let her know that I intend to be the sole master of my money.

I now plainly see why you married me and am very sorry I was blind enough before not to find it out. Understand once and forever, I do not intend now or at anytime to be subjected to indignity from any of your people.

If you think you have any prospect of making money if you remain where you are you had better do so. I can get on quite well and I am happy with everyone around me striving to make me as comfortable as possible. Should you, on reflection, elect to stay in New Zealand then you can return the passage funds to me that I transferred to you yesterday.

I am truly sorry I have to write to you in this manner, but I can bear it no longer. It is better to tell you all and be done with it.

I must now bid you goodbye, with my love.

Believe me,
Yours, as ever

Emily"

Upon reading all of this Jackson became enraged. His anger, fuelled by a Victorian male arrogance and every concept of the position and authority of a husband current at that time was added to by the real possibility of his perceived security being snatched from him.

In his mind's eye Jackson saw the pompous and odious Hartley Baldwin, that old terror Esther Hall and the pseudo respectable Betsy Baldwin all arraigned against him. All set to rob him of his wife and all that went there with. To have attacked him and his relations was truly outrageous. He would show them what he was made of. He would have to destroy this conspiracy against him.

Savagely he grabbed his pen which he proceeded to employ as a weapon in his new found battle.

"Auckland, New Zealand

28th May 1888

My dear Emily,

Your letter is an insult to me and mine. I cannot understand how you dared write to me in such terms.

As to coming home, it was at your request that I gave up starting anything here and have waited until now for the means to return.

I have been ill nearly all of the time. You knew quite well what I had and I did not care to ask my brother Raynsford for more. As to Dixon, if it had not been for him, I should have died.The advice your people have given you is bad and you would have been a great deal better without it.

I never repeated a word of our talk when we got engaged. Your good people must have sent someone to watch us. As you say everything between a husband and wife is sacred, but you have dared to tell your people everything.

Make no mistake, there shall be a perfect understanding between us but I will make it, not you. It is most ridiculous for you to say you will not have this or not have that. It depends entirely on whether I approve or not.

Though Miss Jackson has dared to write to you, she did her duty and was in the right so do not in future be so foolish as to call her "Miss Jackson." Her name is Isabel. I wonder how you dare write to my sister as you say you have done. And how dare you say I married you for your cash when you know it is a lie. If you get a house of your own and I am with you, you will be pleased to treat anyone I care for in a good and kind manner.

I do not care a fig what your people say, think or do. Before I left home, I was told that old Hartley and your people were trying to influence you against me. I did not believe the story at the time, thinking that you cared for me and would shut your ears to anything that might be said.

You say you do not wish to quarrel. Yet you insult me in every possible way.

I believe you to have been deluded by others as only such could cause you to write as you have done,

I remain
Your (still) loving husband

Haughton"

Throughout June 1888 there was a deep silence with no further communications until, en route to England aboard the S.S. Orizaba Jackson despatched the following message from the ship on 7th July 1888:-

"My darling

We expect to be at Plymouth on the 16th or the 17th so any letter addressed to me should be to

C/O I. T. White & Co
Agents Orient Line: Orizaba
Plymouth.

I can hardly believe we shall meet so soon and I feel so happy. We shall be in Naples tomorrow and then on to Gibraltar and then to Plymouth and London. You could meet me either at Plymouth or at London.

Goodbye, my darling little wife

Ever your loving husband

E. Haughton Jackson."

The S.S Orizaba arrived on the due date at Plymouth. There was no sign of Emily at the quayside and no letter from her amongst the boat's mail. Slightly crestfallen Jackson remained on board until the ship docked at London. Though it was July there was a heavy mist covering this part of the Thames and the docks. Haughton disembarked followed down the gangway by a rather tired and subdued Dixon Robinson.

Jackson scanned the dockside, as best he could given the fog. Apart from the stevedores who were busy there were about a dozen or so people gathered to welcome the passengers - wives, parents, lovers or friends. No. There was nothing wrong with Jackson's vision. There was no sign of his "loyal" wife. It was to his mind her duty to be there and she was not. He was now not simply dejected but angry once more.

Dixon had to wait outside as Haughton entered the Shipping Agents' Offices. After a brief delay the man serving behind the counter returned to Jackson and handed over two envelopes each obviously handwritten by Emily.

Jackson felt warmth inside at the sight of Emily's handwriting. He jumped into the carriage having instructed the driver to take both him and his companion to Sydenham.

Dixon slouched in a corner and was soon asleep.

Jackson opened the first letter which had been addressed to the office in Plymouth and then forwarded to London.

"Shawbridge

14th July 1888

Dear Haughton

I received your very insulting and unmanly (I won't say ungentlemanly) letter yesterday and am more than surprised how you dare even think of writing to me in such a vein. From the tone throughout, it is very evident to me that we shall never get on together, husband and wife as we are, in name only.

If you are capable of addressing such a letter to me before we have lived together a single day, it plainly shows me what you will say and do afterwards. I have made up my mind from henceforth to have nothing whatever to do with you. You must go your way and I will go mine and endeavour to forget the unfortunate mistake I have made.

I remain,

Yours truly

Emily Jackson"

In a state of incredulity Jackson rushed to open the second letter addressed to the London agent.

"16th July 1888

Dear Sir

I enclose a copy of the letter I addressed to you at Plymouth and posted on Saturday last, the 14th and which I am quite sure you received. I am more determined than ever to abide by my decision stated in my letter and beg you will not trouble me anymore.

I remain

Yours truly

Emily Jackson"

In that moment Jackson was consumed by a feeling of desolation. He felt insecure. His dreams of New Zealand were gone. His gamble of coming back to Emily for warmth and shelter had seemingly not paid off. He stared unblinking out of the carriage. Looking into the fog he could see nothing. He was lost.

****

The Pursuit - commences

Once she had posted her letters to the shipping agents, Emily became very unsettled. Not that she considered her judgement in terminating her relationship with Jackson as either hasty or in any way an error. No. She had no reservations on that score. She was though upset at how she had so badly misjudged Jackson and been taken in by his charm. Emily was punishing herself at this time. She had failed to see the warning signs that had been signposted along the journey of the courtship. Emily had allowed a desire to settle down and not be alone to cloud her reasoning about a marriage to Jackson. She had also to admit that motivation to marry was in part at least fuelled by the rebel within wanting to spite her own family.

Conversely, having stood up to her family on the subject of Jackson, she now reproached herself for not having asserted herself with them over John. At least then love could have been her vindication.

Emily was also gripped with an irrational fear. She did not trust Jackson. Over all the years since she met him he had so doggedly pursued her. Each and every occasion when she had tried to dissuade him from imagining a future with her, he had persevered. Emphatically his marriage proposals had been rejected by her and yet such rejection appeared, if anything, to have spurred Jackson on.

The psychology seemed to dictate that when she placed herself out of Jackson's reach he became keen and caring and then when, as it were, he had her, he just became disinterested. In the letters she could not have made her position clearer. The pathology of Jackson as she perceived it strongly suggested that he would not take this rebuff meekly or accept it.

She was fearful of what Jackson might do for she had witnessed first hand his sudden mood changes. It was already clear that Jackson's family would not offer him sage advice but would, almost always, defer to Jackson's whims, notions and plans.

Before Jackson was due to come ashore in England, Emily visited Prospect House. There she confided at least some of her thoughts to Betsy. They had been served with tea in the morning room and it was after Charnock had retired from the room that the sisters engaged in the subject on both of their minds.

"Em, it is so hard for you after all that has happened but be assured I have your best interests at heart when I say that you have made the correct decision. No good was ever going to come of your marriage."

"Oh, I see that now. "Why did I not do so before it was too late?"

"Thinking like that is not going to do you any good. Anyway, even I was latterly taken in by Haughton. I started to believe all he said about caring for you when he was last in this house. So there's no need to feel stupid. Plenty before you have been ensnared by a charmer and plenty more will still be in the future. Just be thankful you have got out of it before you were living together or before, heavens above, you had any children."

"Thank you. I know you are right. It is just not easy to understand all that has happened and all that I have done. You know I can sense this is not over. I cannot see him taking this lying down. Yet I have no more to say to him. He cannot see what he has done to me. I mean if he turns up at Shawbridge I fear there will be an awful scene which I cannot bear the thought of."

"Tell me sister if you can. Is it a fear of, as you put it, an awful scene that scares you or that you may succumb to this man's charms yet again?"

"Betsy. In truth I do not know. All I can say is that just now I feel revulsion at the thought of listening to his voice or reading anymore of his letters."

"You know what we are going to do?" posed Betsy in a cheery manner.

"What?"

"You need a bit of peace and quiet. I could do with a change of air. How about we go way to the coast for a while?"

"Are you serious? But, what about Mr Baldwin?"

"Do not worry about him. This is for the good of our family. He will understand."

"Can I stay for supper?" asked Emily.

"Of course you can " said Betsy taking hold of her sister's hands.

Emily had never been away with her eldest sister but knew that Betsy would look after her. Esther would be happy to have Shawbridge to herself for a while. There was another implied attraction. This, though unspoken between the sisters, was that, wherever the two of them went, they would be in hiding from Jackson. This was the start of a game which Emily, for her sanity if for no other reason, was happy to play.

****

Hartley Baldwin returned from the office, as was habit, at shortly after 5 45 pm. He was surprised but pleased to greet his younger sister-in-law. He had been appraised by his wife before this day that Emily had decided to live apart from her husband and Hartley, as always, felt a strong desire to protect her just as he would have felt towards any of the family.

Charnock brought through on a tray a couple of small sherries and a brandy.

"Emily and I have decided to go away for a while."

Hartley raised an eyebrow but he knew Betsy well enough to know there would be a good reason for such a pronouncement. He did not though ask why they were going away but rather:

"And where will you be off to then?"

"We thought the coast."

"Excellent idea. In fact I know a Magistrate who owns a flat in Southport. He rents it out from time to time. Would that be of interest ladies?"

Emily found her brother-in-law's acceptance of the situation quite remarkable. He is quite different from my father, she mused to herself.

"Oh I think that would be ideal Hartley if that could be managed."

"When exactly would you be reckoning upon taking off? I can contact the owner tomorrow."

"Well" said Betsy "I rather think it should be as soon as possible as Mr Jackson is due back in England within the next two or three days."

The reason for this sudden plan dawned upon Hartley and at the mere mention of Jackson's name, he rose and excused himself.

"This, ladies, cannot wait until tomorrow."

Hartley Baldwin re emerged after about ten minutes.

"It's all arranged. I've spoken to the Magistrate on the telephone just now. He is delivering the keys to my office first thing tomorrow. I have agreed to rent the flat for a month."

He then looked across at the two ladies. He picked up his brandy and with a wicked twinkle in his eye said:

"My guess is that the two of you will have to get packing. Do not get up to any mischief and enjoy the seaside."

He raised his glass to his lips.

Emily suddenly remembered why she had wanted to stay for supper. She wanted Mr Baldwin's advice.

"Mr Baldwin, I am so fortunate to belong to such a close and caring family and I thank you from the bottom of my heart. There is though something I must ask you. What can Mr Jackson do about the situation? Can he sue me for money? I gave certain vows when I was married. I vowed to obey my husband. What can be done about this?"

"As you went through with the marriage he cannot sue you for breach of promise of marriage. The vows you made were vows made before God and the law cannot really give effect to obedience. Can you imagine if everytime a wife disobeyed a husband she could be taken to Court? No, until or unless one of you seeks to dissolve the marriage I cannot see that there is anything that the man can do."

"If he comes looking for me what will you say?"

"Emily, I need say nothing at all. Precisely where you are or where my wife is are matters of no concern to Mr Jackson and, if given the chance, I will tell him exactly that. Not that he would ever find out but the flat in Southport will be recorded as leased in the name of my partner, Mr Weeks and Charnock will simply be told that Betsy is away for a rest cure and that you have gone as her companion. The other thing we must ensure is that Esther's coachman takes you to Southport. We can certainly count upon that man's discretion."

"Gosh" said Emily. "Everything seems to be settled then."

"Apart from one thing sister" said Betsy with a smile. "No time for supper now. If you are to be ready by tomorrow you will need to hasten back to Shawbridge. I'm sure Esther will have something delightful for you to eat there"

****

The Pursuit - continues

At Sydenham, the despair Jackson had felt upon setting foot again on English shores was overtaken by the need to recover from the long sea voyage. He felt not only revived by a thirteen hour sleep but found himself in a different mindset altogether. He would not now accept defeat and certainly he would not be defeated by a woman. He had had to explain to Raynsford that he had returned because his wife could not bear to be parted from him. He had "dressed up" the scene to be one of pure romance as he could not bring himself to disclose to his brother that he had now been rebuffed by Mrs Jackson. He could depend upon Dixon Robinson. He found the young man within the back garden of the Sydenham property. Unlike the previous day, the sun shone and it was a fine summer's morning in London.

"Dick. Now that we are back in England, we have to make plans. I have to discuss these with you as they will involve you."

"Yes. Yes." Dixon said eagerly.

"This is rather delicate and I need you to keep all I am about to say to yourself. Can I trust you?"

"Of course you can."

"In my correspondence with Mrs Jackson I had proposed that she and I invest in a Farm and part of the plan was that you reside nearby. Now I had formed the impression at the time that Mrs Jackson was not unfavourably disposed to this plan. This may or may not be the case. The most recent communication from my wife is very confusing. She may not be herself. Alternatively, I would not be surprised if, during our absence, she has had her head turned by her ungrateful family who have never been well disposed towards me. Anyhow, she declares hostility towards both you and myself. "

"I do not really understand."

"Nor, if I may say so Dick, do I. I will not accept what she says and will not be so dictated to. I will confront her but firstly things need to be planned. I need your help."

"Just tell me what I need to do."

"I need you to return to Clitheroe Castle with all speed. From there I want you to find out as much as you can about what is going on. Let me know of Mrs Jackson's movements. Let me know what word is about in local circles. If you find out anything just call me here and reverse the charges. I will square that with my brother."

"You mean I am to be a sort of spy?"

"Exactly, but remember, not a word to anyone."

Dixon was very eager to set off upon his mission.

****

After Dixon had departed for the railway station on the northbound train, Jackson took the opportunity, whilst his brother was absent from the house, to call Isabel. He confided in her totally and played the conversation with his heart very much on his sleeve. The effect upon his sister was predictable. She fulminated over the cheek and disrespect of Emily.

“Haughton, she has had you wrapped around her little finger for long enough. She never stayed with you on your wedding night, let you spend all that money getting to New Zealand and then she demands you return instantly. Now you tell me she wants nothing to do with you. She is a conniving and manipulating woman that Emily Hall. You cannot just sit and do nothing. You cannot allow her to get away with this."

Jackson changed the tone of his voice. He was now quietly assured in his speech.

"Isabel, I have no intention of letting her, as you say, "get away with this". She will not get away with it, mark my words. I am her husband and she has to do as I bid."

"Indeed she does. You should come here to West View. It is no good you remaining in London."

"I will be with you shortly. Oh, that is our brother arriving back. Take care, sister."

Jackson hung up the telephone.

****

He never questioned Dixon's devotion and Haughton's prediction that he would soon "report in" was realised just after supper the following day. Dixon had chosen not to make the call a reversed charge one.

The essence of this report was that Emily had not been seen around Clitheroe. Esther, Dixon had observed personally, had ventured in and out of Shawbridge. Hartley Baldwin had, with his son, journeyed predictably to and from his office. Everything seemed normal but for the lack of evidence concerning Mrs Jackson. Dixon had arranged to meet the next day with his friend in the Post Office whose day off it was. If anyone knew about Emily then she would.

Jackson thanked his friend. He did not dwell on the report he had just had. There could be a perfectly innocent explanation for his wife's lack of visible profile. She could, he surmised, be unwell and confined within Shawbridge for, as he knew and had been told, she was not infrequently struck with a malady.

The next day's report from Dixon did make Jackson become suspicious.

No.The Post Office contact had not seen Emily. There were two things that this lady had imparted. Firstly, that Betsy Baldwin had failed to attend the monthly meeting of the Flower Committee. Mrs Baldwin was the Chairwoman of that Committee. No apology had been provided. Betsy had not been seen around the town. There was a rumour she was away but no one knew if this was true let alone where she was. There was also gossip from the blacksmith. A horse belonging to Esther's coachman had had an accident and lost a shoe. Apparently, the accident happened when the carriage it was pulling en route to Clitheroe had had to swerve to avoid a rock on the coast road.

Jackson was convinced, following this conversation, that Emily was not in Clitheroe for one sister not to have been seen about was unexceptional but for neither sister to be visible was simply not credible. Mrs Baldwin would not simply forget her meeting. He reckoned he was onto something. These two women had chosen to disappear. Jackson discounted any relevance to the story regarding the injured horse. The more he thought, the more he became angry. If all was above board and the sisters had gone away together then it would not be a secret. The possibility that Mrs Jackson had gone into hiding from him was a vision that made Haughton even more determined to assert himself over his wife.

If he was correct and Emily was hiding from him, this conveyed a fear on the part of his wife. Jackson knew he could employ such fear to his advantage. By now, in his mind, Jackson very much took on the mantle of the hunter with Emily his fox. Yet even with Dixon being his hound, how could he best flush out the fox? Whilst aware of the protective shield provided by her family, Jackson refused to admit that any third party would or could get in his way. This was strictly between him and Mrs Jackson. He must take no step that could be perceived as a threat to Emily's welfare for that would make his task even more difficult. He had to act at all times now as though he presented no danger to Emily. He would disport himself as if he was completely unaffected. He had to provide her with no crumb to complain about to her family.

****

The first contact that Jackson made with Emily arrived at Shawbridge in the form of a brief note.

"Sydenham

23rd July 1888

My darling little wife,

I have given up every wish of a life with you. I am leaving Sydenham for Blackburn.

I do not consider you have made any mistake.

I hope to see you before too long.

I remain

Your ever loving husband

E Haughton Jackson"

If, as Jackson suspected, Emily was in hiding from him, the effect of this intimation that he was moving north again would, if anything, serve to heighten his wife's worries. He knew that, wherever Emily was, the terms of the note would be conveyed to her. There was absolutely nothing in the note her family could possibly take exception to. Certainly, he did not expect any response to the note but Jackson's strategy did not require a response.

Jackson duly headed north and again took up residence with his sister in Blackburn. He was soon discussing his plans with Isabel.

"I do not see why you do not simply present yourself at Shawbridge and demand to see your wife. All this pussyfooting about with letters is not your style and is not going to achieve anything."

"Isabel, you do not understand. One has to make preparations. Lay the groundwork. After all one does not attack a fortress or do anything to stiffen the resolve of those defending it"

"Haughton, don't be silly. This is not a war."

"Ah, but the approach to conquest is not that much different."

The phone rang.

Susan "It is Master Robinson for you, Mr Jackson."

Jackson walked smartly to the telephone.

"Ah, Dick. What news?"

"You might have told me you were going to Blackburn. It is not good having to find out where you are from your brother" moaned Dixon.

"Oh, do not go all peevish on me. What has my spy got to report ?"

"Well, I spoke to my father and... "

""You did what?" said Jackson becoming angry.

"No just calm down Mr Jackson. Let me explain. I never let on anything about you looking for you know who."

"Just get on with it, man" said an irritated Jackson.

"You see they were to be having one of their picnics today. You recall their picnics?"

Jackson fought to remain calm.

"Of course, I remember the picnics."

"Well, my father said he was going to the picnic and I said I wanted him to pass a message to you."

"Will you please explain Dixon? I am getting all too confused by this story?"

"I pretended to the Colonel that I had gone and left my silver compass by mistake in Mr Jackson's bag and only realised this after getting off the boat at London. Since then you and I had argued and I felt I could not approach you regarding the compass. So could he inform Mrs Jackson or her sisters of this and get the message passed on to you."

As this unlikely tale unfolded Jackson became progressively nervous. So easily Dixon could have let slip his agency on behalf of Jackson and aroused suspicion. He did though take his hat off, metaphorically, to his young friend for having produced such an invention.

"What happened?" queried Jackson with interest.

"That's just it. My father is not long back. He told me that the only Hall at the picnic was Esther. You will appreciate that my father is quite direct and probably moreso after his usual Malmsey refreshment. Miss Hall informed the Colonel in no uncertain terms that no one should run errands for his son and that she would not run errands for anyone. Imagine that?"

Jackson could well capture the scene in his mind's eye.

"So, after all of that, we have really learnt nothing?"

"Well, not exactly. The blacksmith was at the picnic. He lives quite near the castle here. Anyway, he was overheard speaking to Miss Hall's coachman telling him to take care on the coast road next week as he had heard there had been more rockfalls ."

Jackson tried to analyse what he had just been told. That horse? Yes, indeed. His knowledge of Miss Esther, though not very extensive, did not suggest she would travel far and wide in her carriage on social jaunts. Was the coast road a connection to her infernal turkeys? How could he know? Or did the coast road lead to her sister, his wife?"

"Dick, when is it this coach heads out on the road?"

"Sorry, I do not know." Dixon said a little deflated.

"Thank you, my good man. Keep your ear to the ground. I think we are getting closer."

****

Jackson did feel better. He sensed the fox would soon return to her lair. She would not stay away from her family forever. Certainly, he believed Hartley Baldwin would demand that his wife return to him.

Jackson, the hunter, was quite prepared to wait for his quarry. In fact he would pass more time by adding more of his powder to the perceived keg by writing once more to Mrs Jackson.

"West View
2 Rover Street
Blackburn

25th July 1888

My darling little wife,

This misunderstanding which, I emphasise, is on your part only must be put right. Do not throw away happiness which could be ours for the rest of our lives just because you have heard some abominable untruths about me. Just believe that I love you.

I must see you. I will see you at the house of, say, Dr Irving or perhaps that of your doctor, Dr Musson or wherever you would like other than Shawbridge or Prospect House.

I remain

Your loving husband

E Haughton Jackson"

Haughton Jackson had so quickly forgotten the basic precept of his earlier letter wherein he had represented he had relinquished all hope or thought of them being together.

His mindset had reverted to that which saw his powers of persuasion and his natural allure as irresistible and it was in that mood he continued on a "charm offensive" in a further letter to Emily on 2nd August 1888. In this further letter he asked his wife to gift him the power of "putting this great unhappiness and discomfort right."

****

Showdown

The pivotal day was 13th August 1888. In the game being played by Jackson, by this date, he craved and indeed had expected a response from his wife. He was convinced she would have been privy to the correspondence he had sent to Shawbridge. Yet no mail bearing his wife's handwriting arrived at West View. Now Jackson was beginning to review his strategy. He deserved a respons - to ignore him was the height of rudeness. He then pictured Mrs Jackson laughing at him and mocking him behind his back and such thoughts drove Jackson to go over all of his options. Should he consult his lawyer? Should he turn his"fire" onto Emily's family and by so doing flush her out of her hiding place?

Susan interrupted Haughton's thoughts.

"Excuse me Sir, that is a call for you."

Jackson was in no mood for Master Robinson's conversation for he just sensed it was Dixon on the phone for him. He wanted to refuse to take the call but then changed his mind. He was so glad then that he did speak to Dixon.

"Mr Jackson. She is back. Emily is back at Shawbridge. I have just seen her leave there with her sister and go to Prospect House."

This news was exactly what Jackson needed to hear.

Isabel was right he thought. His "softly, softly" approach had achieved nothing. It was now the time for direct action.

****

The following day, 14th August 1888, Jackson boarded the train for Clitheroe. In his heart he wanted to get to Emily. In his head his fury was focused upon her family. They would be pulling her strings and prohibiting her from writing to him. He convinced himself that this was the case as it was, for Jackson, the only possible explanation.

He left Clitheroe Station on foot for Shawbridge. Jackson told himself to keep calm for losing control would not achieve his aim. He guessed the shock to Emily of seeing him in Clitheroe would be great but she had to learn her place in their marriage. Anyhow, did he not still possess the charm to bring her round?

At 2 o'clock Jackson knocked on the door at Shawbridge. Mary, the maid, answered and informed Mr Jackson that his wife was out for the afternoon. After he had left, Esther sent word to Hartley Baldwin.

At 4 30 pm Jackson again called at Shawbridge to be told that Mrs Jackson had not yet returned. He scribbled a note which he passed to Mary.

The note stated Jackson would return at 6 30 pm and that he expected Emily to be present and available to speak to him.

With military precision Jackson knocked yet again on the door of Shawbridge the very moment the clock in the hall struck 6 30 pm. He was admitted to the house but his route into any of the rooms was barred by the twin bulwarks of the defence. For there, at the far end of the hall stood the reception committee comprising Hartley Baldwin and Esther Hall. There was no sign of his wife. Unbeknown to Jackson Emily was crouching behind the top of the staircase and in a position to hear whatever was said.

Hartley Baldwin stared solemnly at Jackson. Esther's eyes glared into the visitor's face.

"I demand to see my wife, Mrs Emily Jackson" shouted Jackson with little of the control he had promised himself.

Mr Baldwin, in a cold and measured tone responded :

"The lady whom we prefer to call Miss Emily Hall will not see you now or at any other time. You had her letter. She is done with you."

"I have the right to see her. You cannot refuse. Where is she? I must and I will see her."

By now Jackson was shouting loudly. How dare they try to deny the very fact of his marriage to Emily.

"Whatever you have to say to the lady you can say to me. Now say it and go."

Jackson's fury increased.

"I will speak to her and no-one else" shouted Jackson. "Stand aside, I will find her." He made to push forward.

"Not one step further, Mr Jackson. This is **not** your house."

When he saw Haughton had paid no attention and was continuing his advance towards him, Hartley Baldwin instinctively threw a punch at the intruder. This only succeeded in knocking off Jackson's hat. Esther then let loose and screamed at Jackson:

"You are a vile wretch. You are a fortune hunter. You have deceived my poor little sister all along. But it is, thank goodness, ended now."

Jackson had had enough and reason became lost to him.

"Call yourself a lady?" he ranted. "There is not a lady amongst you all. Neither you nor this man's wife and certainly not Emily"

"Wretch." responded Esther "How dare you say so. You are no gentleman that is clear. Emily is well rid of you"

"And what are you, then? You are a lying bitch. And a damned prostitute................and everybody knows it."

"Enough" boomed Hartley his voice resonating above the other protagonists. He threw open the door nearest to him and gave clear instruction to Mary "Call the police."

Through his furied and stressed mind, it was now clear to Jackson that he could not make headway. He would, after all, have to explore legal routes to find the satisfaction he not only yearned for but was entitled to. He was perfectly within his rights to demand to see his wife. They had physically thwarted him on this occasion but, as he continued to glower at those barring his way, he was certain there was more than one way to "skin a cat" and that he would never allow his personal mission to be denied. Not by the Baldwins. Not by the Halls. Not by anyone.

"We'll see who will get the better of this" Jackson was restored to his arrogant self. He put his head to an angle and sneered:

"I know all about you Baldwin. You're known as the biggest blackguard in all of Lancashire."

Esther, who had a hold of her brother-in-law by the arm, felt Hartley tense. She tightened her grip on his arm fearful as to what he might try to do. Her apprehension was though relieved when, before Hartley reacted, the front door swung open.

At the sound of the door opening, Jackson turned around to see two burly constables from the Clitheroe Police standing there. Both constables touched their helmets in deference to Mr Baldwin who then pointed at Jackson and said to the officers:

"Remove that man from this house."

Without resistance, Jackson permitted the police to take hold of him and escort him away.

Once peace had again descended upon Shawbridge, Hartley bade farewell and returned quite shaken and serious in his thoughts to Prospect House. Emily though horrified at the spectre of Jackson and his behaviour had raced down the stairs to see if Mr Baldwin and her sister were alright.

Emily sat for a long time with Esther. They relived what had just taken place. Emily was focused. She was sure now that Jackson would not easily let go of her. Something told her to make a written record of what had been done and said that night, which is what the two sisters proceeded to do.

When she made it to her bed Emily was relieved that the Jackson visit was over with. In herself she also felt embarrassed and, in a way, ashamed. For, it was she who had brought the disturbance upon Shawbridge. It was because of her, her family had had to suffer the humiliation and abuse from Haughton. Now that the police had been called it was fair to imagine the tongues of Clitheroe would once again be wagging at quite some speed.

For this moment Emily's discomfort was confined to the village of Clitheroe. It was as well that this lady did not and could not have foreseen the national notoriety that would, before long, be her fate.

****

To Law - Pt 1

Having been accompanied to the Railway Station by the police, Jackson found himself returning to Blackburn. He felt angry, sorry for himself and that he had been badly wronged. He was now more convinced than ever before that the situation he found himself in was nothing to do with his "darling little wife" and nothing to do with him. No. The meddling and obstruction by Emily's family was the sole cause of all this misfortune. It explained so well for him now why Emily had been so emphatic that their courtship should take place in secrecy.

Jackson regarded himself as a fine match for Emily. No, he reminded himself. This was not yet over.

****

At West View Jackson, as always, found comfort and support in his sister.

After hearing her brother's summary of all that had happened, Isabel was certain that there would be more trouble coming his way. Jackson must not wait for Emily and her supporters to make the first move in any conflict. In her mind it was essential that Edmund take the initiative.

"They called you a fortune hunter? That is defamation of character. You must take legal advice. You are such a gentle silly boy and you cannot handle that lot alone."

Jackson had not obviously confided in Isabel the words he had chosen to use when "debating" the issues with Esther and Mr Baldwin.

Haughton decided he would accept his sister's counsel but not before he had given his confidence in his own powers of persuasion another throw of the dice. Objectively his decision was doomed to failure. He decided to address matters by writing to the man he now saw as his nemesis, Hartley Baldwin.

"West View
Granville Terrace
Blackburn

27th August 1888

Dear Mr Baldwin,

I am writing to you about this unfortunate and most unhappy estrangement between myself and my wife. How it has come about, I cannot for the life of me conceive, and certainly it does not exist on my side. No doubt you know all about it and can, if you will, do much to assist me to set everything right again. Please do all you can to help me and so discharge the promise to make all straight and right in every way on the evening of my marriage.

I know that last Tuesday week, you refused me admission to Miss Esther Hall's house when I called to see my wife to have the interview I so much desire. My purpose and sole intent that I may remove all misunderstanding and persuade her, as I know I could, to come and live with me. Even after I got into the house, you would not let me see my wife, but then all this was in Miss Hall's property and I cannot but think you were acting for her and not for yourself. I am told that my wife is now staying with you. Do therefore all you can for me and send me a letter by Wednesday's post to say that I may see my wife at your house. I shall expect and most anxiously look for your letter. The present suspense is most harrowing to me and almost more than I can bear.

Yours truly

E Haughton Jackson "

Jackson's information was indeed correct. The family had decided after the raucous events at Shawbridge that Emily would be less vulnerable if she stayed for a while with her older sister at Prospect House.

Hartley Baldwin was infuriated by the fact Jackson had had the audacity to write to him and immediately he issued his response:

"Clitheroe

28th August 1888

Dear Sir,

You have displayed a good deal of effrontery in writing to me after your conduct and insolent abuse of me the other night. I will have nothing to do with you in any way and I will not have you in my house.

I give you notice that if you attempt to intrude yourself into my house, the consequences will be very unpleasant.

I am desired to give you this notice also as regards Miss Hall's house.

Your obedient servant

Hartley Baldwin"

In temper, Jackson crunched this haughty and contemptuous note in his right fist and rushed from West View heading for the solicitor's office. Once at the offices of Messrs Ainsworth, Sanderson and Howson who operated from 32 Clayton Street, Blackburn, he was directed to a waiting room. Without an appointment he had to wait.

There was a calm solemnity. The distant "tap tap" of a secretary typing in the background. The clock on the mantelpiece went "tick-tick" with each second. These noises though were not found to be intrusive but rather assisted in relaxing any anxious client about to face an erudite legal practitioner.

In Jackson's case, the practitioner happened to be the junior partner, Mr Howson.

After the necessary introductions and reference by Mr Howson to the Firm having previously acted for Mr Raynsford Jackson, Mr Edmund Jackson was invited to explain the purpose of his visit.

Jackson pulled from his inside pocket the somewhat crushed letter and pushed it across to the solicitor.

After reading the contents, Howson commented:

"Not a nice letter, I grant you but you will have to explain a bit more."

Jackson then regaled Howson with the story of his marriage, New Zealand and the conspiracy against him since he had returned. Needless to say Jackson omitted any parts of the tale which could conceivably cast himself in a bad light.

Howson listened intently but his experience always reminded him that there would be two sides to this story. He already knew how he could be of assistance to this new client.

"So, you want your position put on an official basis, as it were?"

"Precisely"

"There is Court action which I believe you could successfully bring"

Jackson recoiled a bit.

"Is there nothing a little less serious?"

"Well, of course, we can issue formal letters to your wife."

"What about Mr Baldwin? Can we not deal with him first?" enquired Jackson.

"I see he seems to be the primary object of your attention. Why would that be? I thought it was Mrs Jackson you wanted to address?"

"Well, it is Mrs Jackson I suppose. I do want to fire a shot across Mr Baldwin's bows though. I find him a pompous and condescending monster not to mention a solicitor to boot. Oh, I'm sorry. I did not mean that last bit." said Jackson.

"I am glad you did Mr Jackson. You never mentioned before that Mr Baldwin was a member of my profession."

They then spoke quite animatedly about the plan of action. It is true that a solicitor will ostensibly respect another solicitor but at the same time will perceive it a challenge to succeed with that solicitor over a legal point. However, this was even better. A solicitor was at the centre of this dispute and so the incentive to use if possible this Mr Baldwin's personal conduct to secure the result desired by his client could not have encouraged Howson more to become keenly involved in Mr Jackson's affairs.

As this meeting reached a conclusion, Howson made this enquiry of Jackson:

"I assume you are aware that this Firm charges a premium rate for its services. I do not for a second question your credentials and standing Mr Jackson but I cannot have you later complain about our charges."

Jackson stood up and stretched out his hand to shake that of his solicitor.

"Do not harbour concerns on that front, Sir. There will be no difficulty in settling your fees whenever rendered."

Jackson bounded down the outside steps onto Clayton Street. He felt a different man from the Jackson who had entered the offices an hour and twenty minutes previously. His decision to seek advice had been vindicated. He no longer felt alone in his battle.

He had one reservation though. He could not afford solicitor's fees, yet he had given a personal assurance to Howson about these.

On his return to West View, Jackson took Isabel into his confidence. What was he to do to fund the solicitor?

"Somehow, I think I will have to find a job. Even if it is only until this legal business is through with. I frankly do not believe there are positions suitable for someone like myself in these parts. Possibly in London with the diplomatic service or such but not up here. I will have to return to the City."

"No. I will not hear of it. You have to be here. You cannot take on the Baldwins and the Halls from hundreds of miles away. Only by being an imminent threat to them can you ensure they are put under maximum pressure. What happens if your solicitor needs to see you urgently? No. You will not return to London."

"But if I cannot pay the solicitor I will be back where I was without one"

"You should consider asking your brother?"

"I cannot do that Isabel. I am not averse to asking him for funds, after all, I have done so on several occasions. When I left him to come here I pretended to him that all in my marital garden was rosy. To ask him for funds to now fight Mrs Jackson would simply be too embarrassing."

Isabel looked into her brother's eyes.

"Haughton, I understand. Just leave Raynsford to me. I will explain everything to him. I am certain he will be on our side."

****

Mr Howson swung into action almost immediately. The following day Notices were issued in identical terms. One was addressed to Hartley Baldwin at Prospect House and the other to Miss Esther Hall at Shawbridge. These notices read:

"We do hereby give you notice not to receive, harbour or detain Emily Emma Maude, wife of Edmund Haughton Jackson or permit or suffer her to continue in any house occupied or belonging to you, in any other way to procure her to be absent from her husband, the said Edmund Haughton Jackson, whereby he may lose or be deprived of her comfort and society."

The covering letter sent with these notices included the following:

"................we will thank you to acknowledge receipt of these notices on one of the duplicatenotices in the usual way..................
.... we trust our client may have no occasion to proceed against you in relation to the matter in question, but should the necessity arise, you will please regard the notice now given as the final letter **before action**."

Hartley Baldwin was not surprised to receive Jackson's Notice. He assessed it as just another attempt to put pressure on his family. The expression "before action" was more than likely bluff. Even were it not so, Mr Baldwin could see no jeopardy to his sister-in-law just sitting tight. This was again what he advised Emily to do.

"There is no point in becoming embroiled in a litany of lengthy legal correspondence. Trust me Emily, I will look after you. Between ourselves our approach must be "sue and be damned" but with these notices it is best not to respond in any meaningful way."

Emily did not welcome all this legal aggravation. Why could everyone not simply leave her alone? She had no choice. She now relied totally on her brother-in-law to guide her through all of this.

Messrs Hall, Baldwin & Weeks officially responded by confirming they acted for Emily who is their client and duly returned the duplicate notices duly endorsed on behalf of Mr Baldwin and Miss Esther Hall. The contents of the notices were neither accepted nor challenged by the letter from the Clitheroe firm.

A number of weeks then passed uneventfully.

In October Jackson once more tried the direct approach to his wife by way of letter. Presumably this was not sanctioned by Mr Howson. Again, Emily elected not to respond. This led to a further letter being issued by the solicitors in Blackburn on this occasion to Mrs Jackson in the following terms:

"32 Clayton Street
Blackburn

8th October 1888

Dear Madam

Mr Jackson has shown us the correspondence which recently passed between you and our client and it is with deep regret that, in spite of all anxieties and entreaties expressed in his letters for you to come and live with him, you declined to have any communication with him.

Your refusal leaves him no alternative but to commence an action against you for the restitution of his conjugal rights. Our client is naturally reluctant both for his sake and for yours to have recourse to legal proceedings unless you drive him to do so.

We are therefore instructed by him to make a last appeal to you to reconsider your position, and, after doing so, to inform us whether you will or will not withdraw your refusal to cohabit with him.

And we are, Madam
Yours respectfully
Ainsworth, Sanderson & Howson"

The official reply from Hartley Baldwin was to the effect that any proceedings would be defended to the utmost.

Then, one day in December 1888 whilst Emily was out walking in a field, a stranger approached her. He was unexceptional in either looks or dress. He was, she reckoned, about 40 years old.

"Mrs Emily Emma Maude Jackson?"

"Yes." responded Emily.

"I am instructed to deliver this to you in person."

With that the man thrust into Emily's hands a notice from Jackson's solicitor stating that unless she received her husband to live at either Shawbridge or at no 2 Rover Street ,Blackburn and reply to the notice within 14 days then Mr Jackson was going to bring proceedings in the Court for restitution of his conjugal rights.

****

To Law - Pt 2

Shortly before this ultimatum there had been a further brief exchange between Emily and her estranged husband. Once again, with neither the knowledge nor consent of his solicitor, Jackson had penned a very long diatribe to his wife. The tone of this letter dated 12th November 1888 betrayed Jackson's invincible belief in the justice of his cause but also confidence in his personal powers of persuasion in setting out what was best for his wife.

In this letter he stressed a desire on his part for legal process not to grind on and even described the whole prospect as repugnant to him. Haughton wanted Emily to believe he loved her too much to drag her through the Court. His strong desire was to revert to how matters had been before the awful letter she had sent him, to the days of her beautiful and loving writings.

Jackson repeated his incredulity at how and why she had turned so much against him. He even recapped upon his glowing prospects in New Zealand and that he had, at her request, given these up.

"I have done everything you wished. What more could....can I do? What more can I say? I can only ask you to write to me. Ask me anything you like. I shall be only too happy to explain anything.

With love

Your affectionate husband

E Haughton Jackson"

Emily chose to respond four days later. From the icy tone of her reply she had, without doubt, conferred with Hartley Baldwin before composing it.

"Shawbridge
Clitheroe

17th November 1888

Sir,

In reply to your letter of 12th instant I can only say that I have not changed in the determination expressed in my previous letters, and wish you not to write to me, as I decline entering further correspondence.

I am

Yours truly

Emily Jackson"

****

Whilst Jackson had been continuing to use his wiles to woo back Emily on the basis of his proclaimed feelings and, having again rejected in his letters his wife's accusation of having married only for her fortune, the next step adopted by his own solicitor hinted that there was a material motive behind the legal manoeuverings.

There was possibly at this stage a lack of clear communication between Jackson and his legal adviser. For most likely he was acting independently of Howson by writing in the manner that he was and the solicitors, for their part, believed it necessary to address certain matters as being in Jackson's best interests without obtaining his blessing for each and every step they took.

This situation was highlighted by a letter received by Hall, Baldwin & Weeks on 20th December 1888. The letter was addressed to Mr Weeks as he was Trustee under the Post Nuptial Marriage Settlement prepared by Mr Baldwin on Emily's instructions. Jackson's solicitor requested a copy of the Deed of Marriage Settlement and though "dressed up" in legal parlance the demand amounted to "We need to see what the lady has got for, if we cannot get her back, we might as well go for the cash."

The toeing and froing over this request was not atypical of solicitors and "their ways". Firstly, Mr Baldwin responded saying that Mr Weeks was in the south of England until after New Year. Ainsworth, Sanderson & Howson sent a reminder on the express presumption that Mr Weeks had returned to the office and that they were keen to obtain sight of the Marriage Settlement.

Mr Baldwin then alluded to a "snag" when claiming that Mrs Jackson refused to permit the disclosure of the Deed.

The Blackburn solicitors then sent a threatening letter stating, quite correctly, that Mrs Jackson's permission or lack of it was irrelevant, underlining the legal duties upon Hall, Baldwin & Weeks and making it clear that if the deed was not to be forthcoming then they would "know how to act."

Mr Baldwin had no more delaying tactics available to him and duly but reluctantly released a copy of the Deed. The receipt for this discloses that Ainsworth, Sanderson & Howson paid the sum of £2.12.1 for the copy.

By this time Jackson had become resigned to the pursuit of Court action. He could not just walk away from the situation as such a course would be too shameful for him to stomach. Mrs Jackson's inexplicable obduracy compelled him to action. His case had now been passed to Mr Sanderson, the more experienced of the Court Practitioners within the Firm. Jackson gave the green light to initiate the Court action.

Even now Jackson was irrepressible. It is hard to totally understand the workings of his mind. For, after the constant rejection and the negativity and coldness he had endured for all of these months, did this man really conceive he had any power left to prevail upon his wife? Was he deluded or desperate? Was it part of his general amusement? For, but 9 days prior to the Court Hearing, Jackson again put pen to paper in yet another note addressed to the younger occupant of Shawbridge. Jackson was actually unaware as to whether Emily remained at Prospect House or was reinstalled with her sister. He did think it prudent, if it were at all possible, to bypass the gaze of Hartley Baldwin so far as any correspondence was concerned.

In this letter dated 21st January 1889 Jackson tried to respond to any of the objections he perceived that his wife might harbour. The upshot of this latest misguided effort by the "wronged husband" was, on any view, a very pathetic note.

"I came to Blackburn from school and have been known to hundreds of people here ever since. As to my father and mother, no gentleman and lady could be in a higher position than they were. Dear Emily, why will you not let me explain anything? Surely you loved me when you married me? What happiness can there be for us if things are to go on in this way? I have been very poorly lately, but hope to go out this afternoon.

For god's sake, my dear Emily, make things right and let the rest of our time be happy.

Your ever loving husband

E. Haughton Jackson."

Needless to say, given Emily's ultimate caution against any further communication, no acknowledgement of this impassioned plea by Jackson was ever penned.

****

On Tuesday 30th January 1889 before the President, the Right Honourable Sir James Hannan, the Petition on behalf of Jackson was heard at The High Court of Justice. Mr Searle was learned Counsel for the Petitioner briefed by Mr Sanderson whilst Emily's Counsel was Mr Middleton briefed by Hartley Baldwin.

If anyone was expecting drama at this Hearing they would have been greatly disappointed. Applications of this nature had not been infrequent before the Court over the years. There was rarely, if ever, any serious argument in proceedings of this type. Both parties and their legal advisers had no doubt other than that Jackson would succeed with his Application.

Behind the glory of his High Court wig and gown, Sir James Hannan gave the distinct impression of being bored by the proceedings. As for the proceedings they failed to instill any excitement. The only witness to give evidence to the Court was Jackson himself and despite his natural flamboyance and gift for eloquence, he chose or was under strict instruction to give the briefest of answers to the questions put by his Counsel. His responses were both monosyllabic and delivered in a monotone.

Searle: "She persists in her refusal?

Jackson "Yes"

Searle: "And then you presented your Petition?"

Jackson: "Yes."

When the examination of Jackson was over, Mr Middleton wisely said he did not propose to ask any questions for, indeed there were none relevant which he could put to the Petitioner.

There was though a further question put to Jackson by his Counsel:

Searle: "I may ask you this. She has some property of her own, has she not?"

Jackson: “Property of her own? Yes"

The Judge: "I surmised that. Well, I pronounce a Decree for Restitution of Conjugal Rights"

Searle:"We have given notice of our intention to seek costs. Accordingly, I ask for same."

The Judge: "Very well."

Nobody was perturbed or surprised by this result. Everyone though, except Jackson, knew full well that Emily would not comply with the Decree. After the Judge had left the bench, Jackson excitedly engaged with Mr Sanderson.

"Mr Sanderson. What happens now? When does she come back to me?"

"Mr Jackson, I'd be very surprised if she returns to you."

"But what happens?"

"We will get the physical Decree from the Court and then order that she complies with it"

"And then what happens if she does not comply?"

"Well, it is like this, there is nothing then that we can do."

"But, but how can that be?"

"Mr Jackson, it was formerly the case that where anyone refused to obey an order for Restoration of Conjugal Rights that he or she would be in Contempt of Court and would then be liable for arrest and detention. However, Parliament passed an Act in 1884 which did away with this sanction. I'm afraid you cannot legally force Mrs Jackson to return to you and her lawyers will be well aware of this."

Jackson looked dumbfounded and a little crestfallen.

"But what exactly was the point of going through with this if the order is unenforceable? Has this just been a big waste of time and money?"

Jackson's latent vein of frustration and anger was clearly forming and was close to being aimed at Mr Sanderson.

"There were two points to these proceedings. First, there was always the possibility, however remote, that Mrs Jackson would be prepared to at least discuss reconciliation or terms therefor if confronted with this legal action. In truth however the real purpose was to lay the basis for future proceedings. The Judge acknowledged this when Mr Searle enquired of Mrs Jackson's property. You see that by a failure to resume conjugal rights with you, Mrs Jackson provides you with sufficient evidence for separation, and financial claims against her. That, Mr Jackson was what this has all been about."

The colour temporarily left Jackson's face as he absorbed what he had just been told.

"This has never been about the money. I have only ever wanted my wife back. I understand what you have just said but this will merely serve to fortify Emily's belief that I am only interested in her money. I wish I'd never taken her to Court now."

"Mr Jackson, I did explain all of this to you when we last met. You remember - about laying the groundwork, about asserting your legal rights. You clearly instructed the case to be presented."

"Yes. Yes. I know. I guess I was just so angry about the situation at the time I did not fully take in what you were telling me."

“At least, we got an order for them to pay costs" said Sanderson.

As he walked away from the Court, Jackson reflected that indeed the costs order was something. At least he could let Raynsford know he would not need to pay all of the costs.

****

One thing that was neither disclosed nor used in relation to the Court Hearing was a brief prepared by Emily's solicitors for Mr Middleton's interest and in case he would find anything contained within the brief of use in his dealing with the legal matters at hand. The brief contained a resume, accurate or otherwise, in relation to Jackson's character and background. It read as follows:

"The Petitioner, Edmund Haughton Jackson, is not mentally a strong man, nor is he much thought of by men. He has been an active man at picnics and lawn tennis parties, and is in the habit of making himself useful amongst ladies, girls and young people, fetching and carrying etc. A perusal of his letters will give Counsel an idea of the man. No doubt he has always been having an eye to someone that would maintain him."

The brief went on to state:

"We believe that Jackson's parents, who must have died some years ago, were in a respectable position socially, but of slender means. His father was a Captain in the Royal Navy. Jackson has no profession or occupation that we know of. He was, for a time, a book keeper in the Mills of his elder brother, Richard Raynsford Jackson, then a cotton manufacturer in Blackburn.

In 1878 there were alarming riots amongst the factory operatives in Blackburn consequent upon a proposition by the Masters to reduce their wages by ten per cent. In March 1878, some fifty thousand were out on strike in Blackburn alone. Raynsford Jackson took a prominent part on the side of the Masters and became very unpopular with the workmen. On 14th May 1878 a mob set fire to his house which was burnt to the ground and its contents destroyed. Soon after the riots the Master Manufacturers subscribed and presented him with a sum of money, believed to be £10,000.

He then gave up the business and went to Ashurst, West Hill, Sydenham and is a Director there of one or two Companies. He owns the house in which Haughton Jackson lives at 2 Rover Street, Blackburn.

It is suspected that Jackson and his sister have little or no secured income and are dependent wholly or substantially upon what their brother may give them. Raynsford, one can imagine, could be very anxious to get his brother "off his hands" as it were."

****

In the aftermath of the Hearing, Emily felt light hearted and freer than she had been for some time. Hartley Baldwin had taken some time with Emily to carefully explain that Jackson could not employ the law to coerce her against her will to live with him. In many ways the Decree her husband had obtained was a pointless order. Emily had not had to attend the Court. At last she started to believe she had escaped her husband's clutches and that his stalking of her would cease. There was nothing more that he could do. It was over. Emily could breathe again.

Away from Emily, her brother-in-law did though have concerns. He well knew the decree was a pathway for financial claims to be made against Mrs Jackson. He was so concerned he sought the opinion of Learned Counsel. The ultimate sanction would be for sequestration of Emily's resources to recover the monies under the Marriage Settlement. Such an order could attach not only to Emily's current assets but also any future legacies. As the youngest in a wealthy family the prospect of future legacies was, indeed, a real one. To Hartley's mind the optimum would be to ensure that this particular sister-in-law had no assets. He had already suggested to Emily that, from a legal viewpoint, it may be better to try and negotiate a settlement with Jackson's representatives. However, Emily would not hear of it. She was intractable on the subject and refused to pay Jackson a penny until ordered to by a Court.

Hartley did his level best to protect Emily. Nonetheless, he arranged for Esther to be made the sole tenant of Shawbridge, instead of this being jointly held with Emily. The furniture and contents were treated in a similar fashion in order that they were taken outwith the power of any Sequestrator to realise and convert to monies for Jackson's benefit.

Mr Baldwin tried to form a scheme whereby Emily's interests in the settlement were sold, albeit fictiously, and the proceeds secured and paid into an account in Esther's name or in the name of another third party. It was posed to Counsel:

"Could Jackson, motivated by vengeance, rob Emily of all her money and property, present and to come, make her pay costs, honour the Settlement and punish her for contempt of Court in refusing to obey the Decree of Restitution?"

Counsel was reassuring but only to a degree. No. A Sequestration could not attach to future income or property. However, it was quite possible that Jackson could employ Sequestration to bring pressure upon Mrs Jackson to obey the Restitution Order.

Mr Baldwin was warned against any illusory sales of assets. Any sale would only stand up if it were a" for value" consideration. All proceeds had to be accounted for. It was essential for all receipts and vouchers in relation to any sales to be carefully preserved.

In a further effort to frustrate Jackson's potential claims against her, Emily completed a Last Will and Testament wherein she directed that her Marriage Settlement be made void.

****

At this same time, Jackson had met again with Mr Sanderson. Was there nothing he could do to vindicate his position? He was duly advised regarding the possibility of Sequestration arising from the Marriage Settlement. The process and implications had to be carefully explained to Haughton. He was told effectively it could bring him, in the form of money, a measure of justice for his broken heart.

There was something hollow in all of this. Some financial compensation was not the same as securing the lifelong services and security of his wife. He longed for comfort and provision for himself. His object was never to ruin Emily financially or bestow on her an eternal grievance towards him. It was not meant to end up like this.

His conclusion was that, when all was said and done, the law could do nothing for him. It could not bring him his wife back. It could not provide for his long term financial security. It had indeed been a waste of his time.

His rights as a husband were, to his mind, inalienable. This was surely the legal position even if the law was impotent to do anything about it. As he viewed his situation, there seemed no other course open to him. He would have to take the law into his own hands.

This realisation, once more, gave Jackson purpose and motivation. All he had to do was to alight upon a plan, a foolproof strategy to get his wife back.

****

Unexpected Encounter

Two weeks before Jackson was issued with his Decree for the Restitution of Conjugal Rights there took place an event so strange in the context of all that had occurred and so difficult to explain from the aspect of either of the protagonists.

In spite of Jackson having had recourse to law and notwithstanding the appalling things said and done on both sides, Jackson never ceased from appealing for an interview with his wife to "put things straight". For her part Emily had steadfastly refused to entertain having anything to do with her husband let alone seeing him.

The extraordinary fact at this time was that, completely out of the blue, Emily granted her husband's wish.

There is no hint or suggestion that Emily ever considered retreating from her very entrenched position. She knew she would never change her mind about Jackson in that she was absolutely determined not to live with him. There was no antidote to the poison injected into the relationship. She appeared to be free from Jackson in all but name. Her motives then in agreeing to see her husband are devoid of any logical explanation. There is though no such query over Jackson meeting his wife. He simply never gave up hope.

The facts concerning this coming together of the warring parties were never later disputed by either Jackson or his wife.There is however a related shroud of mystery.

Both Jackson and his wife, in narrating how the meeting came about, made reference to "an intermediary", "a mutual friend" as having made the arrangements. Emily's apparent willingness to meet was conveyed to Jackson by this intermediary and Jackson confirmed that the place and timing of the meeting was organised by this self same mutual friend. Commentators have subsequently suggested the intermediary was Dixon Robinson. Possible but deemed not probable. Could the individual have been Hartley Baldwin? It is very hard to believe he would have done anything other that dissuade and more likely he would have prohibited any such meeting. As Esther Hall did not permit the name of Haughton Jackson to be spoken within her earshot she is also discounted as the "helpful friend" who facilitated the meeting.

Whoever was responsible, the one and only occasion the married couple met since Jackson had returned from New Zealand on 16th July 1888 was the day precisely one year later, namely, 16th July 1889.

Emily arrived at the Charing Cross Hotel in London at precisely 9 45 am. Jackson, despite having sought this meeting for so long had been staying again at Sydenham. He refused to travel north on account of his allegedly poor health at the time. Emily travelled to London the previous day and stayed overnight at Wood's Hotel, Furnal's Inn, being where her family tended to stay when in the capital. She would not have travelled to London by herself but was indeed alone when she walked into the Charing Cross Hotel.

She was shown to the room which had been booked for the meeting.

Once alone in the room, Emily waited for Mr Jackson. With all the recriminations and counter accusations what could have possessed her to meet in this grim and impersonal room? It can only be imagined how she must have felt waiting for the door of the room to open. For her to be confined with a man who, to her mind had shown himself, by her standards, to be rude, violent, money seeking and with no true affection for her. The room was chilly. She should have been very nervous but Emily was not so. She was possessed with a steely determination to confront the demon that was Edmund Haughton Jackson and it was not long before Emily's intentions were revealed.

At ten o'clock, Jackson entered the room. There was no shaking of hands and no remark other than a mutual enquiry regarding the health of the other. Each of them took up position in one of the two chairs that were far apart from each other in the room.

Unusually for Emily she chose to try and take control of this meeting which she reckoned was preferable to allowing her husband to get started.

In a formal manner she opened the dialogue:

"I requested this interview to give you any explanation you may require and to prove to you that, contrary to what you have been saying, my people have been willing for me to see you and to show you that I am not under lock and key, as you and your friends have said. Now, understand, I have made up my own mind, uninfluenced by my friends, not to live with you, in consequence of your behaviour towards me."

Inside Jackson felt a little deflated. He had had a wild notion that this was to be a reconciliation meeting. Now clearly it was not. Even so he knew it was still an opportunity for him and he certainly did not want to say or do anything to jeopardise any residual prospects he might still have with Emily.

He rose from his chair and went over to his wife.

"What have I done" he asked gently "to be so unkindly treated by you?"

"You know as well as I do."

"Truly, I do not. I only wish you to live with me. Why do you treat me so?"

"I am not here to answer questions. I am here to tell you I will not live with you. All love and affection has gone. Your letter to me showed me your real character."

"Ah. But do you remember your letter to me?" asked Jackson.

"Yes. I do. And I was fully justified in writing it."

"Well, perhaps we both wrote in irritation and on impulse?" reasoned Jackson calmly.

"Was it impulse that brought you to Shawbridge when you forced your way in and insulted us all in a most vile way?"

Things were not going well. Jackson could see that. He decided to steer the conversation elsewhere.

"What is it you expect from me?" he enquired.

"Only that I may go about without fear of molestation and insult" Emily retorted quickly.

"I have never molested or insulted you" protested Jackson "My solicitor's letters were only the usual ones in such cases. You left me no option but to go to law."

"There are ways and means of doing it otherwise".

In view of Jackson's numerous approaches this comment by his wife was distinctly obscure.

"What exactly does that mean?"

"If you do not know I cannot tell you. But you should know that you cannot win a woman's love or forgiveness by such methods."

Jackson gave way to his inner desperation. He begged her to live with him. She rose from the chair and said she must go. Emily alluded to having other business in London.......only a pretext. Each time she got up Jackson prevailed on her to remain seated and continued with his protestations of love and appeals for her to be with him. Throughout the deluge of utterings from her husband Emily had remained impassive and never sought to interrupt Jackson. Suddenly though she spoke, her voice clear and measured in contrast to Jackson's begging and whining:

"Do you know why I no longer go to Church?"

Jackson was stopped in his tracks.

He then hazarded to suggest:

"I suppose it is because you are heartily ashamed of yourself."

Emily jumped to her feet.

"There you are. Do you think I could live with a man who could talk like that?"

Haughton reached out to take his wife's hand.

"Emily, dear, I am so sorry about the letter I wrote you, but what could you expect after what you wrote to me?"

"I'll tell you this" said Emily now staring with determination into Jackson's eyes "If you had one particle of respect for me, you would never have gone to law about us as you have done." She rose again to her feet and shook off his hand.

"Now" continued Emily "You can do as you like. I have never harmed a man, a woman or a child in my life. It is quite unpardonable of you to have gone to law."

"But, my dear" stated Jackson with an edge of sneer to his tone "you could settle it in a minute."

"You have not been to Clitheroe lately"

"No, I have not."

"I know every time you have been there and every house that you have entered and who advised you......not your solicitors. I know that."

Jackson looked taken aback by this, He said nothing.

Undaunted, Emily continued.

"Another thing, you deceived me saying that you and Dixon Robinson were taking out money to buy land when it turned out you had not even enough to live on from January until April or to pay for your fare home."

"As to the land, the New Zealand Government would have let us have it without money."

Emily was becoming progressively more irritated. She was fired up and any apprehension about dealing with Jackson was, in this moment, not evident at all.

"But you wanted me to provide not only for you but for Dixon Robinson and your sister. And another thing is your abominable behaviour and insults to Mr Baldwin and my sister Esther."

Haughton was duly provoked by this and his hitherto care in his responses was worn thin and beginning to crack and with no regard for its effect upon the conversation he responded:

"Well, I only called her what everybody called her, and are still calling her."

Emily had her voice raised by this time.

"You do not answer me about your insulting letter to me. You have never ever retracted it. I'm not going to run the risk of a cat and dog life with you. After what has happened I should be afraid to live with you. The fact is we are unsuited. I repeat we are unsuited and must live apart. We have made a great mistake."

In contrast to his wife's raised voice Jackson deliberately spoke in a quiet and a steely tone when he replied:

"I do not think so."

To make her point Emily raised her hand and pointed at her husband as she said in her most solemn voice:

"Whatever you may think, I consider that I have. Even when I spoke of my not going to Church, you insulted me. How dare you speak to me so.. I thought I knew you when I married you but I find I was so deceived in you."

"That is nonsense" shouted Jackson beginning to show his temper.

Emily glared at her husband.

"Do not raise your voice, please. Be quiet. We are in a strange house. I have not come here to wrangle with you. I simply came for this interview you said you had so long wished for, and to tell you that I refuse to live with you."

"But.....but I want you, not your money."

"It does not look like that." replied Emily. "If you have no money, why do you not get a job? Let me tell you something. I had prepared for housekeeping on your return to England and obtained lodging for us in Southport. Mr Baldwin had placed at our disposal a house opposite his house. No. If I had lived with you and you had insulted me and treated me as you have done already, I should have left you, and the scandal would have been worse than it is now. Now, I'm going. There is no more to say. But before I leave, I will shake hands with you and bid you farewell."

There was no protest left in Jackson. Without any further word he took her hand and felt the bitter sadness as her finger ends slipped from his grasp and Emily swept out of the room.The bitterness was compounded when he chose to look out of the room window only to observe Emily being greeted outside by Hartley Baldwin and his wife.

****

To any observer the Charing Cross interview represented the final closure of the curtains. The curtain calls had been played out. The characters on stage had all left to go home. The performance of the play was well and truly over. But, not so.

Despite his feelings (well founded on this occasion) as he stood alone in the Charing Cross room that the candle had indeed gone out and all hopes of a life with Emily were irretrievably interred, Jackson, as he so often demonstrated rallied again to his personal crusade within a matter of days.

For a week after the meeting Jackson, penned a note to her requesting another interview. The request was sharply rejected. Jackson repeated his request several times more. No further letters were received from Clitheroe.

It is, as said, difficult to understand the point of the Charing Cross meeting and why Emily's family would have consented to it. The only rationale can be that Mrs Jackson wanted to lay down a ghost. Having hidden from Jackson when he had barged into Shawbridge, it was perhaps liberation for Emily to discover she could face up to him and therefore not fear encountering him by accident at some future date. It is evident that Emily had thought out well in advance of the meeting precisely how she wanted to handle the discourse and what she wanted to say. It was not really, as may have been represented, a case of giving Jackson an opportunity to explain himself. The sole calculation was to convince her husband by seeing her that she meant exactly what she had said in her letters and that she was her own mistress in such decisions. For as long as Haughton could harbour imaginings that she was constrained by the dictates and wishes of her family then he may remain so deluded. Hard as it must have been and hard as it indeed was for Emily to go to and endure the time at the Charing Cross Hotel this purpose, if achieved, would be such reward for the ordeal.

****

Calm Waters

A short time after the Decree for Restitution of Conjugal Rights had been granted, life for Emily quickly settled down. The letters from Jackson had ceased and there was no word of him coming to Clitheroe.

Every so often Emily's stomach would churn if her mind drifted to her "Jackson" experience. He did though rarely feature in her thoughts. Esther had banned his name from being uttered in Shawbridge. Oddly there had been no mention of the Costs Order granted against her in the High Court.

With the passage of each day Emily's traumas became firmly part of history.

Whatever sections of Clitheroe Society knew or thought of her "marriage" no one Mrs Jackson encountered or passed in the street gave her odd looks or treated her any differently now that they had done prior to the marriage. The gossips must have moved on and found another "victim" for their tittle tattle.

All things considered Emily felt that matters had worked out rather well and certainly much better than she would, not that very long ago, have envisaged.

Emily's life was simple, quiet and to her liking. She'd spend time at Shawbridge reading or playing the piano. She would go long walks if the weather was clement. Locally she was normally accompanied by Esther. Emily would always insist upon going to the local antique and curio shops such was her taste in fine fashioned items. Some occasions saw her leave Clitheroe for the day. On these sojourns it was normal for Betsy to go with her. The sisters viewed it as prudent to avoid going near Blackburn so these shopping trips were normally to Manchester. Emily would seek out her favourite clothes shops. Her taste in hand made garments was noticed by all within her circle.

Emily was far less active in the social events that were organised. She did not become a hermit as such but chose carefully to go to only an event organised by her family or by one of her very few close friends. She was still very much of an age and attraction to lure a man but conscious of how she got herself entrapped with Jackson, it was very much a case of "once bitten, twice shy". Anyway, she did not crave more romance. She was not averse to male company and conversation but she had no need for such. Emily had become very content within herself. She still reminisced very much about John. Thinking back to these times no longer made Emily upset. Such thoughts just made her feel warm.

Another reason for Emily's retiral from the round of social outings was their connection to Clitheroe Castle and its occupants. She did not trust Dixon Robinson or, for that matter, Colonel Robinson. Either could easily, for whatever benefit they saw in so doing, report about her to Mr Jackson. In particular her preference was not to socialise at all with Dixon Robinson.

By the end of 1890, a year had gone by and Emily felt content and secure.

****

After the Charing Cross meeting and his abortive attempts to further correspond, Haughton Jackson spent quite some time "licking his wounds." He expected and received comfort from his sister who listened fairly often to her brother's narration of heartbreak and upset.

Jackson seemed to oscillate between Blackburn and Sydenham. It is possible his sister needed a rest from her brother and subtly persuaded him to go to London. Probably the need for funds or a need for a change of routine from that at West View took Jackson to the big city.

It was different for Jackson at Sydenham. He did not dare wear his heart on his sleeve for Raynsford would not entertain such behaviour. Jackson was freer in London. At Blackburn, Isabel would be "clucking" a lot of the time. She would ask him where he was going, when he would return and would he do this or that for her? It could get rather oppressive and yet he was sufficiently astute to do or say nothing to upset this particular woman!

At Sydenham he could come and go as he liked without being asked to explain himself.

Jackson tried to fall into his old ways. He would go out in an afternoon and meander over his old stamping grounds. He was pleased that his powers of charm had not been dimmed by the trauma of his disastrous marriage. With any lady he favourably encountered, Jackson would not, of course, confide his marital status. It was not though long before Jackson became bored with all these "easy" conquests. There was so much lacking in affairs restricted to false charm and lust.

He felt as if Emily Jackson had cast a spell over him and that he was morally tied to her. He sensed that for as long as he felt so bound, he could not contemplate settling down with anyone else. This strange "sense" he described was quite possibly connected to the fact that Haughton Jackson was no more able now than he had been when he met Emily Hall to keep and support a wife.

That vexed subject happened to briefly enter his consciousness. A job. What about a job? The dire routine of work was repulsive to him. His thoughts once more meandered to the haven that was New Zealand. How he wished now that he had never returned to this country. Could he go there and start again? No, he could not. Raynsford would not sponsor him for such a further foray.

Damn it. It was all Emily's fault as she had caused him this grief. It was her command to return that had ruined his New Zealand adventure. It was Emily Hall who had caused him financial embarrassment and, of course, had destroyed his dream.

The latent hostility within Jackson now returned treblefold.

Mrs Jackson, he pictured, would be sitting snugly and smugly in Clitheroe surrounded by her "know it all" relatives. That is so unfair and unjust. Forget this London life. He had been a man of action and he could be a man of action again.

Damn the Baldwins. Damn the Halls. Jackson was again ready for battle.

****

Once more Jackson took up full time residence at West View, 2 Rover Street, Blackburn.

Isabel was delighted to have her brother back especially as he was again his confident and charming self. She looked at him with pride and approval when he declared his new found resolve to get his wife back. From Isabel's standpoint, Emily had dishonoured and disrespected the Jackson family and so deserved everything that she got.

Jackson made a phone call to Clitheroe Castle and the very next day Dixon Robinson arrived at the Blackburn house. Susan provided tea, sandwiches and cakes and then closed the study door. There was to be no interruption. Jackson entitled the gathering a Council of War, his Council of War.

The three of them agreed from the outset that their discussions were top secret and no hint of whatever was discussed or planned should reach anyone outwith their triangle. At this initial point two pairs of eyes stared at Dixon Robinson in acknowledgment that he was, by his track record, the weakest link. The stares only withdrew from his face once he had signified his concurrence with the principle of confidentiality.

Taking charge, Jackson spoke.

"As you know already Isabel, I have, after all this time, resolved to secure my wife to live with me by whatever means that are available. However, I have already waited an age so there is no need for us to rush at anything. Any plan must be detailed and safe."

"What about your solicitor?" queried Dixon,

"No, my friend, there is no legal process that can restore Mrs Jackson to me. Whatever we do, we do ourselves. I tell you one dream I have is to see the smirk wiped off of Hartley Baldwin's face if I succeed in getting my wife back. That would give to me such joy."

Then Jackson joked:

"Why, for two pins I'd pick her up off the street and carry her away willy nilly! Can you picture it?"

Isabel looked alarmed. "You can't be serious. Surely that is against the law?"

Jackson then openly mused in front of his friends.

"Can you not just imagine it? I am the gallant knight on horseback, seizing his maiden, throwing her across his charger and making off to the thunder of clattering hooves? It is chivalry!! It is romance!!"

Isabel could not tell if her brother was serious or simply making fun.

"But Haughton such is, I do believe, against the law."

"No. I beg to differ." interjected Dixon Robinson. Master Robinson had secured a position in his family's law Firm as an Articled Clerk and although in this new found position he was, to say the least, green, it did not restrain him from offering a dogmatic and definite legal opinion.

"Such is not against the law. A man has the irrefutable right to possess his wife's person. It is Emily Jackson who is breaking the law. In my humble opinion, Mr Jackson you can act with impunity."

"You are sure of that, Dick?"

"Oh yes. No trouble on that score"

Jackson was not to be carried away with whims and notions. There was so much to be calculated.

"Dick, I'm afraid I am going to have to ask you to recommence your spying in Clitheroe. This time though it is totally different. You cannot speak to a living soul about any of this. You must be totally discreet at all times and it is essential I have as much detail as possible regarding Mrs Jackson's movements. If you like, keep a diary of where she goes and when. Again this cannot be made up by you asking anyone - most certainly NOT your friend in the Post Office. Everything you report to my War Council must be entirely derived from your own observations. Do you understand?"

"I think so. I am to see but not myself be seen. Something like that?"

"Yes, that sounds right. I do not want letters or phone calls. "

Jackson was, by now, paranoid that his intentions would be discovered and so he no longer trusted telephone operators or those employed by the Post office.

"We shall meet again here in two weeks' time."

When Jackson's War Council next convened the first to speak was Dixon Robinson.

"I've made one or two notes" he said pulling a notebook out of his bag.

Jackson curbed his angst. He wanted to demand where the notebook was kept and who might have been able to look at it. He was though sufficiently concerned about what Master Robinson was to say to overlook the issue of this carelessness as he saw it.

"Well" started Dixon. "Emily tends to be alone at Shawbridge for two hours every morning as her sister is always out tending to her birds at this time. She goes to the library on a Tuesday afternoon with Mrs Baldwin and also has a coffee date with Mrs Baldwin on a Thursday morning. I have seen her out walking - sometimes a country walk - but, so far, she has always been with a companion. I saw her out in a pony and trap with Mr Baldwin's son. The only other sighting that I made was on Sunday when she was going into church."

"Mmm, I see" said Jackson. "We cannot force an entry to Shawbridge and get her whilst she is on her own. That would certainly amount to a breach of the law."

"I suppose it would." the articled Clerk seemingly uncertain about the law relating to housebreaking.

"And, according to you, she is, at all other times, not alone. This does make things rather tricky. I do not want to involve anyone else and, in particular, anyone who would try to protect her. "

There was silence for a while.

Jackson continued.

"It is interesting that you saw Emily going to Church. Now I know it is quite a long time since my interview with Mrs Jackson but she led me to believe she did not attend Church anymore. I really cannot see Miss Esther going to Church so my guess is that my wife will walk to and from the Church by herself. This could well be when Emily is vulnerable. A Sunday? Nothing else is open and few people about. Yes, I can see a plan beginning to take shape."

"Haughton, I do not yet understand how you intend to carry her off. You are not serious about throwing her across your charger? "

"No, not exactly and I can hardly run with her over my back like a sack of coal either. I have to hope that she will come with me voluntarily. The chance to escape from her family and what must, by now, be a dull life maybe an invitation she cannot refuse?"

"But"said Dixon " what is the plan if she does refuse?"

"Mark, my words you two, that woman will certainly refuse. You are both mad if you think she is going to turn around and say "Oh. I am saved. I've been longing for this moment"." Isabel tried to mimic Emily's voice.

"I am hoping that if any physical persuasion is needed, then my friend here will assist me with her?"

"Of course, Mr Jackson you can rely upon me."

Ever the most practical of the triumvirate, Isabel decided to ask:

"So, you have your wife captive. Where exactly do you then intend to take her ? What are you then going to do with her?"

"Yes, of course." said Jackson "Would it be an imposition to take Mrs Jackson to this house?"

"I admit I anticipated you would say that. Despite my loathing of this lady, just like Mrs Jackson, I can also act. So do not worry. When she comes here, I will be the picture of hospitality towards her" •

"Once she is here, I have no doubt I can bring her round to my way of thinking. Well, the facts are she will just have to come around. She will have no other choice. I will give her no other option"

Isabel had a propensity for sarcasm.

"And, I suppose the two of you will just put her on a train at the station and she will smile to the guard and pretend that nothing is wrong?"

Dixon proclaimed "We shall organise a carriage"

"Nice thought Dick. We do not have a carriage though. We do not know when all this will be able to happen. It could be weeks or months hence. We cannot afford to buy a carriage or hire one for such a length of time."

"Haughton, Raynsford, I think, may help us out in this."

"So, we are agreed the plan now is to aim for a Sunday - at the church?"

"Yes" said Jackson's co - conspirators at the same time.

"I have a worry though. I do not want Emily to be injured or hurt."

"What a man you are Haughton. You are so hard in so many things and yet so soft about others."

"Isabel, you misunderstand. I want to give myself the best chance. I want to give Emily the choice. The choice of, at last, being with me. The thing is that all of that will be truly spoilt if she is battered and bruised or breaks an arm or whatever."

"I have the very answer. My brother William is a doctor. I am sure he will help us."

"Can he be trusted?" speared Jackson.

"Oh I am sure that will be no problem. He does not know Emily. I will tell him that she is desperate to be with her husband but needs to escape the vile clutches of her overbearing family, that you are very concerned about her health and well being and could William be in attendance? He is usually at the Castle on a Sunday in any event."

"If you are certain he can be trusted then it is a risk I am prepared to take. Now Dick, you will have to observe St Mary's Church over the next few weeks. I need to know if Emily does or does not attend regularly. I want to know if she goes to and from Church by herself and where all her family is during the service. I must leave nothing at all to chance. And Isabel, can you speak to our brother and organise the carriage and driver? One last thing, I want there to be a nurse who we can summon once we have possession of my wife. Over the first night of her stay I need her watched. I do not think she would try to do anything stupid but I have to have some insight into Emily's mental state when she gets here. Is there anything else?"

"Why do you not just take her to the asylum?" mused Isabel rather cruelly.

"Isabel. Even for you that is rather extreme."

****

It was the night of 7th March 1891. Emily rested in bed about to go to sleep. She had agreed to meet Betsy at the church in the morning. Of late she had rediscovered her interest in the church. She had looked out the attire she was to wear at the service. After the service she intended to go and visit the mother of a good friend. The mother was not at all well by all accounts. Later, as usual, being Sunday she would be going to Prospect House. Such were Emily's thoughts that night.

Not in her wildest dreams would she imagine what the next day held for her. Unaware of what was lying in wait for her Mrs Emily Jackson entered the last good sleep she would enjoy for a long long time.

Henry Hall

Emily & Haughton with the boys.

Hartley Baldwin Jun. Alexander Baikie Baldwin

Haughton Jackson

Clitheroe Castle

St Mary Magdalene Church
Clitheroe

Prospect House
Clitheroe

Esther's Turkey Cup.

PART THREE

To Action - Pt 1

The press continued to lavish space upon the siege, the back stories of those involved and continually sought to whet readers' appetites posing the question "What would happen next?" At this time no journalist ever appeared to contemplate what the lady's side in all of this was. Without exception the newspapers hailed the right of Jackson's position and more than one referred to him in terms as 'the loyal cavalier'.

The Lady's Pictorial which could have been expected to display a degree of emphathy for Emily's position was very reserved and commented on 14th March 1891:

"It is very doubtful whether the law can prevent a husband from compelling his wife to live under the same roof with him; and the upshot is this very incident which seems like a fragment of the 18th century imported to our day."

In response to the mass coverage of the abduction and siege there was generated in some measure letters to the newspapers from members of the public and any sample taken of these reflected almost unanimous support for Mr Jackson.

Some of this correspondence referred back to similar cases and how in these instances the wives had wisely capitulated and that the reconciled partners lived then together in perfect harmony. The authors of such letters implied it was through the husband's no-nonsense attitude and the wife's acceptance of her proper and secondary role in the household that such a state of happiness was established.

The Preston Herald journalist referred to "Woman will always delight in her bondage, given a lord of her liking" and with reference to the specific case suggested that this would be "in spite of the plethora of platitudes of those superior sexless sisters of hers".

The Blackburn Times of 14th March 1891 "In London and the provinces, the papers are full of it, and the besieged house of Mr

Jackson and his bride has been visited by thousands of people attracted by the romance of the situation."

From France a contemporary issue of Figaro declared "We are rather inclined to admire Mr Jackson. He had probably gone the best way to work to gain or regain his wife's affection."

In summary what was conveyed to the reading public was a picture of an ill used, neglected and deserted Jackson, his love proof against every rebuff, forcibly, maybe, but romantically takes his wife into his arms. The wife had stubbornly refused to come to him of her own free will and, therefore, by her refusal, had outraged every good husband up and down the land. "Romance, romance!!" cried the newspapers. "Good man, good man!!" replied the readers.

****

At West View, Jackson was very much in his element and lauding it over his captive wife. Several newspaper managers had jumped at the invitation Jackson had extended whereby he asked them to deliver each morning a copy of their daily issue. Each held out the thought that by acceding to the invitation they would some day benefit from an exclusive interview with the "loyal cavalier". It was a conclusion they each jumped to without any encouragement from Jackson. Of course, there was no arrangement for the Jackson household to make any payment for these newspapers!

Each morning therefore there was a steady stream of paperboys arriving at and delivering "their" newspaper. Susan received them one by one and only when the correct number had arrived were they placed by her on the study table for Jackson to peruse at both his leisure and his pleasure.

In such a short space of time, Jackson had gone from resisting what he saw as an unwarranted intrusion by the press into his private life to a man who could not have enough of the attention. After all he was not responsible for the wild statements that appeared in print even if he wholeheartedly agreed with them. The more these reports boosted his ego, which they most certainly did, the more Jackson construed them as a weapon to bring to bear upon Emily. If he had not been able to persuade her of the error of her ways then surely his wife would be receptive to persuasion by the Court of Public Opinion? She'd perceive her stance could not succeed and then he would make progress with her.

Jackson would sit with Dixon Robinson each digesting the day's reports and the correspondence pages. Then Jackson, having identified those articles or letters which were most damning to Mrs Jackson, would proceed to highlight each of those with pen and ruler before the chosen pieces were handed to Susan to deliver to Emily's room.

****

Emily did try to keep her spirits up. She knew her family would surely arrange somehow, sometime for her release. Every so often though, doubts entered her mind. What if they had really given up on her? Was it a false hope she was clinging onto? If so, how could she endure this captivity?

Yes Jackson now permitted her to stroll about the house if she so wished. Emily had been downstairs a couple of times since she had been struck low. On these occasions she had only done so when she had learnt either from Susan or had seen from the window that her sister-in-law was out. For some reason Emily felt she could handle Jackson not because she was more acclimatised to her captivity, she just seemed to fear him less. There was latent anxiety through ignorance of what he might do to her but no longer did she tremble inside. Isabel was different. Isabel detested Emily. It was Isabel's house and therefore she held a degree of authority there. Emily could not expect pleasantness from her sister-in-law and so only went down when that lady was absent.

When she did go down, she spoke to no one. She nodded to any of the "guards" she saw and smiled towards Robert Birtwhistle - they had not managed to converse and so she remained unaware of his visit to Hartley Baldwin. She would hear Jackson speaking or laughing in one room or another although he did not show any interest in speaking to her. When she played the piano, he would have known that it was Emily yet chose not to come near her. For her, this was indeed a blessing.

Yesterday and this day also she had been delivered of her husband's chosen newspaper extracts. Of course, what she read made miserable reading for Emily who became progressively more worn down with pessimism. Even so, Emily was made of strong stuff for, far from all this "bad news" eroding Emily's spirit and bringing her round to believe in a better life with her husband, she was even more determined to adhere to her views. She adopted a saying that came into her mind

"The more you try to force me into a corner Mr Jackson the farther away from you I will be." Why Emily even composed a little tune for this and played the tune on the piano whilst singing these words to herself. No wonder the piano proved such a tonic for this lady.

****

Though hardly drawn to any of the newspapers since the abduction, Hartley Baldwin was aware of what they were putting into print. He refused to read any of the "rags" but got Hartley junior to summarise all that was being said. Hartley Baldwin knew it was pointless to challenge the mistruths and wicked allegations about Emily and her family. Yes, Henry Hall had had success all these years ago but this was different. The public seemed to thrive on the oxygen that was the press and the press was encouraged by the public to keep pumping the bellows.

No, Hartley had to explore the options available to him at law. Before the revelations from Birtwhistle he had contemplated a number of possible courses to pursue.

He had researched whether it was viable to have Jackson and the Robinsons charged with conspiracy to commit an illegal act. Success at this he concluded was slim and it presupposed the abduction was an illegal act. This latter point was the very essence of the debate in the press. If, Hartley argued to himself, the abduction was illegal but Emily was now reconciled with Jackson then the illegality would hardly be punished severely by the Court and the action would not succeed in having Emily returned to Shawbridge.

Hartley Baldwin had commissioned much research into Jackson's background. The report had identified insanity two generations back and Mr Baldwin contemplated building a case based on some insanity inherited by Jackson from his forebears. Without any qualified report on Jackson himself from a mental doctor, any such argument was indeed doomed to failure.

There only remained one potentially viable course and, as soon as he had heard Birtwhistle's words, Mr Baldwin knew right away this was what he had to pursue and pursue it with alacrity and vengeance he did.

****

The last throw of the dice for Hartley Baldwin was to present to the Court a writ of Habeas Corpus. The purpose of the Habeas Corpus Act which dated from the time of Charles II was "to prevent illegal and indefinite detention". Applications of this nature were predomininantly brought against the State when a prisoner was held in a prison or, back in the days, a dungeon either without proper legal authority or without the prospect of an early appearance before a Court of Law.

In this case Hartley was resolved to attempt to use the legal provisions to have the Court order Emily's release from West View. If the application was successful Emily would have to be brought before the Court. If the application was refused Jackson would have won for there would be nothing left for Hartley to do.

Hartley Baldwin had been scrupulous in retaining anything that could potentially have been of use in connection with Emily's litigation. He had recovered from Shawbridge all the letters which Jackson had ever penned to his wife. He had further come across a torn piece of paper upon which in Emily's handwriting there was a list.

The paper bore the date of 31st August 1888 not very long following Jackson's return from New Zealand.

The script read:

"Sent to E Haughton Jackson a wooden box at 8 10 pm, containing:

1 Indian Basket
1 Indian fancy basket without lid
1 gold bracelet with topaz stones
1 scent bottle
1 Small Ivory ornament
A little horn case
An old fashioned nail brush
1 lead pencil
5 books"

This recorded the return of lovers' presents. This represented a slap in the face, the return in anger of what had been given in tenderness and hope. The gold and topaz bracelet had belonged to Jackson's mother and was given to Emily by Jackson on their first betrothal at Wilpshire Station.

Hartley Baldwin well knew that if it could not be established that Emily was being held captive against her will, then any Application would be doomed to failure. Any document indicating a desire on the part of Mrs Jackson to live apart from her husband could prove to be useful. There was, of course, the note that had been delivered to Esther in Blackburn on the eve of the assault proceedings in Clitheroe. In addition to the letters and other adminicles of evidence, Mr Baldwin obtained Affidavits from witnesses who included Esther Hall, Betsy Baldwin, Doctor Musson and his partner Mr Weeks.

Hartley Baldwin was a clever man and generally his approach to litigation was one of calm detachment and calculation. In this matter his involvement was personal. The action concerned his dear sister-in-law Emily. It involved Mr E Haughton Jackson for whom he held little favour. Also there was the backdrop of his enmity with Mr Wagstaff of the Northern Daily Telegraph. For Mr Baldwin there was just so much riding on the Habeas Corpus Application that he could not but tense inside when he got word that the application had been set down for a hearing on Monday 16th March 1891, exactly nine days after Emily's abduction. All of this and Emily would not know what was happening.

Whilst his wife went regularly to the Church, Hartley was not a particularly religious individual. How would he convey to Emily his failure if the Court refused the Application? That Sunday night Hartley shut his eyes and prayed.

****

The application for Habeas Corpus was to be heard in the High Court in London before Mr Justice Cave and Mr Justice Jeune. Mr Baldwin had instructed Mr Lankester as the advocate to present the case before the Court. Mr Lankester had a reputation for being most eloquent and learned but also persistent. If Hartley Baldwin had any reservations it was that, however learned Mr Lankester maybe, his persistent disposition could engender hostility from this particular bench.

The gathered Affidavits were read to the Court by the Advocate. Esther's Affidavit narrated the whole history of the relationship between Emily and Jackson.It spoke of the refusal on the part of Jackson to allow any of the family to visit Emily. Doctor Musson deponed in his Affidavit as to Emily's tendency to poor health and the rejection he had had when he tried to see his patient at West View. Similarly, Mr Weeks complained that he had not been permitted to consult with his client since the abduction. Mrs Baldwin spoke generally in respect of her sister's often expressed and heartfelt resistance to cohabiting with her husband and the emotional effect upon Emily of Jackson's correspondence to her.

Having listened intently but impassively to this material upon which depended Emily's case, the dual between the judges and Mr Lankester began.

Justice Cave: "Have you an affidavit from the lady herself?"

Lankester: "I have an Affidavit from the lady's sister, Miss Hall, stating that the lady is so placed that she cannot possibly make an Affidavit."

Justice Cave: "She is simply in her husband's custody?"

Lankester: "But the husband has refused access to any of her relations"

Justice Cave: "Well, he has a right to do so. A husband has the right to say whom his wife shall see."

Lankester: "But not the right to detain his wife in such a position as may be dangerous to her health and injure her in various ways. I submit that a husband has no right forcibly to carry off his wife and keep her in prison."

Justice Cave: "She has a remedy before a Magistrate if he is ill using her."

Lankester:"There is no remedy for a wife who is forcibly detained unless your Lordships order that she is brought before you to state her case. I can produce Affidavits by other persons showing the extreme violence with which she is treated. She is constantly weeping and entreating her friends to take steps to release her. I submit that as a matter of right she is entitled to a habeas corpus against her husband, and your Lordships cannot refuse it and by statute law, you would be liable to a serious penalty if you did."

Hartley Baldwin shut his eyes. He could not believe his Advocate seemed to be threatening the judges. He waited for a loud censure from Justice Cave yet none was uttered. Instead Justice Jeune intervened:

"Supposing she was brought here and the Court makes an order releasing her, what is to prevent her husband from seizing her again?"

Lankester: "The Court will, in accordance with usual practice, give her protection until she returns to such place as she wishes, and if forcible removal were then repeated, it would amount to contempt of this Court by the husband."

Justice Cave: "Were the applicant's relations besieging the house?"

Lankester (after having a brief word with Hartley Baldwin): "They were not in any sense besieging it."

Justice Cave: "Were they preventing people going in or out?"

Lankester: "There is no suggestion they were besieging or picketing the house."

Justice Cave: "I know, of course, you would not make the suggestion, but I want to know if it is a fact. People would not take the trouble to get their food in through an upper window if there was no interruption from outside."

Lankester: "Mr Jackson was, it seems, afraid that if the door was opened someone would walk in and ask the reason for the lady's detention."

Justice Cave: "Oh, no. This does not sound right to me."

Lankester: "I don't know why you assume that. Half a dozen men are kept in the house to resist any attempt by force to set her free."

Justice Cave: "Precisely. Mr Jackson expected an attempt by force to set her free. She has all along persistently disobeyed the order of the other Court has she not?"

Lankester: "That does not justify anyone enforcing the order of the Court by illegal means."

Justice Cave: "The means are not illegal."

Lankester; "Not illegal - a removal with violence?"

Justice Cave: "No, not in the case of a wife."

Lankester: "It is news to me that such conduct should be tolerated by the Court."

Justice Cave (sharply):"We shall see about that. You will have to produce authority. There is no point in you saying to me, this is the law. The Court is not to be threatened in that way."

Hartley Baldwin shrank as the Judge bore down on Lankester. At this point Hartley feared the worst.

Lankester: "I hope I have not adopted a threatening tone towards the Court. He then quoted from Esther's Affidavit "Mrs Jackson was locked in her room, continually weeping."

Justice Cave; "If she would not go to her husband, he has the right to use violence if it is necessary."

Lankester: "Do you mean violence by actual striking?"

Justice Cave (backtracking somewhat): "I only mean what you mean."

Lankester: "Upon these Affidavits, I submit Mrs Jackson has been subjected to gross cruelty. The Court must grant a writ of habeas corpus against the husband."

Justice Cave: "I do not see any evidence of cruelty whatsoever. Can you quote any instance in which the Court has interfered by habeas corpus to assist a wife in refusing to obey its order? The Court had made a solemn decree that the husband is entitled to his wife's society and you are now asking us to help her to disobey that decree?"

Lankester: (with sudden passion) "But she is imprisoned."

Justice Cave: "Yes and her sister was so ill-advised as to go and live opposite with a view to molesting her. The lady herself had made no complaint and there is not the slightest evidence of cruelty. We cannot have the lady brought here unless we are satisfied that something illegal has been done."

Lankester: "But let her be heard."

Justice Cave: "Supposing she was brought here and said "I decline to live with my husband, we should have to say to her "You must live with him."

Hartley Baldwin and his allies listened to all this with increasing gloom. It seemed obvious that poor Emily's fate was about to be sealed. The Justices judgement appeared a mere formality. Even so it had to be delivered and Hartley Baldwin could hardly walk out of the Court. He was not a party litigant. He was a solicitor and from a professional standpoint he had to remain as Justice Cave pronounced the decision of the Court.

"I am of the opinion that there ought to be no ruling made. It is necessary before there is any ruling granted to show that something illegal has been done. Mr Lankester has utterly failed to do anything of the kind.

The general law of the country is that a husband has custody of his wife unless he abuses that right, with cruelty or misconduct with respect to her.

Her relatives set themselves to persuade her not to live with her husband. She refused to return to her husband and he took measures, which he was perfectly entitled to do, to obtain possession of her.

The conduct of the lady's sisters is as unwise as can possibly be conceived. They appear to have picketed the house in which she was living with her husband to such an extent that he thought it desirable to obtain persons to keep guard over the house and prevent her being removed by force. A more injudicious and unwarrantable proceeding on the part of the relatives there could not have been.

It was complained that the husband has kept her confined to the house. He was compelled to resort to that course by the very mistaken conduct of the lady's sisters who have persisted in besetting Mr Jackson's house. They never tried the experiment of leaving the husband and wife together to settle their differences and so live as husband and wife should. To bring her here would be to make her think this Court would do what it certainly would not do - take her out of her husband's custody."

With the concurrence of Justice Jeune, the Application for a Writ of Habeas Corpus was dismissed.

To Action – Pt 2

Within the Court Building they found a small ante room where they could exchange views in confidence. Hartley Baldwin's cheeks were flushed red. The tall thin Advocate addressed Mr Baldwin and Mr Weeks who was also present.

"I regret the outcome Mr Baldwin. At least we gave it our best shot."

"Yes, Mr Lankester I am indeed grateful for your efforts but I do not reckon the matter should rest here."

"The Court was crystal clear in their view. They have expressed what indeed the law dictates. I cannot recommend further proceedings. They would, frankly, in my view, be a waste of money."

"I appreciate your advice Sir." said Hartley "It is though, with respect, not a member of your family who is a prisoner." Hartley turned to Weeks and instructed him:

"As Emily's solicitor please advise the Clerk that we are appealing against Justice Cave's judgement."

He turned then to Lankester and looked up at him with steely eye:

"I do not put a price on this. I know that whatever the law says the Judge's comments are, in this day and age, morally repugnant. We may not succeed but even so professionally I am curious to find out the view of the Appeal judges"

****

That Monday the printing machines of the newspapers thundered into action. Justice Cave's decision had been pronounced just in time for the evening editions.

The Manchester Courier commented in its Tuesday edition:

"Old maids who are not already satisfied with their lot will find a great deal of consolation from the remarks made by Mr Justice Cave yesterday.The cynical unmarried woman can flatter herself that she at any rate is a free agent, not subject to the caprice of a man to whom the law allows a perfect right to say whom she shall see, and can obtain her in custody when he pleases" In a less whimsical manner the same writer also penned:

"Considering this matter seriously, however, it cannot be denied that the law as it stands is just and right and the interference of Mrs Jackson's family cannot on any grounds be justified."

The Lancashire Evening Post came out boldly in support of the view laid down by Justice Cave and so in favour of Jackson:

"The public ought certainly to be grateful to Mr Jackson for having carried off his wife in the way he did. It has helped out conversations all over the three kingdoms and it is now going to act as a valuable illustrative commentary on the full meaning of a bride's vow to love, honour and obey"

****

Jackson was unaware of anything that had happened on that day until the telephone at West View rang at 6 30 pm. This was Mr Ainsworth the senior partner of Ainsworth, Sanderson & Howson. For having initially consulted the junior partner regarding his affairs and having dealt then with the middle partner, Jackson was now addressed by the senior partner of the Firm.

"Mr Jackson, Ainsworth here. I'm afraid that Mr Sanderson is on holiday which is why I have to call you."

"And why exactly do you have to call me, Sir?"

"You will find out tomorrow if you consult the newspapers. Mrs Jackson's family brought an Application which was heard in the High Court today."

"What! Why was I not told? What sort of application? This cannot be right." Jackson did not like to be ambushed as he saw it. He was clearly displeased.

"Now, Mr Jackson, calm down. I cannot say we anticipated it but even if we had, we would not have received any notification. What Mrs Jackson was seeking was a Writ of Habeas Corpus."

"I beg your pardon Mr Ainsworth you will have to explain that." interrupted Jackson.

"Such an application represents that a party, in this case your wife, is being illegally detained or imprisoned and asks the Court to order the alleged detainee, against your wife, to be brought before the Court."

"This is ridiculous. My wife is not a prisoner. She has the freedom to move about the house and in fact she was playing the piano this very morning. Mrs Jackson is perfectly well and content here."

"That may well be so Mr Jackson."

"Do I get no say in the matter?"

"If you could just slow down Mr Jackson and listen to me, please. The Court dismissed Mrs Jackson's application."

"Well now is that not just fine and dandy? So, what you are telling me is that I have nothing to worry about?"

"Not exactly....or, should I say, not yet. We did not believe they would dare make such an Application so I cannot therefore discount the possibility they will appeal against the dismissal, any appeal would be to the Appeal Court in London."

"Would they really do that?"

"All I am trying to say is that we must be prepared for the worst."

"What do you mean?"

"By their very nature, applications such as this have to be swiftly adjudicated on by the Court. These are not proceedings which drag out for days and months or years. If there is an Appealthen the Appeal Court may very well dismiss the Appeal at the first Hearing. In fact I'd guess this is quite likely. If, however, the Court does not reject the Appeal it will order you to produce Mrs Jackson to the Court. There you will have the opportunity to present your argument. We must then prepare accordingly."

"How do we prepare?"

"I will have to brief Counsel. We will need Affidavits from anyone who can confirm that Mrs Jackson has the freedom you say she has and that she is in good health."

"I do not see any difficulty there. My sister will help and Dr William Robinson will no doubt provide medical evidence as he saw my wife very recently."

"Mr Jackson. If you refer to the self same Doctor who participated in your wife's abduction I cannot recommend that he certify your wife's health. I appreciate your friend must have subscribed to the Hypocratic Oath but he would nonetheless be perceived to have a bias in all of this. Contact my office tomorrow to make the necessary arrangements."

****

Jackson was annoyed with himself for since the Conjugal Rights matter had proved fruitless for him, he had assumed there was no point in any legal proceedings and indeed had been told as much by Mr Sanderson. Yet he had been so focused upon his exercise of power over Emily and her family, it had never occurred to him to enquire what steps, if any, they could take against him.

Well, at least, he had now been forewarned and he would ensure he was properly forearmed and not be caught off guard. He summoned right away another "War Council" meeting. He did so just in time for Dixon Robinson was due back to work the following day.

Jackson summarised his conversation with Ainsworth.

"Isabel, I need you to speak to someone at the solicitor's office to tell them what to put in your Affidavit"

"This all seems rather hasty when you say it all might not happen."

"I cannot take any risk. Now who is your doctor?"

"My doctor?"

"Yes. We need to get a doctor to check over my wife. Presumably to check she has no wounds, injuries nor shows any signs of physical suffering."

"Dr Wellesley"

"Then get hold of him first thing tomorrow. Who else can we try to use?"

"Susan. She tends to Mrs Jackson. She was present the night of your little party and heard Mrs Jackson singing."

"Yes, excellent. Anyone else?"

Isabel then spoke in a wicked tone "What about your wife herself?"

"No, sister, I hardly think I'd get a glowing reference from that person"

"Can I do anything?" asked Dixon

"Perhaps you can Dick. Upstairs in the attic you will find a wooden box with the letters "EHJ" on it. Within the box are most of my wife's letters to me. They were just thrown in any old how. Perhaps you could sort them out in date order. I will remove any of them that maybe considered damaging to my case and hand the remainder over to Mr Ainsworth."

"Let us just pray none of this proves necessary. I want things to settle down. Anyway who is paying for all this?" enquired Isabel.

"Yes. You are correct. I had better call our brother again."

****

On the morning of Tuesday 17th March 1891 there was the usual delivery of the newspapers to West View. It was a smiling Jackson who quoted to Dixon from the papers certain phrases from the reports. Dixon had contacted his office to declare he was unable to return to work on account of pressing business at the High Court!

Jackson was "cock a hoop". "Emily's sisters' actions unjustified" he laughed. "the Public should be grateful to Mr Jackson"............Of course, they should be!!"

Isabel put her head around the door.

"Dr Wellesley will visit at 11 30 this morning."

"Very good" responded her brother.

Jackson suddenly arose from the chair, took hold of a couple of newspapers and said to Dixon: "Time for a bit of fun, I think"

Jackson took himself off to Emily's room.

Emily knew it was not a good sign when her husband simply opened the door and waltzed in. She had already worked out that when Jackson wanted to appeal to her better nature or was seeking to exercise his charm, he would courteously knock on the door and await permission to enter. When, like now, he effectively barged in she knew to prepare herself for something unpleasant.

At first, she thought she was mistaken.

"Good morning, my dear. I hope you are well. I've arranged for a doctor, Dr Wellesley, to check you over this morning to ensure you are in good health. You know I would not want you to become an invalid"

"What about Dr Robinson, he saw me just the other day?"

"Ah, but he cannot always be in Blackburn. Dr Wellesley is Isabel's doctor. I think seeing as how you are staying in this house, it is prudent to engage a more local doctor."

"Mr Jackson, it is neither my desire nor intention to reside here any longer than necessary."

Jackson immediately reacted to this statement and thrust the newspaper ostentatiously in front of his wife's face.

"Look at this. Read this. You will see what your family has been up to. Even the Court has refused to release you from here. There is now nothing your family can do so resign yourself to being here with me. Your family cannot assist you now. I am complete master over you. If you can deal with this, why, you may even get to like it. It may have occurred to you and, if not, it should have that the colder and more resisting you are to me, the harder this life will be for you."

He then left the room with a flourish.

****

Emily refused to read any of the newspapers. Jackson would not have joked on a matter concerning her misery. Despite her feeling of abject despair, Emily was heartened to know that her sisters were still doing what they could to get her home. If there was nothing else that they could do for her then there was little that Emily could conceive to change her situation. Emily had, by this time, gone from having no feelings for her husband to hating him for what he was doing to her. The suggestion that if she was nicer to Jackson he would make her life easier was not a lure, for she had learned from her relationship with John that if she did not remain true to herself and her feelings, she would be perennially unhappy and more miserable than when subjected to all the privations Jackson imposed on her.

****

It was a very early breakfast at Prospect House that Tuesday. Hartley had endured a troubled night with little sleep. The appeal had been promoted by him despite his Advocate in the lower Court having counselled against such a step. Mr Baldwin was not unduly troubled by any tarnishing of his hitherto good professional reputation. Whilst he would prefer not to be the butt of inevitable sarcasm from the press hounds, he knew he was stolid enough to survive such scurrilous attacks upon him. No. The sleepless hours were caused by the endless circles of his mind. Had he done everything he could for this case? Was there some argument he had overlooked? Any small piece of crucial evidence he had not considered? For he could not forgive himself if, after an unsuccessful appeal, there was a realisation that had something been done which he had not done, Emily could be spared the cruel excesses of her husband.

This was the day of the appeal. It was, he knew, Emily's very very last chance. Hartley had to set off early to catch the London train. Betsy sat with him at the table. She did not speak as she knew her husband was preoccupied and she also appreciated the significance of this day for her and for her sisters.

During the night she had offered Hartley to accompany him to the Court. He had refused this offer. Better his wife stay with Esther. He would report to her as soon as he was able to. He would though take Hartley junior with him. His son was not as emotionally involved in the case and it would be an opportunity for the young solicitor to experience the Appeal Court.

Hartley wiped his mouth with his napkin and rose from the table.

"I must off now Betsy."

His wife put her hands upon his shoulders and said:

"Try not to get too uptight. We are all in this together and whatever happens we need you in one piece. Your office needs you. Do not worry, we all know that whatever happens that you will have done your very best."

Five minutes later Betsy looked out of the front window. Her son was waiting at the gate. Her husband, with his back towards her, walked down the path with his case in his right hand. As soon as Hartley Baldwin was out of her sight, she shed a tear.

****

The sun was out. Jackson was very much buoyed not only by all he had read but also by the way he had handled Emily. It was always the case that Jackson felt so much better in himself when he could exercise control. Not just control over his wife. In the past it would have been control over his soldiers in New Zealand. If he felt he was able, by cunning or charm, to use his brother or his sister for his betterment this also made this man feel good about himself. News of possible Court action the previous night had shaken him but, as was so often the case, it did not take Jackson long to revert to his self - confident and occasionally arrogant manner.

"What a lovely day, Dick." He said as they strolled together in the local park. "Do you realise that we were in New Zealand three years ago? In so many ways I wish we had stayed out there. I'm sure we would have made a good team. I sometimes imagine what we would have been doing out there now? The adventures we would have had."

"Well. Yes. It is a long time ago now."

Jackson had by now and for so long been obsessed with his own battles, his own affairs. Yes Dixon had always done his bidding. Yet, it was only now he saw that, with the years, Dixon had grown up. There was no longer the dewy eyed enthusiasm or the sound of unquestioning devotion in his voice. Jackson could see in this case that this friendship, if not on the wane, was certainly changing. You cannot instill immaturity once maturation was formed and he knew better not to pretend all was as it used to be.

"So you are going to be a bigshot solicitor?"

“I’m not sure about that. I must say from the point of view of my learning, I actually hope that Mrs Jackson does go to the Appeal Court." The Dixon Robinson of not so long ago would not have dared suggest such to Jackson.

"What is this?" said Jackson humorously "less than a fortnight ago you were part of a kidnapping gang and now you want to view the legal process in action. A swifter example of poacher turned gamekeeper I have never heard of"

Robinson made to protest but Jackson put up his hand. "Dick. It is no big issue. Just pulling your leg. I appreciate you have your own future to consider and that that does not involve dashing adventures at home or abroad."

"My father has said I have to think of settling down."

"Oh has he now? Does he mean marriage as well? You should take a leaf out of my book young man. Choose well and marry quick for then you will have them for as long as you want, not as long as they want!!" Jackson laughed some more. Then he continued:

"Now then, as a lawyer of the future, are you telling me that my wife may win any appeal?"

"Oh, I am not saying that. I have not researched all the authority in such matters. I'd just like to see the Appeal Court in action."

"Despite the caution from Ainsworth I've got to believe it will not occur and that Emily and I can live out our lives in peace."

****

After Esther had checked on her turkeys, she made her way round smartly to Prospect House to be with her sister. It was to be a long day.

It was only spring but the day was very like one from summer. The sisters decided to sit out in the garden. Though Hartley would barely have arrived in London by the time they were seated together, Charnock was left the strictest of instructions that they were to be interrupted just as soon as Mr Baldwin or his son telephoned the house.

After a while, Betsy turned to her sister and said softly;

"Esther. Have you thought of how life would be if Emily cannot come home?"

"The thought does not enter my head and I will tell you why. Truth will prevail, if not now then next month or next year. My bones tell me we'll get Emily back."

"I appreciate your faith Esther but what if…"

"There is no "What if?". There is always a way. I have not myself interfered but, if pushed, I will."

"I do not understand."

"Well, this Sydenham place that man goes to, that is a brother I understand?"

"I believe so."

"What I wonder does he make of all this? If that man can barge into my house then surely I can do the same at the Sydenham house? His family has been protected from all we have had to deal with."

"You wouldn't ,would you? You'd get into trouble."

"Maybe I would. I'd not tell your husband though. There's that sister of his. Stuck up piece, I am not afraid of her. I have watched her walking to and from that house with her nose in the air, as if she is Lady Muck. Well, there's nothing stopping me addressing her on the pavement is there?"

"Oh, Esther, I do not like the sound of any of this. I mean the press would paint you blacker than black-worse than they call poor Emily."

Esther looked at her elder sister with a rare glint in her eye, "Unlike my little sister and as Mr Jackson has so eloquently put it - I have no reputation to protect!"

They laughed and then changed the subject. They conversed about their early days as sisters, the inedible scones baked by Mrs Gilchrist at the recent bring and buy fayre, the difficulty in getting a good gardener these days and the general cost of servants. They did their best to pass the time but because of the import of the day time seemed to pass very slowly.

****

Emily had been seen by Dr Wellesley. She was courteous and polite which she might not have been had she been aware of the true reason for his visit. Apart from the doctor's visit it had been for Emily just another day.

She had seen from her window Jackson and Master Robinson go out. She could not believe her good fortune when she saw ten minutes later Isabel also leave the house. She wanted to and needed to play the piano once again.

Emily went downstairs, opened the piano lid and had just started to play a Chopin prelude when she was interrupted.

"Excuse me. I do not want to interrupt. You told me before how much music means to you."

She turned and greeted Robert with a smile.

"It is lovely to see you again."

"It has not been possible to speak to you before now. McAllister has always been here keeping an eye on us. He's not though working this day. You see I promised Mr Baldwin to tell you that I went to see him."

Emily was quite taken aback.

"You went to see my brother-in-law. But Robert why? Why did you do that?"

"It was a bit of a liberty Mrs Jackson. I did not mean any harm or to interfere. But when I read and heard all the rumours that you were reconciled with Mr Jackson and did not want to leave this place... "

"What? You heard that?"

"You cannot say I told you this but it was what Mr Jackson told the press. I knew it was not true. I knew it was wrong. All, I could think of was to tell your brother-in-law seeing as how he be a solicitor and all that. He told me to tell you he would do everything in his power to get you home again."

Emily did not know what to say. She recognised a loyalty within this house and it made her feel not so alone. She also remembered the soiree so she simply smiled warmly, said "Thank you" and then "Would you mind turning the pages for me?"

Of course, she did not need the pages turned but symbolically it emphasised the bond between them.

After the prelude, Emily produced a song by Mendelssohn. A song she had always loved. As soon as she had put the score on the ledge and was about to start, there was the noise of the front door handle being turned.

"I must go." Robert retired quickly from the room.

Emily heard the voices. The men had returned. She played the Mendelssohn confident that her husband would pay no attention and nor did he. Mr Robinson and Mr Jackson, so far as she could make out, went to the kitchen.

She did not want to chance her luck and as soon as she had played the last bar of the piece, Emily replaced the piano lid and retraced her steps upstairs.

She arrived back to her room not knowing that, at that precise moment, the Appeal Court was pronouncing its view in relation to the Habeas Corpus case involving Emily Emma Maud Jackson.

****

Down to London

The Shawbridge ladies after luncheon remained in the garden. With a very slight chill now in the air each wore a large shawl. They were averse to moving back into the house until the clouds covered the sun. Betsy sat reading an historical novel. Esther though indulged in a light snooze.

The back door of the house was left open so that they might hear should the telephone ring. Before though there was any phone call, Charnock appeared from the house. Always so calm and assured he appeared on this occasion a little pressed, a little agitated.

"Madam", he said gathering his breath "This has just arrived by express delivery. It is a telegram from London." Betsy dropped her book and reached out to take the telegram. For the very first time ever Mrs Baldwin overlooked the courtesy of thanking Charnock so anxious was she about the telegram. Charnock retired but only so far as the back door. He did not want to intrude and yet he was as anxious as anyone to know what had occurred at the Court.

The interruption by Charnock was a rude awakening from sleep for Esther but she wasted no time coming to her senses. As Betsy endeavoured to open the telegram Esther was impatient.

"Come on, Betsy. What does it say?"

She saw Betsy's eyes open widely and her mouth opened though no words came out.

"Well. Well" prompted Esther.

"I don't believe it. Emily's getting out. Well, the Court has asked to see her. Hartley will phone just as soon as he can."

She handed the telegram to Esther.

"Betsy, we have to tell Emily. Somehow we have to get a message to her."

"Surely Mr Jackson will have to tell her?"

"I do not trust that man to do anything that any normal person would do. No, I will detail my coachman to make haste to Rover Street. If anyone is able to get something to Emily it is Heston.

****

Meanwhile the telephone rang at West View. It seemed to ring for ages. Isabel never answered the telephone as few calls, if any, these days were for her and because she paid Susan to answer it. On this occasion Susan had been sent on an errand by the cook. It was only after the phone had rung for what seemed an eternity that Jackson, rather irritated, made his way to the instrument and lifted the receiver.

"Yes" he said sharply and without courtesy.

"This is Ainsworth, Sanderson & Howson. Is that Mr Jackson?"

"Who else would it be?" he snapped sarcastically but also with a degree of trepidation in his voice as he feared what he might be about to hear.

"I have Mr Ainsworth for you."

Jackson waited with increasing apprehension.

"Ainsworth here, I have just had word. The Court has ordered that Mrs Jackson be produced."

"How has this happened, Mr Ainsworth? You said the Appeal would fail."

"No, with respect Mr Jackson I said that the Appeal should, in my view, fail. Why do you think I advised that we make preparations? Courts can be unpredictable. At least now we have our say in the matter."

"Well. What happens now?" enquired Jackson still irritated.

"At some point today or tomorrow you will be served with an order requiring that you arrange for Mrs Jackson to present herself before the Court on Thursday."

"Mr Ainsworth, I am doing my level best, believe me, to remain calm but this is outrageous. It is as if the Court has already made up its mind. Surely they cannot ask for Mrs Jackson to be taken from this house

BEFORE they have heard our argument? This is very wrong. This is unfair. Can we not object?"

"Mr Jackson, I have to be serious with you, the Court is not playing games. We are talking about the highest Court in this land. Not just one eminent judge but three eminent judges. Neither you nor I are in a position to object and indeed, were we to attempt to do so such would, I am certain, colour adversely the judges' view of your good self and would hardly help our argument that your wife is not being detained by force and threat. You must ensure she arrives at the Court by the time stated on the Order which you will receive."

"But how do I ensure she does not escape before we reach the Court?"

"That is up to you. If she was so minded, got away and failed to attend the Court then, so long as the Court was satisfied that this was the truth and not a false story, obviously the whole reson d'etre for the Appeal would have evaporated and the case would be dismissed."

Jackson had been listening intently and had again calmed down.

"Then Emily would be back in Clitheroe and I would have to abduct her a second time. That is what you are telling me?"

"It is a fair supposition that Mrs Jackson would repare to Clitheroe, I grant you that. I emphatically make no comment on your notion of what you refer to as a second abduction. My advice is to get the woman to Court. Call me when you get the order. Good afternoon, Mr Jackson."

"Mr Ainsworth. I apologise if I have been abrupt. I find this all very stressful. As always I appreciate your help. "

Yet again Jackson got his "War Council" together. The door of the dining room was closed behind the conspirators and Susan advised to ensure the group was not interrupted.

Having summarised the conversation with Ainsworth, Jackson said to the others:

"The more I have thought about this the more I am convinced that the Court will come down in my favour. I mean Justice Cave left no room for doubt and even my solicitor said an Appeal was bound to fail. My guess is the Court will just want to check that Emily is alive and well and then tell her family that Mrs Jackson is my business and not theirs." Once more Jackson was rebounding from a shock and stress finding again confidence from what seemed his never ending store of such a quality.

The others looked at Jackson in silence not knowing what best to say. Even Dixon was reluctant to pass comment upon the views of the highest Court in England.

Jackson continued:

"We have to somehow convey Mrs Jackson safely and soundly to London. Given her physical resistance when we took her from Clitheroe, I am unhappy she might choose to run away. That would not be good and yet we cannot obviously put her in handcuffs."

Isabel volunteered "I do not see why not. The first Court declared, as I read in the newspaper, that your actions have been perfectly justified so, until any Court says differently, what difference does it make if Mrs Jackson is kept here or kept in handcuffs?"

"There must be something else we can do.? No. We do not require handcuffs. Put yourself in Emily's place. What is the most pleasing notion?"

The room went silent.

Jackson continued.

"I know my wife better than you may think. She will want, more than anything, to see her family. It is a safe bet that some or all of them will be at the Court. So long as Mrs Jackson has no cause to be frightened - for then she will act irrationally - she will sooner go to the Court than take flight by herself without money or access to money and try to reach Clitheroe on her own. If we pretend to be considerate then there will be no trouble. I tell you what Dixon can you see if your brother will come down tomorrow night? He has always had a calming effect on my wife and she maybe reassured by his presence."

"But what will I say?"

"Oh, I'm sure you can think of something. How about that Mrs Jackson is very tense about having to go to the Court on Thursday and out of concern for her well being we would rest easier if Dr Robinson was in attendance?"

"I wish I had thought of that." said a rather sulky Dixon.

****

Upstairs in her room, Emily stood looking out of her window. She thought how suddenly the tidal wave of people had ebbed, so few spectators. The vendor was not seen anymore. Perhaps not surprising given the sunshine these couple of days people would more likely now gather in the nearby park and follow normal pursuits. She was glad she was no longer the focus of attention from the Blackburn residents. In a strange way though the absence of the attention added to Emily's feeling of having been abandoned. Her family had done their very best, of that, she did not doubt for a second. However even her loving family cannot work miracles. The crowds had gone. She was very much alone in this house, in this room. She gazed over to where Esther used to be always at the window. Why even Esther appeared not to be there.

Whilst looking at the empty window of "Esther's flat" a movement caught her eye. A figure had just come into view from the lower part of Rover Street. She could see it was a man. He was waving. Emily's eyes darted this way and then that trying to see who the figure was communicating with. There was no one obviously about at this time. As the figure got nearer to West View, Emily took a step backwards. This could be another of these nosey journalists so she pulled the curtains in front of her in order not to be seen.

The man had stopped right outside the house. With a hand on his brow to keep out the sun's glare his eyes looked upwards. For a moment Emily stood stock still and double checked that she was not mistaken. How could it be? Why could it be that her sister's coachman was there? The man started to wave frantically. She knew he was trying to attract her attention.

As quickly as she could Emily managed to open her window slightly. She smiled broadly and waved back to Heston.

"Miss Hall" shouted Heston (he had never addressed Emily as Mrs Jackson) "I have a telegram here from Mr Hartley Baldwin. You have to go to London on Thursday to the Appeal Court."

At this point McAllister walked along the pavement on his way back to West View.

"You there." he said in a loud voice to Heston.

"If you have business at this house then you must speak to Mr Jackson. If you are present to annoy the other guests (looking up to Emily's window) be off with you."

Heston was never a shrinking violet and he would have given anything to give McAllister a piece of his mind and much more. As he had just heard Emily's window above close and had completed his commission from Esther, he made the wise decision to withdraw.

Heston's announcement to Emily had not been whispered. It had been shouted as if a proclamation to the whole street. Jackson and the others downstairs had clearly heard what had been said. The fury returned to Jackson's blood and despite his control of the previous half hour and his instruction that Emily had to be shown some form of consideration he flew up the stairs and confronted his wife.

Jackson bellowed insults about her family.

"Do not get your hopes up" and with the words spattering out as if they were rounds from a machine gun he continued:

"This will do you no good, all this legal fantasy. You will be back here from London before you know it. You are and always will be in my power. Once you are back, I will be taking your family to Court for compensation. By the time my brief is finished with them they will be ruined. All of the rotten lot will be finished. I will ensure the press knows everything about you... and I mean everything."

Jackson's temper was uncontrollable as he stormed out of the room.

Emily was reduced to tears. She was shaking. When shortly afterwards Susan came to ask if she wanted tea, she found Emily hardly able to speak such were the nervous palpitations she was enduring.

Dr Wellesley was summoned. He was very concerned regarding Emily's well being. He ordered that someone should be with Emily all night to keep an eye upon her. Emily told Dr Wellesley she wanted to see her solicitor but Jackson who was standing by harshly refused this request.

****

Hartley Baldwin was very tired by the time he got back that evening to Prospect House. He announced he was not hungry but would benefit from at least one of his favourite brandies.

As soon as he was settled and whether he had the energy to or not, the presence of Betsy and Esther in the room each desperately eager to learn what had occurred, Hartley proceeded to summarise the proceedings before the Appeal Court. The pressing question from the ladies was how come the Court had not, as Justices Cave & Jeune had done, thrown out the Application? Mr Baldwin proceeded to explain.

Hartley Baldwin had dispensed with Mr Lankester who he portrayed as having failed the day before and had arranged for Mr Finlay, Advocate, to address the Appeal Court. The appeal Judges were the Lord Chancellor (Lord Halsbury), the Master of the Rolls (Lord Esher) and Lord Justice Fry.

Unlike the previous day's proceedings there was a certain air of levity, if not humour, about the proceedings.

Mr Finlay referred in his argument to an historic case whereupon Lord Esher observed that the man in that case had got hold of his wife by a "stratagem". Of this case the Lord Chancellor remarked that this was authority for the proposition that a husband may beat his wife, but it must be with a stick not thicker than one inch." Hearty laughter emanated from the amused onlookers in the public benches.

There had continued to be what could be described as gentle debate with continued reverberations of constrained laughter as the Advocate and Judges exchanged quips and similes about "common people being addicted to ancient privileges".

The discussion then drifted towards the central issue of cruelty so casually dismissed by Justice Cave the day before. For that Judge had pronounced there was not a scrap of evidence to show any cruelty whatsoever. The Lord Chancellor begged to disagree with this, albeit the distinction he drew was not represented as overly significant.

"In this case, the circumstances under which the wife was seized and detained are not such as to negative undue violence and severity."

"No, my Lord, certainly not." said Mr Finlay in total agreement.

The ghost of dejection that had shadowed Emily's supporters for so long now was thereby laid.

The Lord Chancellor then spoke the words that were the sweetest music to Hartley Baldwin.

"The Court reserves the question of jurisdiction, but the writ will go and must be returnable on Thursday."

Hartley explained to his sisters this did not set their sister free. What it did do was force Jackson to bring her out of her prison - at least for a day or two.

"We must be there" spoke Esther on behalf of her sister but without consulting her.

Hartley said "Yes. I think that would be most appropriate. I will book us in to Wood's Hotel tomorrow night."

****

Once again Emily endured a sleepless night at West View. Still tormented by Jackson's earlier verbal assault, all she knew was she was supposed to go to Court on Thursday. What were the arrangements? She had not been told. No one had explained why she had to go to Court but, obviously, her brother-in-law thought it momentous enough to send Heston who had rejoiced rather than proclaim any dire warning which he would have done had this development been bad news. Yet what was it all about? Was she supposed to speak to the Court? How would she know what best to say? She did know that,whatever else, Thursday would be a serious day. It presented like a journey into the unknown for her, so naturally she fretted.

Her husband had once more installed a nurse. The nurse was not unpleasant but Emily had too much on her mind to indulge in much friendly conversation. Just as before Emily found it impossible to sleep properly with a stranger in the room.

****

First thing on the Wednesday morning Jackson came into Emily's room. The nurse withdrew.

He addressed Emily. It was brief and to the point without emotion, without pleasantry.

"You must pack immediately and get dressed. We leave for London in an hour's time."

The nurse was told to rejoin Mrs Jackson and, if needed, help her get ready.

Emily started to get some things together but then stopped suddenly. She turned to the nurse.

"I have no bonnet. Mr Jackson threw my bonnet on the fire when I got here. I cannot go out without a hat."

The kind nurse said Emily could wear hers. Emily cheered up at this small gesture of kindness towards her.

****

Downstairs the papers from the Court were on the table awaiting Jackson's attention. However, he looked beyond the official envelope clearly marked "High Court of Justice, Queens Bench Division- Appeal Court" to a telegram which was partly hidden by the Court papers. He pulled out the telegram and proceeded to digest the contents:

The telegram announced that it had been sent by Mr W.W.Kelly, manager, Grace Hawthorne Theodore Company of Nelson (a theatrical concern):

"Have just heard that your wife contemplates going on stage. If this is correct, I am prepared to offer her £50 per week for the remainder of the tour which lasts till July. Should she accept, I can offer you a post in a business capacity, with additional; salary to accompany her."

Mr Kelly's information was hardly correct. Going onto the professional stage was the last thing that Emily was likely to contemplate seeing that she currently occupied, most reluctantly, a central position on the stage of reality. Even had she the remotest notion of a stage career, she would never in a year of Sundays have selected Jackson as her touring companion. Still the entrepreneur that Mr Kelly was, he evidently thought his proposal was worth a try even if his timing left much to be desired.

The telegram did succeed in bringing a rare wry smile to Jackson's face. This was but a fleeting moment. Jackson was just putting the curious telegram back onto the table when he was approached by the nurse.

"Excuse me, Mr Jackson. I think that is your wife about ready. She did want to ask you if, given the situation, you might change your mind and allow her to write to her sister before we leave the house. I said I would find out."

Nine and a half times out of ten Jackson would have shot this request "down in flames". Whether it was the effect of Mr Kelly's communication or the knowledge that he would vet any letter anyway, he told the nurse he assented to this. The pathology of the man might also suggest it was the power that Jackson always craved so that even in an insignificant matter such as a letter giving permission was an exercise of such power.

****

Emily was joyous when told she could pen a letter. The note she wrote did not take her very long. The relief she felt came across in her words.

"My dearest home friends,

I am, at last, permitted to write to you. I have so wanted to do so ever since I came here, but have been most cruelly refused and have not even been allowed to see or to write to my legal adviser which I have felt terribly.

It is most unjust from beginning to end - I mean the whole affair. I pray God it is soon at an end and that I shall before too much longer be with you all again. It has been a terrible time for me, and I have only had one to look to and he has given me strength to bear it.

I suppose we are going to London today but I do not know anymore.

It has been a great comfort to me to learn and to know I was not forgotten by any of you. I have felt all along a complete prisoner, bolted and barred from the world and from everyone, yet being looked at from outside all of the time.

Under any circumstances I have made up my mind positively that I will not live with my husband. I wish things could be settled but it appears that I am the last person thought about in this matter though I am the one principal person.

I cannot say more, only hoping you are all well and that someday sooner or someday later that I may be amongst you again.

Your loving sister

Emily

PS How it is I am allowed to write? I do not know. Maybe it will be intercepted? I want to come home. Pray for me - earnestly."

How this letter was ever permitted by Jackson is not known. Perhaps, after all, he did not bother to read it or maybe he was so confident about the outcome of the Court case he reckoned it would be all the more painful for Emily and her family when he took her back with impunity to West View.

The occupants at West View had a very early breakfast after which the relevant persons set off by carriage for Blackburn Station. Within the carriage were Dixon Robinson, William Robinson, the nurse and Mr & Mrs Jackson. Isabel Jackson steadfastly refused to travel to London. She saw the Court as a circus. She would keep her own counsel and remain in Blackburn.

As the carriage pulled up at the Railway Station another party was in the course of leaving Clitheroe for the same destination - London. Hartley Baldwin and his wife travelled with Esther. Hartley junior had gone to London the day before.

One night for the opposing parties to wait and to wonder, each party seeking a different conclusion from the Court the next day, yet neither being anything other than uncertain that these Judges would favour their case .

****

Judgement Day

Emily had been installed on the eve of the Appeal Court Hearing at the house belonging to Raynsford Jackson in Harrington Gardens, Kensington. Despite the entreaties of her husband and indeed William Robinson, she had gone straight to her room. More than ever now Emily was determined to give no impression that this gathering was one happy family. Perhaps the lack of sleep the night before or a sense of being powerless to affect the next day's proceedings meant that Emily slept surprisingly well. Having secured his wife safely in London, Mr Jackson dispensed with the nurse who faced an immediate return journey back north.

Emily breakfasted alone. On the journey to the Court Mrs Jackson was at pains to remain physically as distant as she could from her husband.

The heads of both the press and the public did, without exception, turn and stare at Emily, the lady that all had heard about but none had until now seen. In a subsequent report in the Daily News Emily was described thus:

"Mrs Jackson is a lady with pale and refined features, and apparently about forty years old. She is slight and short in figure and has fair curling hair over her forehead. She was wearing a black bonnet with a black lace fall, a short sealskin jacket and a black silk dress. She also wore black gloves and mittens. Her demeanour was remarkably calm and self possessed. She never at any time displayed emotion of any description."

Emily entered the courtroom with her head held high as she had promised herself she would do. A Court usher, having had her confirm to him that she was indeed Mrs Jackson, led her to a seat situated between the spectators and the assembled barristers. As best he could Hartley Baldwin had found seats for his Betsy and Esther but these seats were not particularly prominent and to the side of the main body of people. Emily was so intent upon not being distracted she did not alter her gaze from looking ahead and so did not see her sisters or even know they were present. Betsy and Esther got their first real glimpse of Emily since the abduction and, upon seeing her enter the Court, they grabbed hold of each other's hands and Betsy, in particular, fought to control tears welling up in her eyes.

Emily could see Hartley Baldwin with the legal people in front of her. Their eyes met at which point Hartley nodded but made no attempt to communicate with her. Although his position was to argue for her release through his advocate, Emily Emma was not there as a client but rather as a party ordered by the Court to attend. Whether the Court actually wanted Emily to participate in anyway was entirely for the Court and it would be unprofessional of Mr Baldwin to prompt or be seen to prompt Mrs Jackson as to what she should say, should the Court make any enquiry of her.

The Court was packed with spectators and journalists. There were many more outside wanting to get in but could not. There was much pushing and shoving and the ushers certainly had their hands full.

No murder trial, however sensational, could have evoked more keenness to witness an unfolding drama. The lucky spectators gazed at the figures of Jackson and Emily as if they were persons of legend who had suddenly become real and formed of flesh. The fabulous of the newspapers were now tangible human beings. Could that man there described by the newspapers as tall, grizzled, sunburnt and in one case elderly have done all that to that gentle lady that was said he had done? The Court room contained many ladies of fashion who may have wondered what exactly had gone on in that house in Blackburn and now there were the two characters - the masterful husband, the recalcitrant wife.

The clock approached half past ten. There was a low hum of conversation, silenced for a moment when three chairs were brought in and put on the right hand side of the judge's seats. What could that mean? Extra judges? But no. The mystery was shortly solved by the entrance of three ladies, two of them wives of the Judges. They took their seats genteelly but importantly. Had this ever occurred before? It seems that judges' wives were not immune from the magnetic interest of the case.

At precisely 10.30 am the Court stood as the three Judges entered. The same persons sat as had adjudicated two days before namely, The Lord Chancellor, The Master of the Rolls and Lord Justice Fry. Hartley Baldwin, having brought the Appeal, was again represented by Mr Finlay, Advocate. The player who was new to this drama was Counsel for Mr Jackson, namely Mr Henn Collins.

Nothing of the majesty of the Court, the august surroundings, the stately ritual and the trappings of the legal profession perturbed Emily. The impression given was one of someone possessed of steely determination. There had been several guesses regarding Emily's age.

She was pretty and appeared much younger than her actual age of 46 years.

The public were disappointed at the outset of the argument for learned Counsel had to address the dry and legally uncolourful subject of jurisdiction and whether this Court had the authority to issue the Writ that Justice Cave had so emphatically refused. It was becoming all too tedious until the Lord Chancellor stepped in and stipulated that the power to do so was vest in his office and whether or not the Appeal Court had such jurisdiction was neither here nor there. Mr Henn Collins for Mr Jackson could have tried to take issue but, in deference to the Lord Chancellor, chose not to and moved on.

He then proceeded to recount, at some length, the story of the association between Jackson and Emily. From the viewpoint of the spectators it was a case of deja vu. Most had read of all this in the newspapers or become conversant with the tale from tuning into what was exchanged by gossips in public places. Judges become hardened to repetition and tended to listen to what they already knew themselves with varying degrees of attention. Suddenly though Mr Henn Collins was interrupted by the Lord Chancellor.

Lord Chancellor: "You do not allege any misconduct on the part of the lady?"

Henn Collins: "Certainly not, my lord."

The Advocate continued with the story from Jackson's point of view. How great kindness had been displayed to Emily during her stay at West View with not a single cruel, unkind or ungentlemanly word uttered by Mr Jackson. If only her mind had been left undisturbed and her relations refrained from inciting her feelings against her husband, her old love for him would revive. Jackson had done nothing to forfeit her love, his sole desire being to live with her in happiness. He referred the Court to Affidavits sworn by Jackson, Doctor Wellesley and others which had been submitted to the Court.

The Judges had, of course, had the Affidavits on behalf of Emily read to them on Tuesday. There was a clear gulf between the pictures portrayed in the two sets of sworn Statements.

Lord Chancellor: "Did Mr Jackson read the Affidavits of his wife's witnesses before making his own Affidavit?"

Lord Esher: (before there was a response) "Before his affidavit was made?"

Henn Collins: "No, my Lords for whilst the Affidavits from the other side were sent to Mr Jackson for comment, he chose to make no comment and indeed refused to even read them."

At this point the Judges might well have had an insight into part of Jackson's ways. For they could not be forgiven had they concluded this was a lazy or careless or feckless individual.

Dixon Robinson's Affidavit describing the abduction was then read.

Master of the Rolls: "How old is this person-the attorney's clerk?"

Henn Collins: "Twenty-One my Lord."

Henn Collins did not want to linger on any impression that this particular attorney's clerk was irresponsible and therefore possibly an unreliable witness. He then submitted that no action by Jackson went beyond a husband's right at Common Law.

Gradually there was a general sense that the ears of the spectators had pricked up and interest in the proceedings was now being stirred.

Lord Chancellor: "What are a husband's rights at Common Law, Mr Henn Collins?"

Henn Collins: "At Common Law, a husband had the right to capture his wife and keep her, not in imprisonment, but in confinement. He had a right to take possession of her"

Lord Chancellor: "By force?"

Henn Collins: "By such force as is necessary."

Master of the Rolls: "What do you say about this solicitor's clerk dragging the lady into a carriage and leaving her legs outside?"

Henn Collins: "There is some contradiction in the affidavits on the subject."

Lord Chancellor: "The question is not only the degree of violence used, but whether some account should not to be considered as to the insult received by the lady being seized when coming out of church?"

The mention from the bench of violence, cruelty, insult gave rise within Hartley Baldwin to a vestige of hope that there might be a favourable outcome.

Henn Collins then sought to question whether Emily had ever technically been imprisoned. In this case he represented that the wife was in confinement not imprisonment. The Judges were though unresponsive.

The Lord Chancellor stated he was at a loss to appreciate the difference between imprisonment and confinement. The Master of the Rolls then interjected and asked whether it would be imprisonment if Jackson had tied his wife to the bed post? Laughter then broke out.

The judges turned to speak amongst themselves, whereupon the Lord Chancellor enquired if Emily's solicitor had had access to the lady. Mr Finlay responded that access had been applied for but refused.

The Lord Chancellor thereupon addressed the Court:

"We are of the opinion that we must see the lady herself. The grounds on which we proceed are that there has been no direct communication between the lady herself and her solicitor and the allegation on the other side that the whole matter is attributable to external influences. Therefore, for the purposes of satisfying ourselves whether the lady is a perfectly free agent or not as to what is at present being done, we must see the lady on the subject."

There was an adjournment and the Judges returned to their room. After a pause Mr Mellor, whose title was Master of the Court, appeared and proceeded to conduct Emily through to the Judges Chambers.

Hartley Baldwin leaned back in his chair being overcome with such a sense of huge relief. It may not mean anything at all but, after all this long tortuous journey, Emily was to be heard.

Emily's private meeting with the Judges lasted half an hour. She returned to her place in the Court with the same calm air as she had so far maintained. She then remained seated in the silence of the Court for twenty minutes. There was hardly a whisper, the spectators were silent both in anticipation and in ignorance of how the decision would go. Even the legal teams sat in quiet reflection staring at a clock, pretending to glance at papers in front of them. For the barristers and solicitors maybe luminaries in the profession and well accustomed to all the law and process but here, even these professional gentlemen understood the drama of the moment about to unfold and the import for the husband and the wife of whatever decision was being made.

For different reasons the fame and infamy of this case had drawn people in like a magnet, and it seemed that anyone, legal or otherwise, who had taken an interest in the domestic relations on view felt they had an emotional investment in this couple, even, to an extent, did the reporter from the press who had tracked every twist, turn and nuance of the tale. Yet, whether a lawyer, relative, member of the public or journalist the only thing to do now was wait and wait in the sombre backdrop of this highest of Courts.

****

In their seats but slightly cramped given the numbers crammed into the Courtroom remained Betsy and Esther. The moment the door opened to allow the Judges once more to take their places on the bench they held hands again and Betsy certainly felt a tense knot in her stomach.

The Lord Chancellor went to some length to explain the reasons for the Court having reached the decision that it had. The decision can be succinctly summarised in half a dozen points as follows:

In former years, it had been boldly maintained by leading Counsel that slavery was part of English law. Today, that would be received with ridicule. In the same way, the Lord Chancellor said he should scarcely have expected to hear similar ancient notions trotted out as regards a husband's rights put forward seriously in the present day;

Things had been said to justify a husband in using physical violence towards his wife, which were totally inconsistent with the rights of free human creatures;

He did not find anything in the case that justified the husband in restraining the liberty of his wife;

No English subject had a right to imprison another English subject whether she was his wife or not;

The Lord Chancellor regarded with something akin to indignation the facts that had been set forth in this case, and the absence of anything like the delicacy and respect, which were due to a wife whom the husband had sworn to love and to cherish;

The result, concluded the Lord Chancellor, was that there was no power by law, which authorised a husband to act as he had done. The lady must be restored to her freedom at once, and must be at complete liberty to choose her own place of residence.

The Master of the Rolls concurred adding his own comment:

"The proposition of law sought to be established by the husband would render an English wife the abject slave of her husband, who would own her as a chattel, which he might dispose of as he chose."

Lord Justice Fry also concurred whereupon the Lord Chancellor uttered a stern warning as he looked down and towards Jackson:

After the authoritative declaration of the law by this Court, if the husband should make any attempt to carry out the right which he supposed to exist in him, it would be a gross contempt of this Court."

****

A False Freedom

As soon as the Judges had left the Courtroom, Hartley Baldwin junior ran out of the Court hotly pursued it seemed by a posse of reporters. However, there were separate reasons for them "fleeing" from the Court. The reporters were racing back to their editors. Hartley junior was on a separate mission.

Once Hartley had an inkling as to how the case was to be decided, he had passed a note to his son. It read:

"As soon as your Aunt Emily leaves the Court, I am relying upon you to meet her, protect her from any reporter and get her a carriage to the hotel with all speed."

With the host of spectators who remained in the Court, there was no cheering at the judgement. There was certainly an intense hubbub of conversation but the feeling was clearly one of astonishment.

The barristers and solicitors mingled with each other, handshakes offered and taken out of mutual professional respect. Dr Robinson and his brother had said a brief goodbye as they headed off to the railway station. It was Colonel Robinson's birthday and the brothers were expected back at the Castle for a celebratory dinner.

In that moment the solitary figure of Jackson sat in shock and felt so very alone. He watched his solicitor and advocate sharing a joke with Hartley Baldwin and Mr Finlay. The Robinsons had gone. The public were filing out of the Courtroom. He was in a state of complete shock, unable to grasp how things had gone so wrong. What was left in this life he had?

Jackson arranged to see Mr Ainsworth in the solicitor's office the following week. He did not know why. Perhaps he would, by then, have lots of questions to ask. Perhaps somewhere there would be a thread for him to hold onto. The pleasures of London appealed to him no more. He was very low. He had to get out of this place. He had to get back to West View and to his sister.

Jackson then, like a military scout, checked the terrain of the Courtroom. Hartley Baldwin was still in conversation with Mr Finlay and Mr Mellor had joined them. If Jackson walked along the far aisle and then across the top of the room he could possibly slink away unnoticed. For he could imagine, but could not bear to witness, a smug self satisfied grin on the face of the man, who even now, he blamed , along with the dreadful sisters, for having taken his Emily away from him.

Jackson escaped without being seen. In this somewhat morose state of mind he reached the door of the Courthouse leading to the street. As soon as he appeared a loud cheer went up. He looked behind him but there was no one else. The crowd who had gathered at the entrance made it clear they cared not for the Judgement. The cheering continued and many of the men in the crowd slapped Jackson on the back, referring to him as "good man" and saying "we are on your side."

If nothing else this reception quickly pulled Jackson from the depths of his self despair. He saw himself like a military general who had fought and shown valour beyond the call of duty returning home after a glorious defeat. He appreciated this show of support and waved to the crowd as he approached a carriage to convey him to the station.

****

Hartley Baldwin stepped down from the carriage before helping first Esther and then Betsy down the step. He then had a brief word with the doorman before leading the ladies up to the first floor at Wood's Hotel. He was pleased to have learnt on arrival that his son had organised and reserved this private lounge for the family.

Upon setting her eyes on her sisters, Emily momentarily controlled her emotions and simply smiled. Betsy then embraced Emily and because Mrs Baldwin was in tears Emily also started to cry. A knock on the door led to a tray supporting a pot of tea and a plate of biscuits being brought in by a member of the hotel staff.

Hartley appreciated his son's initiative and so diplomatically said:

"Very nice, I don't know about any of you but I think, at this moment, I am partial to something a bit stronger."

Hartley requisitioned a brandy. Mrs Baldwin and Miss Hall partook of a small whisky suggesting the drink would revive them after such a draining day. Emily though insisted she would have the tea.

"It is very strange" she said to her family "I cannot understand what has happened. It is unreal. I know I am told I am now free and that does make me feel so happy but I do not think it is something for me to celebrate. I cannot explain it."

Hartley Baldwin before raising his glass spoke:

"Emily, I think we all know or have some idea of what you must have been through these last weeks. It will take you quite a while to recover and get back to the way you were. As your family we are here for you as we always will be. Yes, we have, I think, won a famous victory today. However, my toast is not so much to mark the success but to welcome you back into the fold of the family where you truly belong."

He raised his glass then as did Esther and Betsy.

The sisters then conversed with Emily telling her how much they had missed her, how much they had worried about her. They talked about the garden at Prospect House and, of course, the turkeys. It was evident that no one in that room wanted to talk about what had happened to Emily during her detention at West View. All in good time thought the sisters. I do not want to be reminded of it all thought Emily.

Hartley Baldwin said they should enjoy a day or two at the hotel to rest and recover. Esther though said she had to get back to her avian friends and Hartley Junior needed to get back to the office.

****

Emily's bed that night felt so very fine as she lay there, with the curtains in the hotel room open, on crisp clean linen. She wanted no reminder of her "cell" at West View where the curtains were usually closed to keep her away from public view.

How she reflected upon her ordeal. How suddenly she had gone from being a linnet trapped in a bird cage to a swift that was free to fly. Very slowly Emily felt her pent up anxiety ebb and sensed relaxation affecting her nerve ends. She thought she could want for nothing so long as she had this freedom. Very soon it was evident that the freedom she thought she now had was largely an illusion.

With the next morning came the dawning, the first signs that the postscript to Emily's success in Court would not be pleasant.

The Press, or at least a large section of it, was vociferous in their criticism of the Judgement.

An Article in the Modem Society publication ran thus:

"I was much struck with the impropriety of the proceedings in the Appeal Court but nevertheless it would be wrong to suppose that the presence of either of the Judge's wives in any way affected the judgements of their Lords, for I am certain that Lady Esher's sympathies were not with Mrs Jackson. And no wonder, for no one who had the privilege of seeing this haughty and imperious little woman as she sat in state in the well of the Court could doubt that Mr Jackson must have possessed more than an average share of self confidence to intrude himself within so select a family circle. Perhaps the strangest thing of all in connection with this case was the extreme deference shown to this lady by the Judges of the Court of Appeal. For anyone who had the experience of being under judicial censure knows only too well the scant courtesy they may expect when they pass under a Judge's direction.

Yet this lady, who had shown so gross a contempt for the behest of the law, is treated as if she were the Queen of Sheba herself and the Judges were Solomons! At the obedience of an order from the Bench, that Grand functionary, the Superintendent of the Royal Courts, clears a passage for the exit of this contumacious lady, who is thenceforth conducted in great pomp through the doorway leading onto the Bench. And, eventually, she gained egress from the building by the same door as used by the Judges."

The outcome of the appeal, fuelled or otherwise by the initial headlines, provoked a tidal wave of correspondence many of which were printed in the letters pages over the following days and weeks.

Letter to Northern Daily Telegraph- 21st March 1891

"Women have always understood that they undertook, and in fact, expressly do undertake at marriage "to obey" their husbands. If this decision takes away a husband's remedies, husbands can have no rights. In which case I should beg to remain

A Batchelor"

Letter from John Strange Winter- London-21st March 1891

"Is it true that the majority of women in this country look upon themselves as slaves and on men as monsters of oppression?

Where will men be in the future? Perhaps some of them will be tailors still and the rest will write fashion letters. And what a time she shall have.

I am Sir

Your obedient servant

A contented Husband"

The newspapers maintained their tack, no doubt aware that the effect would be to stir up certain readers and provoke them into a state of foment over the perceived injustice.

From the Lancashire Evening post on 25th March 1891:

"It is pretty clear that Mr Jackson has won the sympathy of his wife's neighbours by his forcible yet ineffectual wooing. Plain men and women are saying that the law now expounded by the Lord Chancellor has made an intolerable position for the deserted husband"

In another publication at this time, another letter attracted attention. The letter was signed "A Churchman" and it stated:

"What is to become of the marriage vows, civil and religious? Are they no longer to be considered sacred, or only to be looked upon as a mere farce, to be cast aside whenever inclined? If the ruling of the Lord Chancellor be allowed to pass unchallenged, the religious and moral aspect of marriage becomes no better than a comedy. It is the duty of our Church to speak out with no uncertain voice if the sanctity of marriage is to be preserved."

And so, with each issue of each newspaper the tide of hostility comprising huge venomous waves powered by the Press, the Church and Public Opinion was bearing down upon Mrs Jackson and her family.

Mr Baldwin and the two ladies remained at Wood's Hotel for far longer than initially planned. For, on the second day of their stay, Hartley had received a phone call from Mr Weeks. This call brought the disquieting news of what Hartley's partner called "a local rebellion". Residents of Clitheroe and its environs had, it seemed, decided to give vent to their anger at the decision in Emily's case. Crowds had gathered in the main square in the town and passions appeared to have become very inflamed when they were addressed by a couple of loudmouths. The mob had gone off to Prospect House where they had remained shouting for a while until Charnock persuaded them that Mrs Jackson remained furth of the town and he did not know when his master would return. Mr Weeks had also been obliged to shut and lock the office door for fear the mob may enter and disturb the office."

Hartley was indeed alarmed by this report. He called Charnock to check that he was alright and no damage had been caused.

As if to emphasise the warning given on the telephone, Mr Weeks wrote almost immediately to Mr Baldwin:

"Duck Street,
Clitheroe

22nd March 1891

My Dear Mr Baldwin

I refer to our conversation of this date and regret having to have been the bearer of ominous tidings.

I think it would be well if the ladies stayed away a bit longer. I think if it was known they were coming home, there would be a crowd and they would be hooted. Why not let them go to Bournemouth for a few weeks and either go there yourself or send your son Hartley to look after them?.

I think, when they do come home, you should write to the passenger traffic manager of the Midland Railway Company at Derby and ask him to stop the Scotch Express at midnight. Mrs Jackson would probably get home that way the best, elsewise Heston, the coachman, had better meet the train at Gisburn and drive her to Clitheroe.

I have been wondering whether we should ask counsel to advise whether a jury would be likely to convict Jackson and the Robinsons on a charge of conspiracy to assault and imprison? Not that I advise such proceedings just yet but it might be wise to keep a rod in pickle.

I do not see any reason for you and Mrs Baldwin not to come home but as there are a lot of people about on account of the Fair, I should feel inclined to come back the Hellifield way.

I am most decidedly of the opinion that it would be most unwise for Mrs Jackson to return at this time......at any rate during daylight hours. Without any doubt there would be a hostile demonstration. There appears to be a movement afoot just now in the town to burn an effigy of Mrs Jackson upon her return.

Please rest assured that I do not exaggerate the situation here. I speak from enquiries I have made and what is evident to observe when walking around the town. The people - most of them - seem madder because we won than they were before.

Very sincerely yours

J.H.Weeks"

Hartley sat in his room with his head in his hands. He had never and perhaps never could have anticipated such a public reaction. His sole focus had been to free Emily and to bring her back to peace and freedom at her house Shawbridge. Instead he would be taking her back to a cacophony of abuse from strangers who did not know her. An effigy indeed? How could such insanity have broken out? His wife's dear little sister about to be pilloried as a witch?

He felt he had the problems of the world on his shoulders. Any brief flush of success he had felt upon hearing the Lord Chancellor grant Emily her liberty was now quashed by the black cloud of disdain and hatred that awaited her in her home town.

The first thing he had to do was to prepare Emily for what was ahead.

****

Jackson was seized in a state of depression or certainly gripped by his grievous loss. Isabel had tried to motivate her brother by suggesting that perhaps the siblings (Jackson and her) could go away on a short holiday. It would do them both good and surely Raynsford could stretch to sponsoring such a therapy? Her brother was unresponsive.

Isabel then tried a firmer approach:

"You know I am glad this has happened. Of course, you do not agree but, to my mind, she was a stuck up little madam who never did anything to please you and you are better off without her."

Jackson still did not react.

He generally just moped about the house.

Later the same day Susan found Jackson upstairs in the attic. He was sitting aimlessly thumbing through old photographs from his travels in New Zealand.

“Please excuse me Mr Jackson, it is a telephone call for you."

"Just say I am not in."

"But it is your solicitor."

Jackson dragged himself to his feet. He suspected Ainsworth wanted to discuss payment of his fees.

He got downstairs and picked up the phone.

"Hello, this is Jackson."

" I really have to advise…   "

"What? Who is that? You are not Ainsworth"

"No. it's your other solicitor, Dixon Robinson Esquire!"

Jackson gave out a sigh of despair.

"Dick, I'm sorry I am not in the mood for practical jokes."

"It is not a joke Mr Jackson. No, I just thought you should know and perhaps you will want to come up here?"

"What exactly are you on about? And why on earth after all that has happened, should I want to go anywhere near Clitheroe?"

"The place is alive I tell you. You are a hero here believe me. They are demonstrating and all the talk is of how they are going to let Mrs Jackson know what they think. In fact some speak of driving her out of town."

"Dick. I do not want to hear of that. You do not understand. Mrs Jackson is my wife. She has never been my enemy. Goodbye."

The hurt and the loss pained Jackson greatly. Did he have feelings for his wife? Or was he deluding himself and judging the pain to be associated with feelings that were purely of his imagination?

****

Having gently outlined the climate in Clitheroe to the sisters, Hartley decided after being away for quite a few days to put off the return no longer.

On 26th March 1891 Hartley Baldwin settled the bill at the Wood's Hotel. He paid over the sum of £41.14/9. The chambermaid tip was five shillings, the waiter half a crown and the porter two shillings. The pecking order of tipping was well established for those who frequented hotels.

The three of them set off on their journey.

Would their delayed departure have taken the air out of the wheels of protest? Could these travellers realistically hope or dream of a return to civil normality?

****

Easter Parade

The decision to return to Clitheroe on 26th March 1891 was brought about by more than one factor. Hartley Baldwin took the view that the delayed return in the aftermath of the Appeal would have allowed the worst of the passions stirred up by what he considered misplaced outrage to have subsided. Even if he were incorrect in this opinion, he could not remain away from home indefinitely. Further, although he had implicit confidence in Mr Weeks as his business partner, Hartley Baldwin was a man who liked to have his "finger on the pulse", to be the man in control of the practice and, of course, to be seen about the town. He would certainly want to challenge any suggestion that he was "scared" to be seen back in Clitheroe. Then, there was the date - the next day was Good Friday. Yes, it was Easter weekend. His wife was so eager to attend Easter Service on the Sunday as she had never, not once in her entire life, missed this service.

Mr Baldwin did reckon it was prudent to arrange for Heston to collect the party from Gisburn Station rather than risk any trouble by going all the way to Clitheroe.

Emily with Betsy and Mr Baldwin boarded the evening train from London. They would arrive under the cover of darkness. The sisters were not relaxed with what Hartley Baldwin had informed them and now with all this subterfuge to get home, both ladies could not but be apprehensive.

Emily looked out of the compartment window of the train as the noise from the engine signified the slow acceleration northwards. The coalsmoke fed down from the roof of the train against the window before it diffused skywards. Emily felt the world closing in upon her once more. It was unpleasant for her family yet she considered that she was the object of everyone's disfavour, she felt like a criminal. In some ways this was worse than her imprisonment at West View. There she knew "the enemy". She knew Jackson and could almost predict how far he would go or not go. When she had to deal with her husband, she could still endear him to a degree, if it suited her, with a kind word or that certain look in her eyes. Now though, if rumours were true, she was confronting an army of strangers who did not know her and presumably were not open to consider her or her version of events, so many faces staring at her with despication in their eyes. Emily gave herself a jolt just as the train clattered into the entrance of a tunnel. She had her family, her loyal family. She would be with Esther in a few hours. She must put all these negative thoughts to rest. Emily would enjoy being home.

Sitting opposite Emily was Hartley. He had picked up an early edition of the Lancashire Evening Post. He took note in the Public Notices of the death being announced of an important client of his. There was random news such as the opening of a new hospital in Lancaster, a commentary on the price of spring lambs and a burglary at a mansion house near Fylde. His eyes then alighted on a column at the side of page 4:

"Deafening silence in the Clitheroe Case" was the heading. The article went on:

"There are no developments to report following the Court decision in the Abduction Case.

Our reporter contacted Mr Jackson to ascertain if he was going to attempt to challenge the legal decision. We were referred to his solicitor who made the anticipated response of "No comment."

Meantime the victorious Mrs Jackson has not been seen since she left the Court of Appeal. It is generally understood that Mrs Jackson has chosen not to return to the town in consideration of the furore thrown up by the decision. Our Reporter was abruptly dismissed by Mrs Jackson's sister when he sought to make enquiry there as none of those attending the vigil outside Prospect House had seen any activity suggestive that any of the family were in residence.

The office of Mrs Jackson's solicitors in Duck Street issued a brief statement to the effect that they have not been appraised of Mrs Jackson's movements which are entirely a matter personal to her and that the office will be issuing no further statement on the subject unless instructed to do so by their client.

In short, though the public remain generally in a state of high dudgeon following the Court case, those directly involved in the proceedings are tight lipped and seem unlikely to disclose their immediate intentions."

Mr Baldwin then turned to the letters page of this issue whereupon he saw a letter from a reader resident not far from Clitheroe which read:

"The waiving of the law in favour of Mrs Jackson was brought about by a pretty state of things and if it be allowed to prevail it may be that we shall see ladies in wig and gown on the Bench and their husbands at home minding the babies."

To Hartley Baldwin, as this train reached mile by mile nearer to Clitheroe, it was patently obvious that neither the interest in the case nor the anger in some quarters had died down at all. Now, even Mr Baldwin felt trepidation.

****

The rumour mill which was, more often than not unreliable, suggested to one or more Clitheroe residents that Thursday was when Mrs Jackson would come home. There had been similar whispers in the days now gone by and the protesters' hopes, having been fanned by the winds of gossip, were only to be later dashed. The word this Thursday was more widespread. It occurred quite likely that the "missing family" would seek to be installed home for Easter. Accordingly, from about late afternoon onwards, a crowd somewhat larger than the usual "vigil" amassed in the square at Clitheroe.

Word came round that the party would be disembarking from the 8 30 pm train, whereupon the massed ranks of protesters flocked to the Railway Station. They rallied around the station entrance and packed across the overhead bridge. If not quite a lynch mob they were certainly ready and eager to vent their feelings and disapproval at those deemed responsible for having upset what had been settled law.

No member of the Baldwin "clan" emerged from the 8 30pm train which punctually arrived and departed.

It was then surmised they might get the train via Hellfield and would, instead, arrive at 10 30 pm. This suggestion seemed to gain credence as it spread amongst those present. Many of the demonstrators retired to one of the public houses for a drink before emerging again and taking up position in time for the arrival of the last train.

Once more this service was punctual and, yet again, the Baldwin party failed to alight onto the platform. Another wasted effort? Some of the crowd began to disperse. However, some passengers who had arrived in Clitheroe off the train made mention as they left the station that they had observed Mr Baldwin and his wife leaving the train at Gisburn Station some six miles away. This party of 3 had been the only ones to get off at Gisburn and one very observant passenger had noticed under the station lamp, a carriage and pair which he had assumed were there to pick up the Baldwin party.

The crowd was galvanised. This was surely the moment they had been waiting for for days? This must be it.

En masse, the mob headed out the Gisburn Road cheering and chanting Jackson's name.

The size of the demonstration and the mood of the crowd was not lost upon the police. The Chief Constable, having been informed that it looked like things were going to become ugly, sent some officers in pursuit of the crowd with instructions to observe and only to intervene if a crime was perceived as imminent.

It was dark. After twenty minutes on the road, some of the protestors peeled off and returned to Clitheroe where it was deemed more sensible to wait. However, those more determined including those who had possibly consumed more alcohol than some of the others, carried on along the road in the pitch dark of the night.

About two miles out of the town the noise of approaching hooves was heard and soon the crunch of wheels. Before the carriage got too close some of the mob lit torches made of dried straw. Heston, suddenly aware of people ahead on the road, slowed the horses. As he did so the mob started to hoot and to howl. Heston appreciated it would be folly to stop so did his best to force on yet avoid running over anyone. Members of the mob grabbed the carriage trying to push it over. They banged on the doors with sticks and created more and more noise.

****

The Baldwin party had been relieved to get out of the train at Gisburn. Whether misreading the signs from their fellow passengers or not, there were some in that number who would look into the compartment as they walked past with more than the impression of idle curiosity. Hartley Baldwin had reckoned it would have drawn more attention to them had he pulled down the blind on the door to the passageway.

The three of them stepped onto the platform on this very chilly night in north Lancashire. They were all reassured and pleased to see Heston waiting for them. Heston assisted the ladies into the carriage.

"Make haste my good man." said Hartley.

Wearied by their journey and the stress of it all, Betsy and Emily shut their eyes and tried to sleep as the carriage raced off in the direction of Clitheroe. Even the bumps along the road, of which there were several, failed to cause either of the ladies to interrupt their gentle slumber.

It was when Heston suddenly slowed the horses that they experienced the rudest of awakenings. Hartley Baldwin put his arms across the ladies so they would not be propelled onto the far side of the carriage. Just as Emily and her sister got their bearings, the loud din of shouting filled the air. Next the carriage was rocked from side to side. The sides of the carriage were being banged and amongst the unintelligible vocal noise such words as could be heard clearly were hostile and abusive in nature.

The two women turned into each other, holding tight in their embrace. Hartley was standing between the ladies and the carriage door doing all he could to keep his balance and holding a solid wooden walking stick in his right hand. Mr Baldwin was not a pugilist but he was prepared to use every ounce of muscle and the stick in any way possible to save from harm his wife and his sister-in-law.

Just then there was the sound of whistles and more shouting.

“Get a move on up there".

In the dark, the occupants could not see what was going on. It was Heston who confirmed later that, when the police had turned up as they had, they had fought valiantly to keep a path open for the carriage and that just when the police realised they could not hold their line, the sergeant had bellowed to Heston to move off with all speed.

In a very short time the carriage raced into Clitheroe.

Soon, the raucous noise of more shouting echoed through the night. It was almost midnight.

The carriage reached the gate at Prospect House and was immediately surrounded by a cordon of police to keep back the boisterous mob which, slowly but surely, were joined by those who had been on the approach road not long before.. The Chief Constable was himself present and in command of his men.

After sitting in the carriage for about five minutes and enduring the derogatory insults for that time, the party was signalled by the Chief Constable to leave the carriage.

First to step down was Hartley Baldwin who surveyed the scene as best as he could. Two protesters pressed their heads between two constables and mouthed off in the direction of Mr Baldwin. He aimed his walking stick at them in a threatening manner but brought it downward upon seeing Mr Edwards, the Chief Constable shaking his head.

Mr Edwards and Hartley Baldwin then turned to help and shield the ladies on their short but obviously nervous journey from the street into the house. The spectacle of the ladies was too much for the crowd. Some would have been too befuddled by drink and others simply ignorant, for the truth was that few, if any, there that night would have recognised Emily even had she walked past them in broad daylight. It was sufficient for the rowdy onlookers to see a woman come from the carriage.

The jeering, booing, hooting and baying of the crowd escalated twofold upon the sight of the women. Had either of the ladies chosen to look around, which, of course, they were completely disinclined to do, they would have seen hundreds of faces as far as the eye could see. All with mouths wide open, chanting wildly and inanely like a pack of rabid hounds who had finally cornered their prey.

The hour had passed well into Good Friday. The noise of the rabble outside could not be muffled from those now within the walls of Prospect House.

Hartley had told Charnock to go to his bed. It was beyond the duty of the manservant to wait on the family at this time of night.

The sisters sat on the couch in a state that can only be described as silent shock. The violence demonstrated, the ridicule and embarrassment that had been witnessed or felt had gone far beyond anything that any of them could have imagined when setting off that day for the train. Hartley himself had misjudged the mood. It seemed to him that Mr Weeks had possibly been diplomatic in his description of what had been going on and, if anything, had understated the feelings of the mob.

With singing and chanting still audible the telephone rang. This was not an hour when the phone would ring other than in an emergency. Hartley left the room and headed for the phone. The press would not dare call at such a time. It could conceivably be Mr Edwards who had Baldwin's number. It could, of course, be one of the local miscreants wanting to hurl abuse down the telephone. It was though none of these.

He returned shortly to the ladies.

"That was Esther on the telephone. She's very concerned about both of you. I said we were all exhausted but would talk to her tomorrow. Well, I mean later on today."

After a moment Hartley continued.

"I must say that sister of yours is very different from either of you. Says she shooed away a journalist by holding a pole to his chin and says she has full baskets in an upstairs room at Shawbridge and how if any of the mob go near that house she will shower them with bird droppings."

Betsy smiled at this. Emily was now asleep on the couch.

"Let's get her to the spare room."

****

Outside Prospect House, the presence of the police and the Chief Constable was maintained. Near to the property though was a builder's yard and several of the protesters had helped themselves to slates stacked there. Some of the reckless individuals started hurling them at the house. However, as soon as Mr Edwards announced that anyone launching a missile would be arrested on the spot, the threat of damage to the fabric of Prospect House was, for the moment, dispelled.

As the night dragged on and the passion or stamina of the crowd started to wane, numbers slowly drifted home. Every so often those remaining would reprise "For Jackson's a Jolly Good fellow" but the constant cacophony was no more.

****

With the ladies in their beds, Hartley remained up. He could not settle however exhausted he was. He sat in his armchair having helped himself to a brandy........a somewhat larger measure than Charnock ever poured for him!

He stared into the disappearing embers of the welcoming fire which Charnock had lit for their return. It seemed to him that this whole hard earned victory had, in so many respects, been in vain. For himself, he had never courted popularity. He had only ever sought professional acknowledgment and respectability. As he sat there his concern was not the possible adverse effect upon his business that occupied him. In certain ways, it was not even Emily's predicament as the perceived "major villain" in all of this that pressed upon his conscience. Although he had fought tooth and nail for her freedom and would do so all over again, he could acknowledge deep down that it was of Emily's doing. She had acted impulsively in allowing Jackson to court her and then she'd the folly to go and marry the feckless man against his wishes. No, what occupied Hartley most was what he considered to be his prime duty.

For Hartley Baldwin, this was to provide his wife with respectability, security and protection. He worried that he had somehow now let her down and ruined much of what he had built with and for her. The decision to take Betsy to London had tarnished her with the odium people sought to bring on those responsible for the allegedly unfair decision of the Court.

Now and for that, if tonight was anything to go by, his wife would be vilified, shunned in the street and possibly abused.

As he finished the last drop of his large brandy, Hartley was able to see that he was not thinking straight. The tiredness had impeded his usual clarity of thought. Perhaps things would look different after a good sleep. Perhaps the uncivil hordes, having had "their day" would go back to where they had come from and leave him, and his family, in peace.

****

Saturday

News of the tumultuous return to Clitheroe filtered through to Wagstaff at the Northern Daily Telegraph. In maintaining his vendetta against the Hall family, Wagstaff had ensured that there was a critique of the situation in most editions of the newspaper. The paper's owner though enquired of his editor whether he did not think the readers needed a break, a rest from this story. A hint to Wagstaff to "move on" ....to change the debate to something else ?

First and foremost, Wagstaff was a journalist so he knew full well that his opportunity to show the Halls in the light he wanted to was limited. Further, he had to be very careful. Careful not to offend the owner for that could jeopardise his own position and careful not to put into print anything that could result in a civil suit for, should that occur and the newspaper ordered to pay damages, that would indeed end Wagstaff's career.

To appease the owner he would sometimes relegate reference to the case to a short column on page 5 or thereabouts. Now this was possibly his last chance to fire a serious salvo at the descendants of Henry Hall. Unfortunately, news of the return to Clitheroe came too late for Saturday's edition. Wagstaff was tempted to arrange for a special Sunday issue of the Northern Daily Telegraph but he could not justify to the owner the additional wages that would have to be paid to the lithographers and printers to organise such an extra issue. He therefore resigned himself to going to print for Easter Monday. He would make this a splash on the front page along with his inimitable editorial comment. This was Wagstaff's "last hoorah":

"THE CURSE OF THE CLITHEROE CASE

Since the abduction of Mrs Jackson on 8th March of this year, nothing good has come to anyone connected with the case and it is as clear now as it was at the outset that, had Mrs Jackson followed the examples of all of her gender and been possessed of devotion and respect, if not for her husband, then certainly of the solemn vows entered within the house of God, then many would now be spared throes of anxiety and the removal of domestic structure that Mrs Jackson's reckless obstinacy has led us to.

The husband in all of this has suffered the neglect of and then the abandonment by his wife. The loss of both succour and support he could reasonably have relied upon when entering the marriage contract. Further, given the dictate of the Appeal Court, one can but not empathise with Mr Jackson's certain feeling of impotency.

Having so strived release from her lawful husband what, we ask, of the victor?

Instead of a vaunted heroine of her age, Mrs Jackson has become the object of vitriol, the butt of humour of the most indecent taste and a woman destined to remain in the annals of infamy.

Much was made in reports as to Mrs Jackson's attractive features and the impressive way she held herself before the Court. That may well be so. It is though not cruel we think to pose to our readership, what future for this lady? After all her antics, what man could ever trust this lady? Certainly, none in his right state of mind.

So, for Mrs Jackson the victory must be hollow. Having spurned ardency and romance offered by her husband, she has, we believe, condemned herself to abject solitude without male companionship and the protection thereby afforded.

And then there is the small band of Mrs Jackson's supporters - her family. The loyal readership of this newspaper may well recall the embarrassment brought to the door of this publication by the late Henry Hall several years ago. Is this justice whereby the table of embarrassment is now turned poetic or divine?

What of justice and that previously lauded institution, the Law? Has the reputation of the Law in this country not been seriously tarnished? Has it not been harmed also by the curse of this Clitheroe Case?

Before the lamentable Judgement in this case, it was believed that all men were equal, not just in the eyes of God but in the eyes of the Law also. Yet we beg to write that, in this case, this is not so. Was Mr Jackson equal in the eyes of those judges? One hazards to enquire that had Mr Jackson been a landed gentleman or a man of influence in the establishment then the decision would have been much different.

Even if it could be argued that men are equal with each other, it can be deduced from this Appeal Court that the position of women has now been so escalated as to enfeeble male kind and dethrone them from their natural position as head of the family.

Most certainly, then, Mrs Jackson you have brought a curse upon this land."

****

Whilst Wagstaff was fine tuning his "piece de resistance", the occupants of Prospect House awoke to spring sunshine streaming in through the gaps in curtains.

After the tribulations of the previous night, the silence just after dawn was quite unreal.

Emily was the last to appear. She was ashen faced. In fact not long after the others had put her to bed she had wakened. Her mind, agitated by the events of the journey home, became a living nightmare such as she could not rest. The three of them gathered in the breakfast room.

"I think that until I gauge things today, you two should remain here. Do not go outside." said Hartley. "I shall go to the office this morning."

There was a sudden bang on the window. The ladies nearly jumped out of their skins. Hartley immediately got to his feet. It was though only Esther knocking on the glass with a cheery smile on her face.

Hartley decided to leave the three sisters together. They could share their stories of all that had happened. After twenty minutes he was ready to leave the house but his progress was interrupted by a telephone call. It was Mr Weeks calling from his house.

"I am just heading to the office."

"I thought that you might be. However, I think that that would be ill advised."

"I beg your pardon."

"I have learnt that about twenty people got off the first train this morning. They are strangers to the town. Just before I phoned you they passed my house. They are heading towards the square. I have told the police as I reckon they mean trouble. If there is anything you need let me know but I think it best you stay and make sure your family is safe."

****

The rumour mill continued to produce the story that, on the Saturday, a huge effigy of Emily was to be paraded through the town, along Duck Street and thence to Prospect House where it would be symbolically set on fire. This colourful representation attracted people from quite far away to come to Clitheroe to "have some fun", "watch the spectacle" and generally celebrate the Easter time. As the clock turned with each hour, more and more folk congregated in the streets. Again, the chanting started. There was singing too. Of course, some of the crowds attended in the spirit of fun whilst, for others, the motive remained very serious - to attack the Baldwin family and all they were now perceived to stand for - to cause them as much discomfort as possible.

When it was heard the effigy would appear at the market square, groups ran off in that direction. With another rumour it was to be burnt by the railway station other groups headed off there at speed. A ritual clapping by a section of those attending at some part of the town would be heard by others elsewhere who would by way of curiosity move to find out what was happening.

It is no exaggeration to say that the town was in uproar. The police out and about were like dogs round an errant flock of sheep, all the time trying to keep an eye out for the known ringleaders and watch for any new troublemaker trying to run the gauntlet of the nearby officers.

By midnight the protesters were, once again and almost to a man, outside Prospect House. Stone throwing began. The dark of the night handicapped the police in identifying the culprits. The crowds created the drama. The press delighted in reporting everything vividly and this served merely to inflate the numbers who would invade the town the next day.

Some of the missiles hit home. Three large windows at Prospect House were smashed, the splinters of glass and pieces of tile resting on the fine carpets within.

Effectively, it could be said, that the Appeal had, for practical purposes, simply transported a siege from Blackburn to Clitheroe. This was a far more dangerous situation than there had ever been at West View. Here the crowd was hostile, venomous and malintent. Here the "inmates" were most certainly under attack.

The effigy of Emily never appeared that day.

Following the general lack of order on this Saturday, the Chief Constable advised the Town Council he would need to obtain reinforcements from the neighbouring police forces if he was to prevent further lawlessness.

****

The Fightback

This could not go on. Hartley Baldwin would not submit to being a prisoner in his own home. Whilst he had the fortitude to sustain himself through these dire times............for in time those angry men (and women too) would run themselves ragged and lose heart, shrivel like wallflowers and disappear. It may still take some time but that it would all go away he knew to be true. However, his insight made him concerned for the womenfolk. This all had the potential to cause long term harm to them, particularly Emily. He had to work out carefully what his next move could or would be.

By now it was Easter Sunday. Betsy had long since abandoned thought let alone hope of going to Sunday service. The first half of the day was peaceful again. There were no trains which operated through Clitheroe on a Sunday. Charnock had managed to acquire some much needed supplies the previous day and took the opportunity to bring the provisions to Prospect House whilst the area was quiet.

The family could have imagined everything to be back to the way it always used to be when Esther & Emily would visit for Sunday lunch. Here they all were again enjoying the fruits of Charnock's shopping. A beautiful piece of Roast Lamb and all the trimmings served in the sanctity of the Baldwins' fine dining room.

It was late afternoon when the signs of further "trouble" were first detected. Of course, the annual Easter Fair was in town all weekend. Without the trains, people travelled by carriage or walked into town to indulge in the thrills and spills of the shows and the competitions. The Town Council prohibited the Fair to remain open beyond 5pm on a Sunday in order to preserve the sanctity of evening worship. Unfortunately, whilst the regular parishioners left the fair to attend to their religious devotions, others with no obvious Christian motivation formed a different grouping and went to the foot of Duck Street. Once there a huge cheer went up. For the long awaited effigy, having been constructed of straw in a nearby village, was being pulled into view on a drayman's cart.

The effigy was hardly a replica of its female subject. It could have been anyone but for it wearing an Emily style bonnet (Mrs Jackson's concerns about her burning bonnet had been mentioned by the press) and a large placard hung over the neck which read "The Emily of all decent men" being a pun on the word "enemy".

When the cart was stationary, some younger men jumped aboard and held the effigy upright and continued in that position as the cart slowly set off around the town gathering more followers as it went.

****

The commotion got louder as the Easter revellers got nearer to Prospect House. Resigned to yet another uncomfortable night the residents of the house retired to the small ante room next to the kitchen. This room was farthest away from the front of the house and had no windows. They felt more secure in this "inner sanctum" even though none of them could concentrate on anything or distract themselves from the worry of the ongoings outside.

The barracking was muffled so what exactly was being said was not decipherable by those inside. Perhaps that was just as well for there were references to Mrs Jackson being a coward. She could face the posh judges but what about the Court of the public? A voice shouted "We will give you a fair Hearing, Mistress Jackson" whereupon there was raucous laughter. Another voice went up "Mistress? Whose Mistress would that be? Not our man Jackson - he did not have that displeasure!" - more tidal waves of laughter.

The crowd remained unpleasant but seemed, for some unknown reason, in better spirits than the previous nights. There were no missiles thrown, no trying to break through the police cordon, less vitriol and less threatening. Nonetheless, it was all relative and no less uncomfortable for those who happened to be the objects of the taunting from the protesters.

Hartley suddenly got up.

"Goodness. I left the curtains in the front upstairs room open." He rushed out and upstairs.

Once he entered the room Hartley crept along the side of the wall. He was at pains not to draw attention to himself. His hand reached and grasped the edge of the curtain. Three things then happened within a split second.

He rushed across the window closing the curtain as he went. As he did so his eyes were met by the tall figure towering above the heads of the policemen. The shock of viewing the effigy so clearly from the window and the vision in his head of this being burnt caused him to take deep breathes to regain his composure. The third thing that happened was the voice of a screaming woman who had obviously caught sight of him at the window.

"Old man Balders, you bloody twister"

It was not those words but the effect of the effigy that sent Hartley Baldwin back downstairs on a mission. This all had to stop.

Upon resuming his position with the ladies, he discussed with them his plan. With their concurrence and with the crowd still agitating outside, Hartley made what he considered to be the last throw of his dice. His professional motivation was his belief that when the mob rules, the law dies. His personal motivation was to liberate his family from the yoke that now constrained them.

Mr Baldwin proceeded to write a letter. The same letter was issued to Joseph Smithers, Mayor of Clitheroe, to James Garnett, Chairman of the Watch Committee, John Eastham, Town Clerk and to John Edwards, Chief Constable. The letter read:

"Gentlemen

A mob of some 400 people or more assembled in front of my house last night – Saturday - from 11 15 pm until 12.30 am (Sunday morning) and during that time conducted themselves in a riotous tumultuous and threatening manner to me and the inmates of my house, throwing stones and doing other hostile acts and jeopardising our family and our property. Chief Constable Edwards was there with several of his men but was totally unable to deal with the mob. The mob, by their shouts, intimated they would come again and keep on coming. Indeed, they have returned this very night.

I am in fear of my life and further injury to my property and request you, being in charge of the peace of the town, immediately to procure such police or other additional force as may enable any future mob to be properly dealt with and the persons of my household and my home and property protected from injury.

I remain

Your obedient servant

Hartley Baldwin"

Was Hartley Baldwin truly in fear of his life? Or was it more likely that his view of the proper order of society dictated that he apply whatever ploy to the situation to have it sorted once and for all.? Either way, he chose to address a further letter to the Mayor on the following day and this read:

"I am incredibly informed that it is intended to burn one or more effigies in the streets before too long. I witnessed one such effigy this very last evening. There is therefore every basis to believe that the riotous behaviour will be revisited in even greater measure ere too long if not this very night.

It is now not so much the issues between Mrs Jackson and her husband or of even the merits of the controversy that is at stake, but rather one of the preservation of the peace of the town. I must again press upon you the necessity of taking such means as will enable the police effectively to deal with any attempts at violence or rioting. I am sure that I need not point out to you that after the appeals I have made to you, any personal injury or damage to property will rest on the shoulders of those entrusted with the maintenance of the peace of the town.

I remain

Your obedient servant"

Whether this second appeal by Hartley Baldwin was a threat he would have followed through on had any injury occurred, his standing in the echelons of Clitheroe's official classes and the possibility that this wily old fox of a lawyer may try to sue for compensation did prove to be effective.

Police reinforcements were found and a round the clock guard placed at both Prospect House and Shawbridge.

Hartley Baldwin's gratitude for this was illustrated by a rebuke he later received from the Chief Constable. This read :

"Chief Constable's Office
Clitheroe
1st April 1891

H Baldwin

Dear Sir,

I have to request that for the future you will not supply the officer or officers on duty near your house with anything to drink, as the man on duty tonight-10 30 pm - I found under the influence of drink and would be unfit to perform his duty if any disturbance arose."

****

Postbags

It was now more than ten days since the Appeal had been heard and the implications of the decision were still being distilled on many levels of society. There were those who gave vent to their views in private circles. Others such as old school politicians and bankers would debate the issues over supper or a gin and tonic at the Gentleman's Club. Of course, there were hundreds and more who felt strongly enough to put pen to paper.

Despite a modicum of dust having settled, Jackson had still not regained his humour, charm or confidence. He would never really be the same man again. He was still possessed of no sense of proper direction.

The first hours of his day were spent sitting around the house. At some point Isabel would join him. She would indulge herself in reading the newspapers and, in the hope she could instill the old bravado in her brother, she would read "suitable" extracts to him. Haughton, for his part, could hardly refuse to listen.

On this Easter Monday Isabel was thoroughly taken with Wagstaff,s article.

"You see Haughton, the press is still on your side."

Jackson did not respond.

"Look here" said Isabel. "It says in this paper that Prospect House was besieged for a third night running. The mob was throwing stones. My, my, I wonder how it made that lot feel. Getting a piece of their own medicine!"

Jackson winced inside. It had never been his intent to terrorise Emily or place her in harm's way. The vestige of a noble spirit brought to his mind the thought of trying to rescue his wife from the danger she was in and the horror she was now experiencing. Now that was a gesture that would prove his love, would it not? He could not do this on his own and yet even if he concocted a rescue plan, what was the point of it? His wife had made it clear she wanted nothing to do with him.

"You are not listening to me" scolded Isabel.

"Sorry. What was it you were saying?"

****

In late morning Jackson left West View. He would not neglect exercise and, despite his woes, this dictated a brisk daily walk along the Common. Easter Monday was no different. He put on his large hat and took a scarf off the stand. The collar of his coat was pulled up. Jackson made his way to the back door. He checked the window before slipping outside. The last thing he wanted was to be recognised, to be accosted by any of those reporters and, although the focus of press and public attention had shifted from Blackburn to Clitheroe these days, he could not take the chance.

He took in the spring air as he walked quickly towards his usual spot, a wooden seat positioned on a slight bank which looked out over unspoilt fields. The seat was not of the most comfortable, for one of the lateral planks had been broken. However, it was where Jackson headed to on his daily outing. It had the advantage that it was part hidden by a large tall green hedge and, so long as no one sprang out from behind the hedge, he had a clear view of anyone approaching from either side.

He still asked himself what was he doing? He was conscious of the distant noises of industry from the workshops and saw the smoke from the mill chimneys. The populus all busily occupied, earning corn to maintain their living. That was and never had been his life. Perhaps when he got back to the house he would read some of the newspapers but only to look for inspiration. Would there be any appealing positions advertised, perhaps involving foreign travel? He was not minded to expend a huge effort, but if there was something available that involved payment, then that would, however temporarily, extricate him from his lethargy and would all be to the good.

As always Jackson reached no conclusions and soon found himself walking back to West View. His thoughts drifted again towards his wife. Another repeating question - why was he so aggrieved and upset at her current grievous position? Was it possible it was jealousy? Jealous that someone other than him now exercised control over Emily? Or that she was now "public" property as opposed to his private possession? No, he told himself. He could not agree he would be like that. No. The truth was and had to be that he loved Emily.

The next picture that entered his head was that of Hartley Baldwin. Jackson could feel badly regarding Emily but he had no such reservations about her puppetmaster. With Baldwin's house under siege and attack the vision of this so respectable citizen and power broker caged and frantic within four walls did provide some solace to Jackson.

Haughton Jackson was so wrapped up in his thoughts at this point that he was not conscious of the figure which had crossed the street near to West View. The first he knew was when the voice of the figure spoke to him:

"Hello, Sir. I was hoping we would meet ."

"What do you want? I have nothing to say."

Jack Jones would not be so instantly dismissed.

"Please hear me out, Sir."

Jackson reluctantly stopped walking and turned to face the young journalist.

"Well?"

"It is just that my boss has had this idea - nothing really to do with the paper. The paper is willing to put up the money for a proper writer to write a book. You know, to put forward your story to the general public. There is an author in mind. All you would have to do is to see the author and tell him everything that happened. My boss says that such a book could make a lot of money. Course, the paper would want its money back and we'd need to agree a reasonable division of the profits. Think about it. My boss will call you soon."

"He can call me if he wants but I assure you I will be doing no such book."

Jackson then completed his journey back to the house.

****

Susan brought in lunch.

Isabel politely enquired:

"How was your walk?"

"Okay"

"You know I wish you would read some of the mail. There are so many letters we get every day. I know you say you are not interested but I do believe that having read them all myself, it would be good for you to see them. In fact, it is a discourtesy of you not to. If someone has gone to the trouble of writing to you, you should have the decency to read what they say. Of course, there is so much, no one would expect you to reply but at least do some reading."

Jackson was used to his sister getting onto him.

She continued.

"You will see how fulsome people are in their support of you. That will improve your spirits. Then there is correspondence from clever sounding folk who sound as if they know what they are saying and urge that you appeal the case to the House of Lords."

"We cannot afford that......and do not suggest Raynsford for I doubt that even you can persuade him to invest anymore into this matter."

"Haughton but that is just the point. If you read some of the letters you will see that many of the subscribers are willing to contribute to the legal costs."

"Is that so indeed?"

****

West View was not the only address in England inundated with mail. For each day brought an avalanche of letters and postcards to Prospect House. The tone of all but a very few of this correspondence was anything but solicitous or supportive.

The duty of vetting the mail fell to Betsy. She had to read the often poisonous notes, notes maligning Emily's character and notes cautioning her to leave the town. These types of letters which were most common she put to one side, for her husband counselled that nothing should be torn up or thrown out. The few envelopes that contained anything akin to support for Emily would be shown to her.

During that Easter weekend, Hartley Baldwin received the following from the Chief Constable:

"Chief Constable's Office
Clitheroe
2nd April 1891

H. Baldwin Esq.,

Dear Sir,

There are some nasty anonymous postcards flying about. They seem to be trying to whip up more fervour and violence. They are being posted all over the place but are being sent from Clitheroe.

Keep quiet about them. I shall find out who is sending them.

This is strictly private, for God's sake.

Yours truly

J.Edwards"

****

In his study, Jackson had spent more than two hours going through most of the opened but previously unread mail. He had only intended to glimpse at one or two of them in order to appease his sister. Before long the heap of letters commanded his assiduous attention.

Could he really appeal? What if these philanthropic correspondents did manage to raise the necessary funds? He had lost the case anyway so what was the worst that could occur if he did indeed bring an Application to the House of Lords? Another loss? Well, he had survived the trauma thus far. There was no prospect of getting Emily back anyway. He was resigned to that. However, what if, what if the House of Lords did overturn the decision? There may perhaps only be the slightest chance of such an outcome but, if so, Jackson would find himself a hero among all right thinking gentlemen. He would be lauded and applauded. He would have no need to worry about his future.

When he appeared from his study, Isabel noticed an obvious change in Haughton's demeanour.

"Isabel, I do not want to make any announcement as such. Not yet. I do though want it spread about that I am resolved that, as soon as circumstances permit, I will present my case to the House of Lords. I'm sure I can rely upon you to make this known in certain quarters?"

"I am so glad and, of course, you can rely on my absolute indiscretion!"

****

Rumour soon spread like wildfire around Blackburn of the decision by Jackson to appeal. The rumour reached the ears of his solicitor who immediately tried to speak to Jackson. He was told Jackson was not available but, through Isabel, Mr Ainsworth was told that Mr Jackson had made no such decision but that the solicitor would be the first to know. The standard response to the press was that Mr Jackson would be making no statement on the subject.

So why was Jackson so coy about his intentions?

It was symptomatic of the "post - Emily" Jackson that he had become so much less decisive. He had lost much of the previous "devil may care" attitude and had been chastened by the appeal outcome.

It was as if he had set the hare running at a greyhound race. He wanted to see what reaction there would be. It would give him a bit more time before he committed to such a course. Yet how long would the hare take to spring the traps?

In the perceived decision to go to the House of Lords, Jackson, though ignorant of the fact, had the support of a committee of gentlemen of whom a foremost personage was the Vicar of Blackburn, one Bishop Crane-Roberts, who felt particularly strongly that the current decision represented an horrific assault upon the sanctity of marriage. This committee then arranged for the following advertisement to appear in a number of Lancashire newspapers:-

"QUEEN -v- JACKSON

Intended Appeal to the House of Lords"

This advertisement sets out the arguments at length for making an appeal to the Court of last resort and remarked:

"The question is no longer a mere personal one as between Mr and Mrs Jackson; it concerns every married man and woman in the country, and the moral well-being of thousands of households.

Donations to well known banks to the credit of the Jackson Appeal Fund or direct to Mr F.W.Vernon, Hon. Secretary of the Appeal."

If indeed Jackson was running a hare, it seemed to be running rather well.

****

Easter 1891 was now over. A week after the return of the Baldwins to Clitheroe and things, as Hartley Baldwin, had predicted, quietened down. Yes, most nights a hard core of demonstrators would keep a vigil outside but, unless any were drunk, the house inmates were barely aware of their presence.

They chose not to go out after dark as this was still likely to be dangerous but with Clitheroe back to virtual normality during daylight, Hartley Baldwin was able to venture again to and from his work unmolested. Betsy also restarted her routines. She decided to ignore or not to respond to folk who were intent on staring at her. Former acquaintances were, for the most part, renewed without difficulty though, like a very large elephant in the room, the court case and the hostilities were subjects of conversation avoided. The kindest of acquaintances would enquire of Emily's well being but beyond that they would not go.

It was viewed as safe now for Emily to return to Shawbridge though whether anyone actually saw her go back there is doubtful. Very apprehensive about facing the world, Emily only left the house at this time to walk into the countryside and again would only go if Esther was able to accompany her.

At the offices of Hall Baldwin, & Weeks the junior partner there knocked on Hartley Senior's door and, when invited, entered holding a newspaper.

"Have you read this?" enquired Weeks

"Mr Weeks, if it is just a continuation of the usual onslaught against my family I have no need of reading it."

"No, Mr Baldwin. This is different."

Hartley Baldwin took the paper and read the Advertisement.

"This cannot be serious. The House of Lords would never entertain this. He will never get the money for another such legal escapade."

"I agree Sir that the Appeal would not be likely overturned but, as to the money, I am not sure. By default, possibly, because Mr Jackson does seem to have a great number of sponsors."

"Nothing I can do to stop him trying."

When Weeks had gone from his room, Hartley mulled over something in his mind. Something he had, days before, discussed with both Betsy and Emily. There was no guarantee it would work but it seemed that if this card was to be played then it should be played now.

Hartley Baldwin then, having told his secretary that on no account was he to be disturbed, picked up the telephone.

****

The confirmation Hartley Baldwin had prayed for, was delivered by messenger that afternoon. The message read:

"Lancashire Evening Post
April 2nd 1891

To Mr Hartley Baldwin: Clitheroe

Dear Sir

I have told our Editor, Mr Marchmont, what you told me this morning in reference to Mrs Jackson's case and, in accordance with your request, I have asked him if he would be willing, were he to be asked to do so, to go through Mrs Jackson's manuscript in order to prepare it for the press. He has instructed me to say that he would be willing, and that he should be glad to come to Clitheroe to see you on the matter.

I think therefore, the best thing would be to write to him direct if you want his assistance.

A letter addressed to him at the Guardian Office at Preston would find him.

I remain

Yours very truly

Jas. Roston."

The momentum from the start was unstoppable. Mr Marchmont was not about to lose the scoop as he saw it. Everyone connected with this case whose notoriety had gone way beyond the boundary of the kingdom had remained tight lipped and had refused to put even a waft of hair "above the parapet". Out of the blue, he had been offered an exclusive and with no fee involved. His newspaper could steal a march on all the other more well resourced and national publications. Of course, by way of popularity, he might have preferred the Haughton Jackson exclusive to that of the wife. Nevertheless, as soon as Hartley Baldwin confirmed the arrangements, Marchmont set off with all speed to Clitheroe having ensured before he left Preston that the few who knew where and why he was going there, were sworn to utmost secrecy. Not a whisper of this could be leaked.

This first meeting was a purely business meeting with Hartley's focus on ensuring that his rules would be understood and agreed to. It took place at the offices in Duck Street.

After the formal handshake and introductory pleasantries, Hartley called his son through to the room. He wanted to ensure a witness to these discussions.

He addressed the newspaper editor:

"Mr Marchmont, as everyone is familiar with the background here..............or think they are.............I do not need to beat about the bush. My sister-in-law, Mrs Jackson, has been very wronged. Very understandably, she has always viewed her relations with Mr Jackson as personal and not matters which belong in the public domain. Despite the phalanx of lies, half truths and outright fantasies appearing in the press throughout these weeks, Mrs Jackson has maintained a course of, how should I put it, private serenity - until now."

"What, may I enquire, has made her change her mind?"

"Several things I believe. The realisation that if she can now record her own explanation for everything that has occurred, she can maybe free herself from the present and reach for a future and that she no longer has to live under a lie. If you ask me, but do not quote this, I believe it is because Mr Jackson no longer holds any fear in her. I would ask how you'd intend to progress with this assuming we reach an accord today?"

"Obviously, it will be necessary for Mrs Jackson to tell her story in her own words."

"Indeed so. I must insist though that it is Mrs Jackson's unadulterated version that is printed and not any false construction put on her words by anyone else."

"I have already identified the most suitable journalist we have who can undertake this. I presume Mr Baldwin you would be satisfied if we agree that anything that is produced is first vetted by Mrs Jackson and possibly yourself?"

"Yes, we can agree to that. As much as possible I would want any piece to be as much in Mrs Jackson's own words. Any reader needs to believe it is Mrs Jackson and not simply "reporter speak" if you will pardon the expression?"

"No apology necessary."

"One more thing, Mr Marchmont, I accept of course you can have no control over any comments in other newspapers regarding what my sister-in-law writes but, to have the effect I want it to, I need it agreed that Mrs Jackson's story will stand alone in your paper without any editorial comment or interpretation by any of your journalists. Any reason for the article will be put forward by Mrs Jackson herself - not by anyone else."

"I do not see any problem with that. Do we have an accord?"

Hartley Baldwin sat a moment, checking in his mind he had not omitted anything important and then suddenly stretched his hand across the desk.

"We certainly do Mr Marchmont."

As he stood to leave Mr Marchmont sought an assurance.

"I need hardly say that up until we have publication this is all strictly confidential. I do not believe it serves either you or me and certainly not Mrs Jackson for word to get out as to what she has now agreed to do."

"I understand fully. You have my solemn word."

****

Exposure

Andrew Hugh Livingstone was Marchmont's chosen journalist. Known by his middle name "Hugh" he was not employed by the newspaper but rather was a freelance operator. Whilst Hugh would tend to look for stories and then hawk them to one or more papers he was not, as on this occasion, averse to being conscripted for a story of the newspaper's choosing.

In a way Hugh could not believe his good fortune when, having signed a confidentiality bond, the task being presented was explained to him. For so many reasons, not all of them honourable, hundreds or thousands of men would, at that time, have given their back teeth to meet with Mrs Jackson - the anti- heroine of so many and an icon of others especially within the growing suffragette movement. Yet what did anyone actually know of her?

Hugh was in his forties so not much different from Emily. It helped him that he was not judgemental. Of course, he had read so much that had been written about her but none of that would cloud his vision going forward. Like all things in his line of work, Hugh had to and was able to embark with a blank canvas and without preconceptions.

One thing though had stuck in Hugh's mind that he could not divorce from his consciousness and that was the image he derived from the vivid description of Emily when she attended the Appeal Court. The words "attractive", "calm", "with no sign of emotion" and "serene" had burnt an impression that simply made the task presented to him even more appealing.

Hugh visited Emily on several occasions. At the initial meeting, Betsy was in another room just in case there were problems. There were none. Hugh's approach to the subject was one of genuine interest, perception and empathy. Whilst Emily had been schooled by Hartley on what he believed she should say, Emily was still reluctant to divulge personal matters to a stranger despite having given her word to her brother-in-law.

Hugh quickly put Emily at ease. He drew her out of herself so much so that she rapidly forgot Hartley Baldwin's "script" and spoke freely and naturally about everything.

After the first meeting, they met together always at 10 in the morning whilst Esther was absent from the house. Hugh helped Emily express certain things in a way he thought would appeal to the readers without compromising the truth of what he heard from her. At times, Emily became emotional whereupon Hugh offered to retire. If Emily said something that Hugh thought reflected badly or was open to misinterpretation, he suggested that such be excluded from the piece. Emily disagreed as she wanted the truth told whatever that truth was, good or bad.

To say that Hugh was impressed with Mrs Jackson would be an understatement. There became so quickly between them a bond of trust and a healthy intimacy. Emily was able to disclose things to this stranger some of which she had never told her sisters and, in so doing, trusted Hugh not to ever share anything he was told with anyone other than what they agreed the public should read. For his part, Hugh trusted Emily not to mislead or make up anything. He had not a shred of doubt that he was being told the truth and nothing but the truth.

At his house, Hugh had regular calls from Marchmont and from Roston. Always it was "How is it going? What is she telling you? When will you have this ready?"

Even though these people were, in this matter, his paymasters Hugh refused to divulge anything. He would not break faith with his subject.

"It will be ready when it is ready. Other than that you did get me to sign a confidentiality bond?"

"But not from me. Not from the paper!"

"Well, that is the way it is. You will get your story. Do not worry on that score."

About a week after the last of his interviews, Hugh returned to Shawbridge.

Upon being invited into the sitting room so familiar to him by now, he sat down and then produced to Emily a notebook.

"That contains what I have prepared for publication. You will see Mrs Jackson, that I have prepared four separate articles. There is such a lot of ground to cover. Readers, I'm afraid, may lose the way if your story were to go on over a number of pages. This way, a shorter article will hopefully not only give the reader time to digest what you are trying to tell them but make them keen to read the next instalment. Now, I know this means you will be "big news" for more than just a day and I can but apologise for that. It is, I urge you, for the best."

Emily, even now, baulked at being front page, back page, any page news for even part of a day but she was able to place her trust in this man whom she had now come to regard as a friend.

"Yes. That will be fine."

"Now, do you want me to get Mr Baldwin to look over the narrative first?"

"No, indeed, Mr Livingstone. I think not. I have decided this has to be me in my words or at least as we have agreed. I alone will check this over and let you know."

In this one moment Hugh identified with the calm and serene woman of the Court report and yes, as he rose to leave, she was very attractive.

"Goodbye Mrs Jackson"

As he turned in the path to head off, he stopped as he distinctly heard Mrs Jackson say:

"You can call me Emily"

Briefly he caught her soft eyes. He smiled and left.

Twenty four hours later, the telephone in the small flat rang. The receiver was picked up.

"Mr Livingstone, it is Emily. I'm happy with all you have written. Thank you. Please go ahead with it."

"I so much hope it serves the purpose you want it to. Thank you, oh, next time you can call me Hugh!"

And so, this next step in the Jackson saga was about to be taken. Hartley Baldwin could not foretell where this may lead. Mrs Emily Jackson was relieved that so much she had been keeping to herself had been loosed even if barely half of her "confessions" were to appear in print. She was unconcerned and gave no thought to the consequences of the imminent publicity. Unlike her brother-in-law, her sole motivation had been to portray her truth.

As regards Mr Haughton Jackson, he was totally unsuspecting. The wind of change was heading his way with a force that proved powerless for him to resist.

Revelation

Jackson's propensity for "playing games" never really left him. It could be hard to decipher whether, in working things out in his head, he saw these games as an essential strategic move in the military sense or if they were not simply designed for self amusement.

For those clamouring for word, for a commitment from him about an appeal they were simply kept waiting. This was possibly to nourish his personal need to feel in control of events rather than submit to the will of others, no matter how much attraction the lure held for him.

Dismissing the proposal for a biography of events to be composed and published is another conundrum.

Jackson throughout this time refused to take any phone calls. He wanted to remain aloof or to appear distant from all goings on. So it befell to Isabel for the most part to deal with incoming calls for him. Accordingly when Edwards from the newspaper called to confirm the offer outlined by Jones, it was Isabel's instruction to explain that Mr Jackson did not believe it "befitted" his position to agree to any "kiss and tell" publication.

Isabel was all in favour of the idea. Haughton made out to her that he felt he had reached a "truce" with Mrs Jackson and, given her present predicament in Clitheroe, he must refrain from causing her any further grief. Given the history of such a marked absence of any sensitivity towards his wife, Isabel was, understandably, sceptical about this explanation.

However, any sense or notion of a "truce" was soon dispelled.

In the course of that day, Jackson refused to take three phone calls - the call from Edwards in the morning, a call from his solicitor in the afternoon and one later on from Raynsford. He remained in his "ivory tower". Not only was Jackson keeping out of view but he was occupying himself in an attic room at West View, looking at photographs and memorabilia from New Zealand and South America. Press cuttings from the Antipodean press, a commendation from the Post Office. He enjoyed reliving the exploits that instilled pride. When not indulging in such retrospection Jackson would examine various objects and artefacts. There were properties belonging to Raynsford there and other items from his predecessors that had been left untouched for so many years. His interest was in value and provenance.

Could he realise funds he so much needed from anything here? This was a treasure hunt which he approached with both motive and thoroughness.

It was early evening when the attic door swung open. Jackson assumed he was being summoned for supper but when he turned round it was not Susan in the doorway but Isabel. His sister was possessed of an alarmed look.

"What is it?"

“It is that woman. Did I not tell you to do something? Did I not say you were too soft?"

With an air of controlled seriousness Jackson stood up and faced Isabel.

"By "that woman" I can only assume you mean Mrs Jackson. What exactly has my wife done that has wound you up so much?"

"It's the Evening News. My friend Poppy along the road read it out over the phone. The paper says that they have had an exclusive interview with Mrs Emily Jackson which will feature in tomorrow's edition."

Jackson was thinking rapidly. Inside he feared the worst but to try and appease his sister he said:

"Well, we had better wait and see exactly what that lady has to say for herself. What is for supper?"

****

The following day in Clitheroe, the impending article by Emily Jackson was the talk of the tea shops, the Post Office and every corner or space used by the animated tongues of the gossips. Why even individuals averse to such conduct were so intrigued as to allow themselves a break from their normal principles. What on earth would be revealed?

For some so hostile to Emily the heralding of an article caught them off guard. Brainwashed into believing Mrs Jackson to be a coward, a frightened mouse so ridden with conscience that she had to hide away or a simpleton puppet of a cruel family, the publication of her words did not accord with such profiles.

Betsy had supported the idea but was suddenly nervous for her little sister. What if it all backfired? Would it not prove the worse for Emily? Betsy did though share one thing with Esther, a personal interest. Certainly, they had known of Emily's general unhappiness with Jackson and they had formed their own views of that particular gentleman. However, Emily had never confided in much detail at all. There was still a whole lot that the sisters could not understand. There had been no advance disclosure to either of them by Emily as to the contents of the article. So, for possibly very different reasons than anyone else, the sisters were as impatient as every stranger was to learn whatever was about to be laid bare.

****

The delivery of the evening paper from the printworks was always made between 2pm and 3.30pm depending upon where the retail outlet or news stand was located. On this day it was immediately evident that something unusual was happening. For queues started to form at the likes of paper shops long before the delivery was due. People who had never before bought the evening paper stood in orderly fashion in the hope not to miss out on this moment.

Within a very short time it was obvious that demand was far exceeded supply and a great many who regularly bought the Evening News were left disappointed.

****

Jackson paced up and down the lobby.

"She will arrive as soon as she is able." Isabel said as she, for her part, made her way along to the kitchen.

Jackson had allowed the foreboding he detected to consume him. He stared at the clock and continued to walk from one wall to the other.

He detected the footsteps and rushed to the front door. Before she had put one foot into the house, the newspaper had been snatched from Susan's hand by Jackson without a word being said. He took himself off to the study and remained there with the door firmly shut.

After twenty minutes Jackson appeared. His agitation reflected in him shaking as he grabbed the telephone, dialled and impatiently waited for his call to be answered.

By now Isabel had reappeared. She stood a bit away from her brother but noted the conversation or rather one side of it:

"I must speak to Ainsworth now. Sorry, I mean Mr Ainsworth."

"I cannot wait for him to become free. I must talk to someone now it is extremely urgent."

"Ah, Mr Sanderson……..Jackson here. What?"

"You know why I am calling?"

"Yes. This article. It is scandalous. It's got to be stopped. Mrs Jackson cannot do this?"

"What do you mean she can?"

"Yes, I know she has done it. That's a facile comment. We must be able to sue her? I have to be able to protect my good name."

"Now, let me get this right. You are telling me that the law allows this? At no time has the law been of any use to me. A waste of time. No, sorry, Mr Sanderson I did not mean that you are a waste of time. No. I meant the law is a waste of time, in my case at any rate."

"Oh and one more thing, Mr Ainsworth has been waiting for my instructions on a House of Lords Appeal. Tell him I can confirm that this has to proceed now with all speed."

"The funds? Oh, they are all in hand."

"What? You need payment now. I do appreciate the work that would be involved. I will get the monies to you."

****

"Is it that bad?" enquired Isabel.

"Read it for yourself. It could hardly be worse. What is more is that this is not a one day wonder. Emily's supposed interview is to be continued over the next three days."

"Why Haughton, do you say "supposed" interview?"

“This is not her. Emily would never put herself forward like this. It is Baldwin and the Battleaxes. It is they who cannot but conspire against me."

"I'd better tell Susan to ensure she gets the paper every day this week then."

"Not on my account. I have no desire to read another word of Mrs Jackson's fiction"

****

It could hardly have got worse for Jackson but it did.

As the Lancashire Evening News had underestimated the demand for the issues containing Emily's interview, it was announced that the following week they would feature the interview in full as a special insertion in Wednesday's copy of the paper.

In truth, it had proved to be a masterstroke on the part of Hartley Baldwin albeit with the commendable expertise of Mr Livingstone. For, in these articles was presented Mrs Emily Jackson as a woman, a woman possessed of the feelings and hopes and thoughts of any normal woman. She was a person not a monster and certainly not an effigy worth burning.

How swiftly the tide turned. Emily's tormentors dissipated and newspapers up and down the land received flurries of mail in praise of or supporting Emily. Such correspondence was published in most newspapers. Not though the Northern Daily Telegraph. Wagstaff was not stupid. He had to acknowledge that public opinion was now firmly with rather than against the Halls. He would never sanction any approbation through the columns of his newspaper!

****

By now Jackson was desperate to act.

He wrote to Mr F W Vernon. There was no response. He then tried to seek out this man. To Jackson's surprise the address for Mr Vernon was a branch of the North & Midland Bank. He approached the desk:

"I would like to see Mr Vernon."

"Mr Vernon. I do not know of him."

"Mr F WVernon. His name was in the newspaper at this address."

Jackson handed over the advertisement.

The Bank Clerk disappeared and then returned along with one of the Assistant Managers of the Branch.

"You are Mr Jackson. The Jackson named here in the paper you gave my colleague?"

"I am indeed" stated Jackson proudly.

"Well, Mr Jackson. This is all rather unfortunate. Mr Vernon just used the Bank as an accommodation address. It was convenient when the account was set up to receive any donations at this branch. I feel this is all rather awkward but, you see, at the end of last week, Mr Vernon resigned as a Trustee of the Fund as did the other Trustees."

"Why would that be?"

"No reason was given nor was any reason necessary."

"But the money in the account was for my benefit surely I can access the funds?"

"Not when it was held in trust you cannot. Only trustees can sanction the use of the funds?"

"You say they have all resigned? So what happens?"

"It would be necessary for the Court to appoint new Trustees."

"You mean I'd have to go to Court for that?"

"It is, I think, a matter for your solicitor to advise you on."

"How much is in the Account?"

"I'm sure you will understand, Mr Jackson. I am not at liberty to disclose that information to you."

Jackson had had enough of this. In a sarcastic tone he thanked the bank officers for all their help and strode out onto the street in disgust.

He could not believe what was happening to him. Why was he being thwarted at every turn? Why was the world so against him? Two months ago, he had the control of his wife under his roof at Blackburn and crowds were singing and chanting his name. He had been something of a military hero and then become a national celebrity. How had it all come crashing down?

As he walked the streets with his head held low, he saw another mirror image. For this while he had been the hunter and his wife was the one who was hidden from view. With this turn of events, he now felt the knives were out for him, that he was the hunted and that he could no longer show his face, certainly not in Clitheroe.

****

At Prospect House, Hartley Baldwin could not have been better pleased with the situation. Surprised indeed at the complete change in the tide of public opinion, but still very satisfying. He was wise enough and sufficiently perceptive to know that Emily may never fully recover from the psychological and emotional trauma she had been through. At least now he firmly believed she could find the peace that would bring her some recovery. When all was said and done he thought the thing that brought him inner contentment was the fact he had, by his actions, carried out the request made to him all these years ago by Henry Hall when he had said "Hartley, please look after my girls. Please keep them safe."

****

At Shawbridge, Emily always knew the decision to go to the press was a correct decision. It was obvious from all that had happened since her articles appeared. She felt she could, once again, hold her head up high and that she had got her life back. It no longer belonged to Jackson. It was not now possessed of by the great British public and yet she had given away to all these anonymous readers an inner part of herself. That made her unhappy. Forever she would be associated with the scandal and whilst, with Hugh's assistance, she was no longer a black and vile witch, her reputation would be forever tarnished. In all the years ahead of her there would be a mother in the street, or a grandmother looking after a grandchild who would say to the young person "Look over there. See her. I will tell you a tale about her. And it is all true."

Emily knew that she may have the quietness restored and indeed the freedom to do as she chose but she can never ever have restored to her the privacy that had always been her blanket, her protection from the world.

****

Coda

Haughton Jackson was though not quite finished. When his anger had died down and the mists of his downcast mind had cleared, he alighted upon something that he was determined now to do. His approaches to the newspapers to interview him for the purposes of his "exclusive" had met with a lack of enthusiasm. For having themselves seen the effect of Hugh's articles in the Evening News, it was reckoned the public were satiated and had little further appetite for this couple. It had run its course.

It was then that Jackson brought to mind the proposal Jack Jones had made to him and that he had so clinically rejected. He then justified to himself the rejection on the basis of "why should anyone else make money out of my story?" If he now set about writing his own book then his benefit therein was two fold. Not only may his story bring round some of the public back to his favour but his book could generate money which, as always, Jackson was in great need of.

He busied himself away in the study at West View, writing both furiously and frantically. He tried to ensure that this would be the perfect riposte to all Emily had broadcast. This was though not Jackson's forte. Lapses in spelling and deficiencies with some grammar made the finished work less than impressive. The book was actually more of a booklet. It contained many short sharp statements and was noticeable by its bright orange cover. Prominent on the cover was a sketch of Jackson himself.

The publication was entitled:-

"THE TRUE STORY OF THE CLITHEROE ABDUCTION

or

WHY I RAN AWAY WITH MY WIFE"

The booklet was offered for sale at a price of 1/6d.

Though offered through the usual channels of the day, W H Smith who had the largest chain of shops, bookstands and railway bookstalls banned the sale of it.

A Mr Burnett, thinking he would not be outdone by the Evening News agreed to serialise Jackson's underwhelming book in the Evening

Express and Blackburn Standard. However, as Jackson's original required much editing, Mr Burnett not only corrected the grammatical errors but took it upon himself to include long monotonous commentary passages of his own and thus anything of moment within Jackson's text was very much lost in the jungle of the surrounding verbiage.

Circulation of the Evening Express was not noticeably enhanced by the Jackson exclusive. Similarly the level of Captain Jackson's overdraft was not significantly reduced by the booklet's proceeds.

Upon the appearance of Jackson's book in the press, Hartley Baldwin again prevailed on Emily to respond and she was more than pleased to have to see Hugh once more.

On this occasion Emily's response to Jackson's grossly false representations was printed in several newspapers. As before the text produced by Hugh portrayed a lady without any axe to grind, who could logically and calmly dismiss each allegation of Mr Jackson without any hint of rancour. Then in what transpired to be the final statement that either would utter in the public print Emily stated:

"That what I have done, and my motives for doing so and it having been understood, is shown by the scores of letters that have reached me and continue to reach me by every post from all parts of the kingdom, from all ranks of men and women. I desire to thank them affectionately and gratefully from my heart for their sympathy.

I am free, though at such great cost, and when I think of this, and of all that I have escaped, I am sad but I am content."

This was a veritable coup de grace. In its way it was a heartfelt appeal to the public. There was just such a gentle finality to this brief piece. Even the bold impetuous Jackson realised he could not compete with the case so eloquently being put forward by his wife. Even had he begged, borrowed or stolen funds to access the House of Lords, he knew he could not win. He had seen what had occurred before the Appeal Court. After meeting with the Judges for twenty minutes she had encharmed them to her case. Now, through the press she had done exactly the same but with the public. Mrs Jackson would, he was certain, bring the House of Lords to her cause as well.

Jackson rummaged in a drawer and found what he was looking for. It was the only photograph he had ever had of Emily. It was a photograph taken by one of Colonel Robinson's friends at a picnic not long after he had been introduced to her. He held up this photograph and stared for so long at the face looking back at him before he suddenly cursed with a hint of both spite and love;

"You and your damn soft blue eyes"

****

Aftermath

The signs reflecting the waning of interest were clear. The volume of mail delivered to both Prospect House and to West View dwindled.

There were still from time to time reminders in the newspapers. Letters regarding what could be called the vulgar aspects of the drama had been replaced with correspondence from serious people debating what were regarded as serious issues.

A leading article in the Times remarked (as would prove to be all very prophetic):

"All interest in the Jackson case has not died down, nor will it for many a day, if we may judge from the copiousness , variety and vivacity of the comments on it. The decision of the Judges in the Jackson case must be the beginning of far extending changes. Sooner or later, some part of our marriage laws must be reviewed."

The Daily Telegraph, again in a leading article, urged the passing of a Bill to make desertion by a partner to a marriage for four years a basis for divorce.

The essence of the pressure for change rested on the basic question :

"If it is accepted that a man could not force his wife to live with him must the deserted spouse then live a celibate life for the remainder of his days?"

There was reference to the Jackson case in August 1891 with an announcement in the Public Notices of the local press:

"The Abduction of a Wife" a new drama will be produced at The Grand Theatre in the town of Nelson. Unfortunately the enterprising show biz people were thwarted in their scheme as the Town Chamberlain's Office refused to grant a licence for the play."

These occasional references and discussions evaporated by the end of 1891. The spotlight which had focused so intensely upon Clitheroe, upon Rover Street and the individual protagonists for these nine months was turned off and those caught up in the whole affair were left to get on with their lives.

****

The Northern Daily Telegraph was bought over by the Daily Telegraph. Wagstaff was prevailed upon to retire and within a very short time Mr Jack Jones was appointed assistant editor of the edition for the North West.

Hartley Baldwin Junior was assumed a partner in his father's business which became the Firm of Baldwin, Weeks & Baldwin and continued to practice from the offices in Duck Street.

Edmund Haughton Jackson sought anonymity in the city and, once more, took up lodgings with his brother. He had a few acquaintances in London which he renewed and somehow succeeded in passing the years, as he had hitherto, without occupation. Raynsford owned an Irish wolfhound which Jackson befriended. Long walks with the dog across the nearby heath helped to make him feel alive. Some evenings he would play cards though not with any money involved. At other times, he would look for female company but had to accept now that the vintage of any female companion was not as youthful as they had been in his earlier times in the city.

Jackson presumed, probably correctly, that no one was interested in anything he had to say about the year of 1891. There were though sudden flashes of the "old Jackson." For on two or three occasions when in the company of a younger person and it became clear that he or she had no knowledge of the abduction, Jackson became enthused by the captive audience. In fairness, Jackson had perfected the tale and, without any cutting insults or self-pity, was both amusing and entertaining.

What of Emily?

Mrs Jackson, for the most part, kept herself to herself. Her pursuits were of the simple kind. If she was encountered out walking nothing in her demeanour could have suggested she had been the victim of such popular hatred and violence. Indeed, she presented as the very same self possessed lady that had so impressed none other than the Lord Chancellor himself.

In conversation Emily did not once make complaint about her life or anything that had occurred. She would never make mention of Jackson, more because there was no need to rather than to protect her from pain. If solace she sought or if pleasure was required Emily had to go no further than to her piano.

It took Emily several months before she felt she could return to Church for she had had to question her faith in the light of Jackson's allegations and the charges from the mob of her being a witch. She had much to reconcile. For when all was said and done and even although the law had rescued her, she accepted she had broken the vow she had made in Church. It was only after several long conversations with Betsy that Emily was persuaded, if she needed forgiveness, she should look for to God for it..

On the first couple of Sundays back at St Mary's, she clung tightly to her sister as she left. Her eyes transfixed on the spot Jackson's carriage had been lying in wait for her.

****

Thursday 10th March 1898 was just over 7 years since the abduction. Emily was 53 years old. She came downstairs at Shawbridge and as she placed her right foot on the floor she winced.

"What's happened?" enquired Esther "Pulled a muscle?"

"Oh, something like that." responded Emily with no obvious sign of concern.

****

Late on the evening of Saturday 20th March 1898, Jackson arrived back at the house in Sydenham. Any observer would be in no doubt that the man had been drinking. He had hardly made it half way along the hall when Raynsford's manservant, Allinson, appeared.

"Mr Jackson, Sir. There is a man asking for you on the telephone. I told him it was very late but he insisted that I try to find you."

Normally, Jackson would have been suspicious or simply refused the call. Not on this occasion.

"Excellent, I say, excellent." With a hand attempting to go around the servant's shoulders he proclaimed "Lead the way."

"I took the call on the phone by the pantry."

"How clever of you Allthorpe… is it? Allisoness? Oh whatever. I am starving so the pantry is a superb idea."

Haughton stumbled a bit as he reached the wall mounted telephone. He took the receiver in his hand. After a brief silence he said:

"Hello. This is Captain E Haughton Jackson at your service. To whom do I have this pleasure of talking to?"

"Mr Jackson. It is me."

"Come on now. No games. Who is me?"

The solemn voice then announced "This is Mr Dixon Robinson"

"My goodness. Is that really you, Dick? After all these years my old playmate. Are you in London?"

"Can you listen to me Mr Jackson?"

"Why so formal? You turned into a stuffed shirt? Let's... "

"Jackson" shouted Dixon "I'm phoning about Emily. Not sure I should have but I just thought you should know."

"Emily? My Emily. You mean Mrs Jackson? Why should I want to hear anything about her."

"Mrs Jackson is dying. She has not very long left"

The phone disconnected.

Jackson slid down the wall. The sobering words he had just heard were like bullets into his heart or his soul. His life of pretence and bravado, shattered by this real awakening.

****

All these years ago Jackson had vowed never again to go anywhere near Clitheroe. Yet on this Sunday that was precisely where he was heading. For in the fitful slumber as the alcohol diffused Haughton had once more discovered his headline role of the romantic hero. If he could now, at this eleventh hour, prove to Emily that all along she had been wrong about him, then he must go. In the agony of the night he had,for the very first time possibly discovered contrition. He was prepared to seek his wife's foregiveness.

It was not a good journey for, of course, there were no trains to Clitheroe on a Sunday. From Manchester he had to hire a carriage but then a horse became lame and he had to wait in the middle of nowhere whilst the coachman handed a message to another carriage to get help from the next village along the road. The weather was grim and it was wet.

Once on the road again, Jackson realised one thing he had given no thought to. There was Baldwin and the "Ugly sisters". Surely, at this time, they would yield and not cause either him or his poor wife distress?"

Jackson got the coachman to stop and drop him off near the station. The coachman was detailed to wait for his passenger in the inn next to the station.

The rain had not abated much. Jackson walked slowly in the direction of Shawbridge. With the terrible weather and it being a Sunday, there were no persons anywhere to be seen. The rain and his tears formed rivers on Jackson's cheeks, his shoes splashed in the puddles on the road.

He reached the end of the street where, just round the corner, Shawbridge would come into view. He stopped and gathered his breath, his thoughts and his courage.

Jackson took the one step necessary before he then froze to the spot. The carriage at the house was draped in black. There was no mistaking that it belonged to the undertaker. He could not move. The water now seeped through his clothing. He was too late. His Emily was gone.

****

Mrs Emily Emma Maud Jackson nee Hall died on Sunday 21st March 1898. The death certificate signed by Dr Musson confirmed she was aged 53 years and that the cause of death was "Failure of the heart following septicaemia caused by injury to the foot accidentally caused when cutting a corn." It became apparent that dye from her stocking had contaminated the wound on Emily's foot.

From so humble a cause then did the heroine of the famous Jackson case leave a world, which had been so unkind to her, the better for her life.

Reflections

There is much to look back upon and yet on the matter of both the motives and the actions of the principal characters there is so much that will never now be capable of anything other than conjecture.

Neither Emily Hall nor Haughton Jackson ever married anyone else. Indeed they could not do so as neither of them was able to obtain a divorce even were they minded to try and dissolve the marriage. In England at this time the sole ground for divorce was adultery. In order to gain some perspective into the deeds of either of them (some of which today would be viewed as preposterous or without reason) their actions need viewed through the prism of the age - the Victorian era with its inherent deference to paternal views and instruction, respect for the Church and, of course, the subordination of women within marriage.

By maybe the middle of and certainly by the latter part of the twentieth century, the climate of the tabloid press and attendant paparazzi was well established and, though rarely pleasant to be caught in the crosshairs of the rifle of such publicity, there does now exist advisors, representatives and media savvy people to guide and support innocents trapped in the glare and generally offer protection to any unwitting victim. When Emily in particular but also Jackson was suddenly faced with the blazing limelight of the press exposure, there was no established way of dealing with the unexpected and, in Emily's case for certain, the unwanted sensation of it all. Perhaps with his sense of divine importance and having been used to "playing to the gallery" Haughton Jackson was better able to handle the public curiosity and intrusion into his affairs. It is though not very hard at all to put oneself into Emily's position and realise just how distressing and uncomfortable it all was for her to have her life floodlit across the nation and beyond for all to see and to speak about.

Socially, the decision in the Jackson case was a milestone.

In and around the Manchester area in particular, the stirrings of what would become the Suffragette Movement were already detectable. Statutes had been passed to afford women more control over their own income but these bands of dedicated women sought much more. In the eyes of the early day Suffragettes Emily was seen as something of a torch bearer and was promoted by way of inspiration to the cause of emancipation. They acknowledged her courage and lauded her achievement in loosening the shackles of a male dominated institution.

When I reflect on it all I see clearly how very fortunate my Great Great Aunt Emily had been. It was by dint of fate that her sister was married to a solicitor for elsewise what would have been her fate? That Hartley Baldwin had an emotional and professional interest in her situation and, to an extent, could "pull strings" and ensure that every legal path was pursued, meant that he created Emily's freedom and that he became responsible for facilitating an amelioration in the legal interpretation of a spouses rights.

I can then sit here in my Croft as I do and look over at the armchair opposite me. The armchair emblazoned with "H.B. 1882" For Emily Emma, for my family I can raise a glass and say "Thank you, Mr Baldwin. I salute you."

Meliora J Schoenberg

****

APPENDIX-1

Extract from Article by Mrs E E Jackson in Preston Guardian May 2nd 1891

"My husband says that I have compelled him to speak because of what I have before said and he allows it to be said that I was the first to make our unfortunate troubles public. This is not true. Mr Jackson authorised the publication of an article in the Pall Mall Gazette, full of misrepresentations about me and giving a completely false colour to the whole story and full of false charges against me. That interview was published in many newspapers and I felt bound in consequence of it, to break silence.

Mr Jackson quite fails to understand my feelings. He has endeavoured to show that I was influenced in the change of my feelings towards him by my relatives. This is wholly untrue. I did not tell of Mr Jackson prior to the engagement, because, in the first place, they did not like him and, in the second, because of the many reasons which influence a woman not to talk of such things before anything is settled. But as soon as the engagement was fixed, I told him it must be announced to my friends. As the engagement was fixed, I told him it must be announced to my friends.

I caused him to come to Prospect House on the Sunday, three days after the engagement. But all that happened before the marriage is beside the point. The fact is that my friends were reconciled after it had taken place. And Mr Jackson admits it. My sister wrote to him in very friendly terms, and he replied thanking her.

Mr Jackson says my letters were affectionate at that time. That is exactly the case because they reflected my feelings towards him and that my love continued until I found out, as I believed and still believe, that he had not married me for myself but for my money.

My letters continued to be affectionate to the day when he showed me by his demand for money, and his penniless condition in New Zealand, that it was not for myself that he had married me.

He thinks and says my changed feelings were caused by my relatives. I know and say it was the opening of my eyes to his real character and the fact that my letters were to the full as affectionate as ever up to the moment of his letter reaching me, begging for money, shows the falseness of his belief.

He persists in thinking I had no reason for my change of feeling towards him, despite the fact that I had told him in my letters and at the interview at the Charing Cross Hotel what the reason was. From the first to last his whole demeanour seemed to show that he had no affection for me. It is the truth rather that he cannot, even now, understand that a woman would be shocked and repelled by such conduct as his. By his letters, his masterfulness, his foul language and his gross personal violence.

He has laid much insistence upon his assertion that he offered to remain in England if I wished. This is not true. It is an afterthought with him and seems to have grown gradually upon him.

On the meeting which took place at West View, he said "During our conversation I offered to give up my intended trip to New Zealand and remain at home. My wife said "No, go. Carry out your plans and I will join you in six months." He further said "My wife virtually sent me abroad."

I declare emphatically that he never once offered to stay in England and, I repeat, what I have said that I should have been glad if he had stayed.

I had repeatedly said in my letters, which Mr Jackson quotes, that I considered it a mad journey, that I hoped it would be relinquished and that he ought not to go. More than that, I actually broke off the engagement on the advice of his own lady friend, because he refused to stay in England.

I had repeatedly expressed my desire for him to stop. Much more than this, also, if this was in his mind, he certainly would have mentioned it (which he did not) in the letter in which he asked for money or again when he wrote me the angry insulting letter so full of overbearing and violent reproach. All his complaint was that I was not going out to join him. There is not a word about his having gone because I sent him or because I did not bid him to stay. Is it possible that he would have been silent about it if it was then rankling in his mind against me? I say- no. It is an afterthought and nothing more.

Mr Jackson has said that in the interview in London he showed affection for me. This is absolutely incorrect. His manner throughout was chilling and reserved. He seemed afraid to say much and I thought that as the proceedings were pending he feared to compromise himself. From first to last his whole demeanour seemed to show that he had no affection for me. On parting, he refused to shake hands with me as he says and then let my hand fall from his. I was convinced he did not care one jot for me.

He introduces some slanders about some alleged mistress and illegitimate children of his. I never mentioned anything of the kind. I never heard of it until I saw it in his own letter.

THE SIEGE

West View

His version about what passed at West View is in many respects inaccurate but, even so, he has in no way disproved what I have said as to his violence and cruelty to me and he even goes so far as to say this "When we got into the drawing room she was rather obstreperous and would not say anything. When her relations came I wanted her to go upstairs, but she would not so I took her up in the same way as you would carry a bundle."

It is not true to say we were as he says "at times fairly intimate." Whenever he came to me it was a disagreeable intrusion and I was always relieved when he left me.

That I did not resent his approaching me was because I was afraid of him and his violence. That I "chaffed him about his running off with me and complimented him on his pluck" is a wicked untruth. I thought he had acted like a coward with his cruel violence in attacking two women so savagely as he had attacked my sister and myself with two strong men to help - and so far as complimenting him I loathed him for what he had done and told him so. His presence offended me and when he forced his "caresses" upon me, I dared not resist, because I was in his power and I feared worse might result if I did. But I never ceased to long to be free. To say that I put up my face to be kissed is the statement of a coward who compels a woman by violence to yield to his caress and taunts her afterwards for not daring to resist him. He says he refused my offers of money if he would let me out of prison and that he refused to "look at it in this mercenary way". The truth is that he was in constant communication with his lawyers who would be astute enough to tell him, what my lawyer has told me since, that any arrangement I had made while under duress would have been invalid. But he omits to mention that no sooner was the Writ of Habeas Corpus granted than he took quite a different view of the matter, authorised me to communicate with my solicitor (although he had forbidden me strictly to do so) to see whether an arrangement could not be come to on a money basis, without our having to go to London. While I was in his power the thought was he could keep all my income by keeping me; but when he felt he might lose me, he was willing to come to an arrangement. A telegram from my solicitor stopped this negotiation.

Settlement of Property

Mr Jackson takes credit for having signed the settlement of my property. He says "I signed the settlement, as requested by my wife's solicitor. It was wholly in her favour and I made no stipulation on my own behalf. I did not read it but afterwards found it was in her favour."

This is wholly incorrect and misleading. This settlement was read over and explained to Mr Jackson by my solicitor. It was, as I am told, in the form usual when all the money settled belongs to the wife. Mr Jackson was not in a position to make stipulations because of the Married Women's Property Act, and his consent was not at all necessary. It is the fact however that Mr Jackson profits by the settlement as he will get the whole of my income if he survives me. Seeing that he settled nothing upon me, I do not see where his magnanimity in this matter is shown.

He says I misinterpreted his letter when I thought he wished me to provide a home for him and his friend and his sister. His letter speaks for itself.

This is what he said:

"When we get home we can settle what will be done. What Dick and I should like would be a nice little farm, near a town anywhere you like and, if it can be managed, a little place for Isabel near and Dick would stay with her. We should then be so happy."

On this Mr Jackson said :

"I never had any notion of either my friend, Mr Dixon Robinson (who is a younger son of another family resident at Clitheroe Castle, the stronghold of the De Lacies) or my sister going with us. That is an entirely false construction placed upon my letter.

This I leave anyone to judge from the passage I have quoted. Who, but I, was to find the money for the farm? Seeing that my husband had gone out as an emigrant settler and had been writing for money to bring him and his friend back, what other conclusion could I draw?

He said that his demand for the £100 was as much in joke as anything else. He asked for£100 and more to be sent out-though when his brother sent £50 afterwards it was found enough to bring him and his friend home. His sister's letters importuning me about the money show that she, at least, thought the matter earnest enough. When he wrote his next and insulting letter he asserted that I was the proper person to apply to for him. He has repeated this since and the only escape he now has is to say he was joking. What he said at the time was "I did not care to ask Raynsford for more and you were the right one to ask."

I believed that my husband had cared for me, and had married me for myself and not for my money. I loved him on my part and I looked forward to a happy life with him. All my letters which he has so needlessly published show this and show that my affection for him remained unaltered until I saw that it was not myself but my money he wished to get.

From that time on, he showed to me as a man capable of violence but incapable of affection. His masterful and overbearing letter showed his domineering character. What was I to think of a man who, because I would not send him more than twice as much money as was necessary to pay for his and his friend's return to England, could write me a letter containing such phrases as these.

"Your letter is an insult. I cannot think how you have dared to write me such a one. Do not make any mistake - there shall be a perfect understanding between us: but I shall make it, not you. How dare you say I married you for your trash, when you know it is a lie. I am very sorry you are happy... you insult me in every way you can."

He wrote "I was the man, she the woman, and apart from her money which I called trash and meant it, she ought to have been willing to have acquiesced in my wishes. She does not believe what she has put upon paper. I'm slow to temper, but a woman who loved me could manage me as easily as a child. She could have made me her dutiful slave, if she had fulfilled her vow. She has broken her vow and seeks to vindicate herself before the world by writing about "trash". But she never tried me. She never sought to mollify me. She forbade me to come near her as though I were an unclean thing. She took me to the altar and then turned her back upon me. Made mouths at me and then mocked me."

His visit to my friends exactly confirmed my opinion.

But his account is not the true one. He was not struck by Mr Baldwin, nor did my sister say anything to him to provoke him. He was provoked because I would not see him. He seemed to be beside himself with passion at being thwarted in this and the foul and horrible language he used - which I will not repeat again - and the loathsome charges he hurled at my sister showed me what kind of man he was. He never retracted his words either.

Even now he can find nothing harder to say of his conduct in calling my sister a "prostitute" than that he was provoked and said something uncomplimentary.

A month later he had written many letters to me. Does he think that in barely a month I could be brought to forget that he had said he would be my master and had sworn at my sister and that I could consent to see him just when, without a jot or tittle of regret, he asked me. If so, he greatly mistakes me and, as I believe, the vast majority of my sex.

I was not to be conquered by force, whether of the law or of personal violence. Thus, when within a bare month of his return, he got his lawyers to order my relatives to turn me out of their houses, my feelings against him hardened, as would those of any woman. His order was disregarded and then, almost immediately, began his law proceedings. It was force, force, force, always force. And I would not and will not be driven by any man's whip. It is wonderful to me that he does not even now seem able to appreciate what he did.

Thus, having determined upon a scheme for seizing me he says "I wished to spare my wife all possible publicity, notoriety or discomfort" Can anyone believe this to be true when he chose Sunday morning for the abduction and aided by two strong men, seized me at the door of the Parish Church in the face of the whole congregation, just as they were coming from morning service?

If he had designed to seize me in the most public and disgraceful manner, he could not have chosen a time more suited to his purpose.

I have been accused of having painted him in false colours. I have not done anything of the kind. I have merely shown in what light he appeared to me and I have given his letters in order that the public may see in what colours he has painted himself.

His letters, his language, his oath, his force, his threats and his personal ill treatment of me. They are the witnesses against him and, as I have shown now, he does not, because he cannot, attempt to explain them away.

Mr Jackson's statements are nowhere more misleading than when referring to the decision of the Court of Appeal setting me free. He says that what the Court did was to give me "to the very people who have been imprisoning us" and he even goes so far as to say "I never made a prisoner of my wife."

This is totally untrue. He claimed in the Court of Appeal the right to deprive me of my liberty and he tried to lead the public to believe that I was taken away from him and given up to my friends, whereas what the Court did, after satisfying themselves that I freely refused to live with my husband, was to go where I chose."

****

APPENDIX II

Publications & Reports

From the day following the kidnap until long after the final decision of the Court, the press had many a field day reporting the developments, opinions and letters concerning the "warring" couple a selection of which are replicated verbatim here. The impact and confusion brought by the decision for the public at large and indeed the legal profession is reflected in the following extracts.

April 28th 1892 : The Editors of Punch posed two situations to reflect the consequences of the Jackson Case:

"Possible Romance

Scene: A dungeon beneath the Castle Moat. Wife chained to a post with bread and water beside her.

Enter husband with cat o nine tails.

Husband : "And now after ten days seclusion will you make over your entire property to me, signing the deed in your life's blood?"

Wife: (in a feeble voice) "Never. You may kill me but I will defy you to the last."

Husband: "Then die"

He is about to leave the dungeon when he is met by a Messenger from the Court of Appeal.

Messenger: In the name of the law, release your prisoner."

(Joy of wife, and tableau as curtain falls).

Probable Reality

Scene: The church door of a fashionable Church. Wife bidding adieu to Husband

Husband: "Surely now that my name and fortune are yours, you will reconsider your decision, and at least accompany me back to our wedding breakfast?"

Wife: (in a firm voice) "Never. You may will me but I will defy you to the last."

Husband: "This is rank nonsense! You must take my arm."

He is about to leave the Church porch when he is met by a Messenger from the Court of Appeal.

Messenger: "In the name of the law release your prisoner."

Husband: "Sold."

(Joy of Wife and tableau as curtain falls.)"

****

April 13th 1891: Manchester Guardian

"An eloping Wife and her property The Jackson decision again

At Westminster Police Court on Friday before Mr de Rutzen, William Cranmer Lloyd, aged 26, described as a valet and Henrietta Anne Fenn, a tall good looking stylishly attired woman, aged 28, were placed in the dock together on remand, charged with being jointly concerned in stealing furniture and jewellery value £350, on 24th ult. from 125 Church Street, Chelsea, the property of Arthur Richard Fenn, the husband of the female prisoner.
The facts have already been published - yesterday afternoon Mr Dutton said that since the last examination he had ascertained that there would be difficulties to be got over as to the ownership of the property and therefore he asked his worship's sanction to permit the prosecutor to withdraw the charge - Mr Abrahams agreed with his friend that, as the law laid down in the Jackson case rendered the husband's position a little uncertain, the better course would be not to proceed with the charges. Mr de Rutzen allowed the withdrawal of the charge and the prisoners were discharged "

****

April 6th 1891: Lancashire Evening Post

"In the case of an alleged wife beating at Luton today, the Bench refused to grant the wife a judicial separation order and intimated that after the decision in the Clitheroe case, separation orders would not be made, a wife being able to leave her husband at choice."

It was further reported:

"Magistrates seem to be losing their heads over the Jackson matrimonial decision. At Luton on Saturday, in a case of wife beating, the woman asked for judicial separation, but the Bench refused and it was initiated that after the decision in the Clitheroe case, separation orders would not be made, as a wife could leave her husband if she chose. The Bench also refused a maintenance order. It may be the law that a woman can refuse to live with her husband, and, if so, it must also be the law that a man can refuse to live with his wife, but this power is quite different from the question of maintenance. Husbands as well as wives are freed by the Jackson decision as long as it stands, and if pecuniary obligation also ceases there will soon be a large number of free wives and husbands in the country."

****

11th April 1891: Manchester Guardian

This edition of the newspaper contained a letter submitted by Elizabeth Wolstenholme Elmy. Ms Wolstenholme Elmy was a friend and colleague of Emmeline Pankhurst and had, in 1891, founded the Women's Emancipation Union. Her letter read as follows:

"The famous decision of 1772 declared slavery to be contrary to the law of England. There had been three previous cases brought before the Courts, in each of which the learned judges had taken the side of the slave owner and affirmed his rights over the person of his slave.

It would seem, nevertheless, when the precedents are more carefully examined, that however brutal the manners and customs of a past age and however helpless a wife from want of means and other causes may have been to avail herself of legal remedies, there is no justification whatever in law for the broad statement of Mr Justice Jeune, but that the opinion expressed by the Lord Chancellor is absolutely and strictly correct, that "no such right ever did exist in our law" as the alleged right of a husband to seize by force and imprison his wife. Unjust and harsh as the law has been, and in some respects still is, this crowning barbarity has never been sanctioned by the law of England. How unjust and even cruel that law was to the English wife less than a quarter of a century ago may still be read in the indignant words of Mr John Stuart Mill in his "Subjection of Women" published in 1869. "The wife is the actual bond servant of her husband, no less so as far as legal obligation goes than slaves common so called. She vows a lifelong obedience to him at the altar and is held to it through life by law.

Causists may say that the obligation of obedience stops short of participation in crime, but it certainly extends to everything else. She can do no act but by his permission - at least tacit. She can acquire no property but for him. The instant it becomes hers, even if by inheritance, it becomes ipso facto his. In this respect the wife's position under the common law of England is worse than that of slaves in many countries. The daughters, indeed, of rich men were, to some extent, protected by special contracts setting aside the law; but as the system of marriage settlements did not and could not extend to the mass of the people, nine tenths of the marriages in this country were governed by the common law, under which the English wife had virtually no civil existence whatever. She had forfeited by marriage those elementary civil rights which the law carefully safeguarded in the case of all other persons. She had no property and no means of acquiring any."

****

April 25th 1891: Manchester Guardian

Her continued indignation at the plight of women compelled Ms Wolstenholme Elmy to write once again to the same newspaper.

"It is obvious that since husband and wife are not to be compelled to live together against the will of either but are free to depart at pleasure, the relative claims of the parties to the conjugal relation will have to be considered and established in accordance with the rule of personal freedom. It would be a monstruous injustice to hold either husband or wife permanently bound to a partner who refused to accept the relations and obligations of the partnership.

An amendment of the divorce law enabling the deserted wife or husband to become free from matrimonial obligations is imperatively and immediately necessary. The conditions of divorce must, more than ever, be just and equal between husband and wife."

****

APPENDIX III

John Edward Anderton

John Edward Anderton was born in 1842, the only son of The Reverend Joseph Heywood Anderton and his wife Ann. Joseph was, at the time, the vicar at St Mary's in Clitheroe. His son John became a solicitor. Upon his father's death on 3rd January 1878 (his mother having predeceased 4 years previously) John inherited his parents' estate including the title of Patron of the Living of St Mary's Church.

John died on 2nd October 1885. He bequeathed his estate including the Patron of the Living to Emily Emma.

The Patron of the Living

The title along with Emma's estate ultimately fell to the Peel family and the title in particular was bequeathed to Robert Peel. Following Robert's death the title was returned by his widow, Angela, to the Church and the current incumbent is the Bishop of Blackburn.

The Ribble Valley Line

The railway between Blackburn and Clitheroe and beyond was part of The Ribble Valley Line. This stretch of what would become part of the London, Midland & Southern Railway was opened on 27th July 1846. The line north of Blackburn closed in September1962. Following a public campaign the line was, once more, opened so far as Clitheroe in 1994.

Hartley Baldwin

When Hartley Baldwin died six years after Emily, he was 83 years old. The legal practice he had assumed from Henry Hall was in rood health. The connection with his family endured through his son Hartley Junior with Mr Weeks assuming a senior role. To this day the office at 2 Duck Street, Clitheroe is maintained through the offices of Houldsworth, Solicitors.

Betsy Alice Maude Baldwin

Hartley's widow was left comfortably well off and she remained at Prospect House until her death in 1912.

Esther Anne Maude Hall

Esther was a spinster her whole life. She never moved from Shawbridge. She passed away in 1909.

Edmund Haughton Jackson

Of all the main protagonists in this tale, Jackson survived them all. At the age of 84 years he died in London of carcinoma of the bowel.

Frederick Dixon Robinson ("Dick")

Dixon was born at Clitheroe Castle in 1860. After his escapades with Jackson, Dixon Robinson secured a position within the family legal Firm of Robinson & Son. This firm maintained a close connection with the Robinson family until 1966. Dixon settled down. He married Ada Gertrude Robinson and they lived in Chatburn in Lancashire. Dixon Robinson died in 1931.

Richard Henn Collins

The barrister who represented Haughton Jackson before the Appeal Court was soon elevated to the Bench and in April 1895 he was the judge presiding at the first trial of Oscar Wilde. In 1897 he became an Appeal Court judge and a Privy Counsellor. In 1907 Henn Collins was created Baron Collins of Kensington in the County of London. He died at the age of 68 years and is buried at Brompton Cemetery.

Colonel Robert Raynsford Jackson

Raynsford Jackson was born in 1823. He was an Honorary Colonel in the 3rd Brigade of the Lancashire Voluntary Artillery, an honour bestowed in recognition of his original thoughts upon the organisation and training of Voluntary Artillery. His marriage to Mary Haughton Whittaker produced eight children. Following the arson attack upon his property in Lancashire Colonel Jackson spent the rest of his life at 31 Harrington Gardens, Sydenham, London. He developed a keen interest in telephones and was Chairman of the National Telephone Company.

APPENDIX IV

Acknowledgments

I am indebted to Fern Hudson whose research and patient work built the bricks necessary to bring this book together. To my sister-in-law Angela Peel for her contributions and to the late Robert Ashe, who, as a descendant of the Jackson family helped in relation to some of the background from the other side of the fence.

I appreciate also invaluable help from Valerie Birkby, Caroline Ward-Dutton and Avril & Kirsty of Ellon Library.

My special thanks also goes to Paul of Silver City Surfers in Aberdeen.

Sources

"Why I ran away with my wife".............Edmund Jackson/Burnett.

"The Abduction of a Wife"...........................G.Fielden – Hughes

List of Illustrations

Printed in Great Britain
by Amazon

59212813R00225